32489109016508

**921
CHA**

Cesar Chavez

$38.50

DATE DUE	BORROWER'S NAME	ROOM NO.

32489109016508

**921
CHA**

Cesar Chavez

DISCARD

**PEIRCE ES
CHICAGO PUBLIC SCHOOLS**

573011 03850   35229D   0005

Recent Titles in
The Ilan Stavans Library of Latino Civilization

THE ILAN STAVANS LIBRARY OF LATINO CIVILIZATION

CESAR CHAVEZ

Edited by Ilan Stavans

 GREENWOOD

AN IMPRINT OF ABC-CLIO, LLC
Santa Barbara, California • Denver, Colorado • Oxford, England

Copyright © 2010 by Ilan Stavans

All rights reserved. No part of this publication may be reproduced, stored in a retrieval system, or transmitted, in any form or by any means, electronic, mechanical, photocopying, recording, or otherwise, except for the inclusion of brief quotations in a review, without prior permission in writing from the publisher.

Library of Congress Cataloging-in-Publication Data

Cesar Chavez / edited by Ilan Stavans.
    p. cm. — (The Ilan Stavans library of Latino civilization)
  Includes bibliographical references and index.
    ISBN 978-0-313-36488-4 (hard copy : alk. paper) — ISBN 978-0-313-36489-1 (ebook : alk. paper)
  1. Chavez, Cesar, 1927–1993—Juvenile literature. 2. Labor leaders—United States—Biography—Juvenile literature. 3. Mexican American migrant agricultural laborers—Biography—Juvenile literature. 4. Agricultural laborers—United States—Labor unions—History—Juvenile literature. 5. United Farm Workers—History—Juvenile literature. I. Stavans, Ilan.
  HD6509.C48C473 2010
  331.88′13092—dc22
  [B]

                              2009047441

13 12 11 10 9   1 2 3 4 5

This book is also available on the World Wide Web as an eBook.
Visit www.abc-clio.com for details.

ABC-CLIO, LLC
130 Cremona Drive, P.O. Box 1911
Santa Barbara, California 93116-1911

This book is printed on acid-free paper ∞
Manufactured in the United States of America

CONTENTS

SERIES FOREWORD

The book series *The Ilan Stavans Library of Latino Civilization*, the first of its kind, is devoted to exploring all the facets of Hispanic civilization in the United States, with its ramifications in the Americas, the Caribbean Basin, and the Iberian Peninsula. The objective is to showcase its richness and complexity from a myriad perspective. According to the U.S. Census Bureau, the Latino minority is the largest in the nation. It is also the fifth largest concentration of Hispanics in the globe.

One out of every seven Americans traces his or her roots to the Spanish-speaking world. Mexicans make up about 65% of the minority. Other major national groups are Puerto Ricans, Cubans, Dominicans, Ecuadorians, Guatemalans, Nicaraguans, Salvadorans, and Colombians. They are either immigrants, descendants of immigrants, or dwellers in a territory (Puerto Rico, the Southwest) having a conflicted relationship with the mainland U.S. As such, they are the perfect example of *encuentro*: an encounter with different social and political modes, an encounter with a new language, and encounter with a different way of dreaming.

The series is a response to the limited resources available and the abundance of stereotypes, which are a sign of lazy thinking. The 20th century Spanish philosopher José Ortega y Gasset, author of *The Revolt of the Masses*, once said: "By speaking, by thinking, we undertake to clarify things, and that forces us to exacerbate them, dislocate them, schematize them. Every concept is in itself an exaggeration." The purpose of the series is not to clarify but to complicate our understanding of Latinos. Do so many individuals from different national, geographic, economic, religious, and ethnic backgrounds coalesce as an integrated whole? Is there an *unum* in the *pluribus*?

Baruch Spinoza believed that every thing in the universe wants to be preserved in its present form: a tree wants to be a tree, and a dog a dog. Latinos in the United States want to be Latinos in the United States—no easy task, and therefore an intriguing one to explore. Each volume of the series contains an assortment of approximately a dozen articles, essays and interviews by journalists and specialists in their respective fields, followed by a bibliography of important resources on the topic. Their compilation is designed to generate debate and foster research: to complicate our knowledge. Every attempt is made to balance the ideological viewpoint of the authors. The target audience is students, specialists, and the lay reader. Themes will range from politics to sports, from music to cuisine. Historical periods and benchmarks like the Mexican War, the Spanish American War, the Zoot Suit Riots, the Bracero Program, and the Cuban Revolution, as well as controversial topics like Immigration, Bilingual Education, and Spanglish will be tackled.

Democracy is able to thrive only when it engages in an open, honest exchange of information. By offering diverse, insightful volumes about Hispanic life in the United States and inviting people to engage in critical thinking, *The Ilan Stavans Library of Latino Civilization* seeks to open new vistas to appreciate the fastest growing, increasingly heterogeneous minority in the nation—to be part of the *encuentro*.

Ilan Stavans

PREFACE

I remain bewildered by the fact that Cesar Chavez, the labor activist, is arguably the most important Latino figure in the history of the United States yet his work remains unknown by the majority of the country's citizens. The work done by the Chicano leader for the betterment of labor conditions during the Civil Rights era and beyond laid the foundation for a more equal society and was a stepping stone to the 2008 election of Barack Obama to the presidency. But his name is seldom mentioned. This is due in part to the decline of political capital he suffered in the later part of his life, as he survived his own legacy and ceased to be able to mobilize people. But the true blame must be placed on the keepers of that legacy. The United Farm Workers is a shadow organization, besieged by an incessant internal power struggle. Instead of furthering his mission, his successors—relatives and pupils—have wasted precious time in petty rivalries. The result is a face without a message. At present it is utterly impossible to imagine a Latino president of the United States. But when such possibility takes hold, the words of Cesar Chavez will resonate—not without generating welcome discomfort—in the nation's chambers of government.

This volume offers a kaleidoscopic view of Chavez as a multifaceted, if imperfect, agent of change. It starts with a sustained profile of his life and work in the context of the Civil Rights upheaval in general and the Chicano Movement in particular and a scholarly analysis of his ideas and ideals. These are followed by reflections on his rhetorical talents, his capacity to connect with average people, his religiosity and his connection to the Catholic Church, as well as assessments of his decline in the eighties and accusations of the nepotism he received. I've also included fragments from classic reports on his quest for justice by John Gregory Dunne (from *Delano*, chapter 11) and Peter Matthiessen (from *Sal Si Puedes*, epilogue to the University of California Press edition). Tributes by La Raza Party co-founder José Angel Gutiérrez and snapshots by John C. Hammerback and Richard Griswold del Castillo, among others, add to the picture.

My objective in this volume is the opposite of hagiography: an invitation to look at Chavez critically, e.g., constructively.

A note on accents: César Chávez carries acute orthographic accents in Spanish. Some authors include the accents while others don't. I've respected the author's wishes.

PART I
CONSIDERATIONS

Reading César

Ilan Stavans

Once upon a time there were duels; nowadays there are clashes and pitched battles.
——Michel de Montaigne, "On Cowardice"

"The rich have money—and the poor have time." Those were the words of César Chávez in 1991, two years before his death. Is it sheer fancy to suggest that this sentence alone summarizes the dominant concerns of his life? Chávez's life was defined by patience. Patience was his weapon against the grape owners and the Teamsters, against the abuse of the downcast. He had plenty of patience, much more than a normal person, and it was proven in his nonviolent marches, fasts, and petitions "We don't have to win this year or next year or even the year after that," he told his followers. "We'll just keep plugging away, day after day. . . . We will never give up. We have nothing else to do with our lives except to continue in this nonviolent fight."

Of course, there is such a thing as too much patience. How long will it take for Chávez's message to penetrate the American psyche? He's been dead for almost a decade. His name and face adorn schools and public parks. He pops up in advertisements for Macintosh computers, along with John Lennon and the Dalai Lama—"Think Different"! But these ghostlike appearances are empty of all ideological significance, it's a tame Chávez, not the quixotic knight he was; a brand name, as disposable as any celebrity in Hollywood.

My generation is too young to have witnessed Chávez's odyssey from obscurity to legend. My appreciation for his courage and forbearance came indirectly. I learned about him from books, documentaries, and schoolteachers. Every reference to him was cloaked in an aura of sanctity. But as with most saints, it was hard to figure out exactly what he had done on the road to beatitude. No doubt Chávez was the most important Hispanic-American political figure of the twentieth century. But for someone like me, born at the apex of his career, outside the United States, it was almost impossible to lift him from the junk box where icons are stored away and reinsert him into history. Somehow Chávez

---

Ilan Stavans: "Reading Cesar," first published in *Transition 84*, vol. 9, no.4, (2000): 62–76.

the man had become Chávez the statue: pigeons sat motionless on his nose and hands, his beautiful bronze skin corroded by the passing of time.

How can he be rescued from this eclipse? Do his words still have an echo? Have we lost the capacity to appreciate not just a fighter but a true duelist, a crusader capable of reevaluating our preconceptions of the world? What is meaningful about him today? Can his message still speak to us? Americans are obsessed with the radicalism of the 1960s, as epitomized by Malcolm X and the Black Panthers. This obsession is concurrent with a Latin boom, a sudden embrace of Latino music and culture north of the Rio Grande. And yet most Americans couldn't care less about Chávez—especially Latinos. The new Hispanic pride is a profoundly middle-class artifact. It replaces radical politics with consumerism, the gun with the Gap, fasts with Taco Bell. Chávez's face on a billboard goes down easier than any of his injunctions about courage, resilience, commitment. Chávez is not alone: other Latino activists have been shelved as well, from Bernardo Vega and Jesús Colón to Dolores Huerta, Rudolfo "Corky" Gonzáles, and Reies López Tijerina. Even Arthur Alfonso Schomburg, the black historian whose Puerto Rican identity was crucial to his work and life remains a forgotten oddity.

But none of these figures is more emblematic than Chávez. Rumors of a full-length biography surface and then disappear. Very few of his countless speeches have been transcribed, and his occasional writings remain scattered, lost in remote, often inaccessible corners of libraries. Why has no one published a *Portable César Chávez*? Are his politics still too dangerous? Or are they simply irrelevant?

Chávez came from a humble background. He was born in Yuma, Arizona, in 1927, and his family lived on a 160-acre farm not far from town. His grandfather was from Hacienda del Carmen, in Chihuahua, Mexico. He had a slave-like life under authoritarian landowners close to dictator Porfirio Diaz. He was rebellious. The fate of those workers unwilling to cooperate was the draft. But Papa Chayo ran away and crossed the border in El Paso, Texas, eventually moving to the North Gila Valley along the Colorado River. Chávez never quite spelled out his relationship with Mexico, but it's clear that it wasn't colored by nostalgia. Arizona was his home. His father was a businessman. The second of five children and his Dad's right hand, Chávez helped in the crops, chopped wood, and helped with the animals. As he recounted his childhood in the early 1970s, it was a life of hard work, under pressure from heavy taxes. The family was a close niche. But things turned for the worse when Chávez's father lost his holdings during the Depression.

Like many other families, the Chávezes eventually moved to California in search of better opportunities, only to find jobs picking cotton, grapes, and carrots, following the sun and the season from one migrant camp to another. Chávez never finished high school. Segregation was a fixture in the landscape. He once recalled:

> We went this one time to a diner. There was a sign on the door "White Trade Only" but we went anyway. We had heard that they had these big hamburgers, and we wanted one. There was a blond, blue-eyed girl behind the counter, a

> beauty. She asked what we wanted—real though you know?—and when we ordered a hamburger, she said, "We don't sell to Mexicans," and she laughed when she said it. She enjoyed doing that, laughing at us. We went out, but I was real mad. Enraged. It had to do with my manhood.

The education he got was unstable because of the itinerant life that field labor carried with it. He once said he attended some sixty-five elementary schools, some "for a day, a week, or a few months." At the age of nineteen, he joined the Agricultural Workers' Union. The Union existed in name only—the organizing drive to create it was unsuccessful—but the struggle gave him a taste of the challenges ahead. After a couple of years in the Navy during World War II, Chávez returned to California, where he married Helen, whom he met in Delano—her parents had come from Mexico and one of them had fought in the revolution of 1910—and with whom he eventually had eight children. He returned to the migrant's life but also found the time to read about historical figures. It was around 1952 that he met and was inspired by the work of organizer Fred Ross, a leader of the Community Services Organization, which was supported by the Chicago-based Saul Alinsky. Ross and Alinsky channeled important ideas and concepts to Chávez, from which he developed his own philosophy of struggle. Many had already tried to organize the Mexican migrant workers to improve their miserable working conditions. But it took Chávez's charisma—*su simpatia*—to move mountains. By the time he was 33, he was organizing families in the grape fields and persuading growers to increase wages. His strategy was simple: straight talk and honesty. If he was to become a spokesman for the workers, he would also be a model for them. And role models require commitment and sacrifice.

The National Farm Workers Union was created in 1962, with Chávez as its president. It was the year of the Cuban Missile Crisis, and U.S.–Latin American relations were in peril. The organization grew quickly and changed its name a few times in the 1960s before christening itself the United Farm Workers. Chávez solidified the organization's Chicano base, opened up membership to the Filipino community, and forged links with other like-minded groups, most notably the small community of black farm workers. By the mid-sixties, he had become a beloved folk hero to the poor and to the boisterous student movement, and public enemy number one to conservative California businessmen and politicians—especially Governor Ronald Reagan. Unlike many other leaders of the civil rights era, Chávez combined activism with environmentalism—a combination that would make him a darling of the contemporary environmentalist movement, if only they cared. His struggle to improve labor conditions was also a fight against pesticides.

It has often been said that Chávez wasn't a rhetorician: unlike Martin Luther King Jr. or Julian Bond, Chávez had little talent for highbrow oratory. Still, he had an astonishing ability to redefine audiences, to make them act in a different way. He had an inspired message, a clear vision of his place in history, and faithful listeners to whom he gave a sense of shared history. With the listeners he embarked on a crusade idealistic yet practical that attempted to redefine labor relations in America. He lived life spontaneously, and he responded to every occasion with speeches and responses that were neither preconceived nor sophisticated. Yet he was eloquent, precisely because his improvisational, pragmatic mind always found what was needed. "[You] are looking for a miracle, a leader who will do everything for us," he once said. "It doesn't happen. People have to do the work." Elsewhere, he said, "Nothing changes until the individual changes." And indeed, Chávez was an astonishing teacher, a true role model of the kind that comes along only once in a generation.

Chávez's strategic approach to leadership was symbolized by his confrontation with the Teamsters. The Teamsters and the UFW had forged an uneasy peace: in 1970, they signed a pact that gave Chávez jurisdiction over the fields, while the teamsters had control over the packing sheds. But in 1973, when Chávez was at the height of his powers, the liaison collapsed: the teamsters signed a contract with growers for lower wages in the field. It was a major blow to the Chicano leader; his support fell precipitously, from some fifty thousand followers to fewer than fifteen thousand. Suddenly, Chávez's simple, honest speeches seemed empty. There was talk of financial mismanagement; conventional wisdom held that the UFW was finished. Chávez himself was losing hope—he referred to those years as "the worst of our times." But he was nothing if not determined. The smaller UFW continued to march, and the grape boycott began to make an impact. Within a few years, Jerry Brown was the progressive governor of California, and Chávez was again a hero.

Chávez's patient heroism struck a chord in America, a nation that loves underdogs. He once received a telegram from Martin Luther King Jr.: "As brothers in the fight for equality," it read in part, "I extend the hands of fellowship and good will and wish continuing success to you and your members. . . . We are together with you in spirit and in determination that our dreams for a better tomorrow will be realized." But Chávez's heroism did not win him much of a following in Mexico, where militancy of any sort makes the government nervous. Of course, Mexicans love revolutionaries, and there were those among the left-wing intelligentsia who idolized Chávez. They saw him as a guerrilla leader on the order of Emiliano Zapata, a man of the people, a prophet—North America's Mahatma Gandhi. But most Mexicans—especially those in the middle and upper classes—never thought much about Chávez; the UFW was simply irrelevant, a footnote in the history books. No attempt was made to reclaim him as a Mexican. Chávez was a leader of the Chicano movement of the 1960s, the first sustained bout of Hispanic activism in American history, but Mexicans have never really identified with Chicanos. Chicanos are traitors; they are the Mexicans who left and never looked back, the ones that put themselves, their ambitions, before everyone else. (This attitude toward Chicanos is hypocritical—Mexico's economy depends heavily on its emigrants. Where would the country be without that endless flow of precious U.S. dollars?)

Why didn't we embrace him? It wasn't just apathy; the rise of Chávez on the world stage coincided with the rise of the Mexican counterculture—and the government's fumbling yet brutal attempts to subdue it. In 1968 thousands of students were massacred in Tlatelolco Square. The American civil rights movements, black *and* brown, received an icy reception from official

Mexico. As for the Mexican people, our attention was focused locally, on the events that were tearing our own country apart.

It was only in my early twenties, after I came to the United States, that I began to understand Chávez's urge to change the world. In streets and public schools along the Southwest, his name was ubiquitous—a legend, a myth. I wanted to get to know him, to recognize the scope and nature of his revolution. I read everything about him I could find. Sometimes, I saw myself in the pages, and sometimes I found myself overwhelmed by a sense of detachment. An outsider looking in, a north-bound Spanish-speaking Caucasian. Could I see myself reflected in Chávez's eyes? Or was he an icon for another Mexico, another me? Why hadn't I learned more about him in school?

I was glad to find that the story of Chávez and La Causa, as his movement became known, had been chronicled dozens of times, by any number of interpreters. But many of these books felt disjoined, even apathetic. Several authors scrutinized the Chicano leader with academic tools that turned him into an artifact. Then there was John Gregory Dunne's *Delano: The Story of the California Grape Strike*, a highly informed if somewhat detached portrait; Jacques E. Levy's pastiche of memories and anecdotes, *César Chávez: Autobiography of La Causa*; and Richard B. Taylor's mesmerizing *Chávez and the Farm Workers*. But the book that brought Chávez home to me, the one that allowed me to share his dreams, was Peter Matthiessen's *Sal Si Puedes*—an honest, lucid picture of the internal and external upheaval that marked the Chicano leader in his most influential years. In later accounts of La Causa, Matthiessen's journalistic portrait is held in high esteem—panoramic yet finely detailed, knowing, and elegant. Nat Hentoff said the book offered a view of a battlefield where the fight is not only for the agricultural workers but for the redemption of [the whole] country."

I recently reread *Sal Si Puedes* and felt a sense of exhilaration. The book is a kind of aleph that allows the Chicano movement to come alive again, and it gives Chávez's message a much-needed urgency. Somewhere in its early pages Matthiessen admits that he knew he would be impressed by Chávez, but he didn't foresee how startling their encounter would prove to be. After a few weeks in his company, Matthiessen realized the organizer was also organizing him. The author has the same feelings the reader does: first admiration, then awe.

It was the summer of 1968 when Matthiessen first visited Chávez. They were the same age: forty-one. Matthiessen lived in New York City, and he was introduced to Chávez by a common friend, Ann Israel, who had been helping to organize East Coast farm workers. At one point, Israel asked Matthiessen to edit copy for an advertisement about pesticides—not only what they did to crops, but also what they did to the people who worked in the fields. The ad was for the *New York Times*, and Israel wanted to make sure the English was perfect; she was very pleased with Matthiessen when she saw his draft. They struck up a friendship, and one day, she mentioned César Chávez. Matthiessen said he was a great admirer, so Israel took him to Delano, California, where Matthiessen met the Chicano leader. Chávez's grace and intelligence were seductive. It turned out that both men had been in the army around the same time. They shared many passions, including boxing; they both favored

Sugar Ray Leonard. Matthiessen would later write a description of Chávez that has become a landmark:

> The man who has threatened California has an Indian's bow nose and lank black hair, with sad eyes and an open smile that is shy and friendly; at moments he is beautiful, like a dark seraph. He is five feet six inches tall, and, since his twenty-five-day fast the previous winter, has weighed no more than one hundred and fifty pounds. Yet the word "slight" does not properly describe him. There is an effect of being centered in himself so that no energy is wasted, an effect of density; at the same time, he walks as lightly as a fox. One feels immediately that this man does not stumble, and that to get where he is going he will walk all day.

Upon his return to New York, Matthiessen got in touch with William Shawn, the editor at the *New Yorker*, and suggested a profile on Chávez. Shawn had sponsored Matthiessen's earlier trips to South America and Alaska; he was receptive to the idea. Matthiessen returned to California, this time to Sal Si Puedes, the San José barrio where Chávez lived and where his career as a union organizer took off. The result was a two-part article, published on June 21 and 28, 1969. It was one of the first pieces on social justice ever to appear in the *New Yorker*, and one of the first articles in a national magazine about César Chávez and the Farm Workers' movement. When Matthiessen gave his *New Yorker* fee to the UFW, Chávez was deeply grateful.

I felt inspired when I first read Matthiessen. For some years I had been infatuated with the California counterculture of the 1960s—the hippie movement of the Haight Ashbury, Carlos Castañeda's fascination with *peyote* and his quest for Don Juan Matos, the music of the Beach Boys. Through *Sal Si Puedes* I discovered the seething political underground, the world in which César Chávez came into his own. It was a revelation to me: California was not all about alternative states of mind but, more emphatically, about courageous political alternatives and attempts to redefine the social texture, about racial and class struggle. From there, I was able to trace other radical figures in the Chicano community, such as Oscar "Zeta" Acosta, who appears as a three-hundred-pound Samoan in Hunter S. Thompson's *Fear and Loathing in Las Vegas*. Of course, there is a huge gap between Chávez and Zeta. It may even be sacrilegious to invoke the two in unison. Physically and mentally unstable, Zeta was a lawyer and activist, the author of *The Autobiography of a Brown Buffalo* and *The Revolt of the Cockroach People*, a brilliant outlaw, a *forajido* never quite ready to put his cards on the table. He might have done more harm than good to the Chicano movement. Chávez, to whom he paid a personal visit, was a full-fledged revolutionary, the true fountainhead of the Chicano movement.

For César Chávez, patience and sacrifice are siblings. He pairs them in a way that only American prophets can, mixing utopian vision with an enviable sense of practicality. The essayist Richard Rodriguez once described Chávez as "wielding a spiritual authority." It is that spirituality—his use of prayer in marches, the realization that the power of his followers' faith is stronger than anything else—that is so inspiring. When his betrayal by the Teamsters brought him low, Catholics around the country rallied for Chávez; church leaders supported him. What did they see in Chávez? A Christ figure, perhaps; a modest man of overpowering charisma; a man unafraid to speak the truth. In 1974 a reporter for the Christian Century wrote that she was "puzzled at the power of such an uncompromising person to command so much loyalty from so many." The entire quest for social justice and commitment, for patience and honesty, cannot but be seen in these terms. Chávez came from a devout Catholic background and he often invoked Christ in his speeches. "I can't ask people to sacrifice if I don't sacrifice myself," he said. Or, "Fighting for social justice is one of the profoundest ways in which man can say yes to man's dignity, and that really means sacrifice. There is no way on this earth in which you can say yes to man's dignity and know that you're going to be spared some sacrifice."

That Chávez allowed a perfect stranger like Peter Matthiessen to enter his life for a period of almost three years—making room at his own dinner table, bringing him along to union meetings, introducing him to friends—is proof of his generosity. But there was also self-interest: Chávez saw an opportunity to compound his notoriety and consolidate his power. Matthiessen did not disappoint. He portrays Chávez critically but responsibly; the leader is seen as enterprising, the owner of an unadulterated vitality, capable of minor lapses but overall a prophet ahead of his time.

More than thirty years later, Sal Si Puedes is less reportage than living history; a whole era comes alive in its pages: Black Power, backlash, the antiwar movement, the browning of the labor movement, the greening of the browns. Taken with Joan Didion's The White Album, it's an indispensable guide to the 1960s, when America was changed forever. The 1980s were difficult for Chávez. He had grown weary and depressed. The media alternately ignored him and attacked him. He still lived in the Gila River Valley. The grape strike and the confrontation with the Teamsters were buried deep in the past. People in general had grown impatient with activism. His home was with the migrant workers, to whom he had devoted his life. But the heyday of the labor movement was over, overwhelmed by the conservative avalanche that brought Reagan and Bush to power. Scholars such as John C. Hammerback and Richard J. Jensen define that last period as "the unfinished last boycott." The cultural climate was different. Chávez, like a chameleon, ceased to be a leader speaking to his constituency and assumed the role of lecturer. In speeches given in the college circuit, he emphasized the power of teaching and amplified his message so as to encompass not only Chicanos in the Southwest but people from all racial backgrounds anywhere in the country. In doing so, though, he watered down the message. "How could we progress as a people," he claimed in a 1984 speech, "even if we lived in the cities, while farm workers—men and women of colors—were condemned to a life without pride?"

From Chicano to men and women of color, the politics of language was actually more treacherous. A growing Latino middle class—what historian Rudolfo Acuña, in his book Occupied America, defined as "the brokers"—embraced ambivalence as its worldview. It got closer to Spanglish and began to see itself as the owner of a hyphenated identity, a life in between. The shift was perceived as a ticket toward assimilation. This middle class, eager to cross over, started to be courted by savvy politicians and by a merchandise-oriented society. It was clear that the mainstream was ready to open its arms only if Chicanos were ready to define themselves elastically enough so as to become "Hispanics," the rubric that predeceases "Latinos," large enough to also encompass those hailing from Puerto Rico, Cuba, Ecuador, and El Salvador, for example.

But as time went by this polycephalic minority ceased to be acquainted with César Chávez. It no longer recognized the leader's struggles as its own. One comes to America dreaming of a better world, it was announced loud and clear, and in the process, one learns to consume and be consumed. I once heard a friend of Chávez say that he'd had "the fortunate misfortune" to have avoided martyrdom. Unlike Martin Luther King Jr. or Malcolm X, he had outlived himself, outlived his message. His exuberance and self-confidence were replaced by a strange silence. Rumors from within the UFW described him as sectarian. Those that had not stayed and fought were received with indifference; Matthiessen felt some of that reticence when he told Chávez that he was thinking of writing a sequel to *Sal Si Puedes*. Chávez's response was ambiguous, even reluctant. The effort went nowhere. Perhaps we should feel fortunate that it didn't, for the best of Chávez had already been recorded.

Survival, sacrifice. When Chávez died in 1993, thousands gathered at his funeral. It was a clear sign of how beloved a figure he had been, how significant his life had been. President Bill Clinton spoke of him as "an authentic hero to millions of people throughout the world," and described him as "an inspiring fighter." And Jerry Brown called him a visionary who sought "a more cooperative society." In the media Chávez was portrayed as "a national metaphor for justice, humanity, equality, and freedom." Matthiessen himself wrote an obituary for the *New Yorker*. "A man so unswayed by money," he wrote, "a man who (despite many death threats) refused to let his bodyguards go armed, and who offered his entire life to the service of others, [is] not to be judged by the same standards of some self-serving labor leader or politician. . . . Anger was a part of Chávez, and so was a transparent love for humankind."

It is left to us, though, his successors, those who never had the privilege to meet him, the millions of Latinos capable of realizing that middle-class life ought not be a form of blindness, to ponder his legacy. Yes, the rise of consumerism and the disenfranchisement of reformism might have pushed Chávez to the fringes. At first sight his ethos in the field might have little to say to our angst, the one that colors the way we zigzag ourselves through Hispanic history in the United States. But it is an outright mistake to let our class differences obliterate the bridges between us. It is true that toward the end of his sixty-five-year-long career, César Chávez and America parted ways. Yet it is the leader valiant enough to redefine his roots, devoted to make America more pliant, that we most reread and thereafter reclaim, a dreamer that proved that wealth and a formal education aren't everything, that humankind is not about getting ahead of everyone else but getting ahead together. Not Chávez the myth but Chávez the ordinary man—neither the name nor the face but the message, "Let's enable common people to do uncommon things"—awaits attention. In the attempt to agglutinate us all under a single rubric, his Chicano self must be opened up to embrace all Americans, particularly all of those with diverse Hispanic backgrounds. Perhaps it was diversity that killed him. But we can reassess his message, for plurality is inspiring only when the whole doesn't devour the parts. The fact that Chávez was Mexican is significant but not confining; his Mexicanness, he showed us—and now I see—is a lesson in universality.

Toward the end of *Sal Si Puedes*, Matthiessen records a few lines told to him by a black migrant farm worker: "But you know what I—what I really think? You know what I really think? I really think that one day the world will be great. I really believe the world gonna be great one day." This was Chávez's own view as well: a better world, built one step at a time, without exclusionary laws, one harmonious enough for every person. He believed democracy to be the best political system of government, a view he learned to appreciate not from his ancestral Mexico but from and in the United States. He was a great advocate of it, even though his foes at times portrayed him as anti-democratic. What he learned about democracy he learned in the hard way—through punches and clashes. But he was patient. In order for democracy to work, Chávez liked to say, "People must want it to." And he added, "To make it work [for us all], we have to work at it full time."

Negotiating César

Jorge Mariscal

We want radical change. Nothing short of radical change is going to have any impact on our lives or our problems. We want sufficient power to control our own destinies. This is our struggle.

—César Estrada Chávez

An aggressive militancy, symbolized by the ubiquitous image of Ernesto Che Guevara, pervaded the discourse and activities of the Chicano movement in the late 1960s in the Southwest. This militancy is visible in the fiery rhetoric of Reies López Tijerina, the charismatic leadership of Rodolfo Corky Gonzáles, and the paramilitary formations of the Brown and Black Berets. In this context, the figure of César Chávez and his philosophy of nonviolence strike us as incongruous.[1] Armando Navarro writes: "The militant actions of Tijerina and Gonzales, coupled with the nonviolent direct action of Chavez, provided role models for both students and barrio youth" (1995, 23).[2] Navarro is surely correct, yet in retrospect we are struck by the incompatibility of the different leadership styles practiced by *los jefes*. F. Arturo Rosales notes as much when he points out: "Interestingly, the leader of the farmworkers, César Chávez, contrasted sharply with other Chicano leaders. The former farmworker . . . did not possess an imposing figure; he did not swagger or project a tough persona as did many militant activists of the era. Chávez's short stature and soft-spoken, quiet demeanor was often mistaken for the stereotypical look of passivity rather than forceful leadership" (1997, 130–31).

For some contemporary observers of the Movimiento, Chávez was the necessary complement to the more traditional "warrior" styles of Corky Gonzales and López Tijerina. Three weeks before he was assassinated by law enforcement agents on August 29, 1970, *Los Angeles Times* reporter Ruben Salazar offered this analysis of the Chicano movement: "César is our only real leader . . . [Gonzáles and Tijerina] rant and rave and threaten to burn the establishment down. That's good because most people won't listen unless you rant and rave. But this provides the community with little more than emotional uplift;

Jorge Mariscal: "Negotiating César," reprinted with permission of The Regents of the University of California from *Azlan: A Journal of Chicano Studies* 29, no. 1 (Spring 2004), UCLA Chicano Studies Research Center.

nothing palpable" (Gómez 1982, 501). In retrospect, Salazar's assertion that Gonzales and Tijerina produced no concrete gains for their communities and functioned merely as a rhetorical sideshow is open to debate. Ironically, even as moderates like Salazar designated Chávez as the only authentic Chicano leader, young activists criticized him for being too narrowly focused on one issue and too conciliatory toward traditional liberal organizations such as the Democratic Party.

In this essay I will trace the complex and often contradictory relationship between César Chávez and the various sectors of the Chicano movement during the crucial period of the American war in Southeast Asia.[3] To do so, I will draw upon the entire field of discursive practices that contributed to the construction of multiple images of Chávez and the ways in which these images were put to political use. Chávez's own self-fashioning, his public statements and actions, will make up one area of inquiry, but this will be complemented by journalistic, artistic, and literary representations of the leader as well as critiques from both the political right and the political left. By mapping the broader cultural field in order to understand what the figure of César Chávez signified for various groups, I do not adhere to the naive empiricist notion that so-called historical sources (archival documents, testimonials, and so forth) are somehow more authoritative (that is, "real") than cultural materials. A passage in a novel or a poem dedicated to La Causa, for example, may have had as much to do with the construction of Chávez as a powerful sign for the Movimiento as did the actualized practices of the fast and the march, themselves to a great extent political and artistic interventions rooted in Mexican cultural traditions. Rather than seeking access to "what really happened" during the movement period construed as a totalized and objective historical whole, I am interested in charting the ideological systems that generated a diverse array of organizational styles, political languages, and leaders.

The reinsertion of the public figure of César Chávez into the rich discursive archive that was the Vietnam War period will help us to understand the interplay among various sectors of the politicized Chicano/a community and the ways in which these sectors negotiated with Chávez as both leader and symbol. The contrast to which I alluded above between Chávez's public figure and those of other movement leaders, for example, produces on one level "points of incompatibility" (following Michel Foucault's archaeological method). However, what seem to be incompatible historical agents are in fact all consequences of the same general set of social relations or discursive constellation that I will call the "critique of liberalism." That diverse movement figures and organizations assumed different forms in their realization of that critique does not signify a "weakness" in the movement. According to Foucault's concept of discursive formations, the relationships among cultural and political objects or statements that appear to be in conflict are not gaps or flaws: "Instead of constituting a mere defect of coherence, they form an alternative . . . [and] are characterized as link points of systematization. . . . One describes it rather as a unity of distribution that opens a field of possible options, and enables various mutually exclusive architectures to appear side by side or in turn" (1972, 65–66). At issue, therefore, are not historical figures as metaphors or images created by subjective "perceptions" but rather the manner in which discursive objects participate in political projects and thereby exercise a direct impact on material conditions, in this instance as part of a major social movement created by ethnic Mexicans in the United States.[4]

By the time of the Delano grape strike in late 1965, the political, cultural, and economic project that was the National Farm Workers Association (NFWA) and later the United Farm Workers Organizing Committee (UFWOC) and the United Farm Workers (UFW) had already established the groundwork for the multiple forms of Chicano/a activism that emerged in the final years of the decade. Years before the full-blown Movimiento burst onto the historical stage, the NFWA had become a classic version of what Raymond Williams (1989) called a "militant particularism"—in which a group of workers in a specific geographical locale, faced with intolerable conditions, organize to change those conditions for the better. But the particularities of the farmworkers' struggle spoke to a wide range of related issues that affected virtually every Mexican American community in the United States during the Vietnam War period. As other militant particularisms developed across the Southwest, the UFW functioned as an affective link and practical training ground for movement organizations with diverse agendas. In a dialectical and often contradictory process, the union's project fed into an emergent cultural nationalism and provided it with a repertoire of symbols and tropes even as it worked against the construction of a sectarian ethnicity-based identity by insisting on multiethnic coalition building and international solidarity with workers around the world.[5]

By both underwriting and destabilizing a "resistance identity" designed to create a collective subject based on shared cultural traits ("our essentially different life style" invoked in the Plan de Santa Barbara [Muñoz 1989, 191]), the UFW indirectly assisted in the formulation of a more radical Chicano/a "project identity" that critiqued the entire structure of U.S. capitalism at home and abroad (Castells 1997, 8). I will argue, therefore, that just as the Movimiento is inconceivable without the UFW, the most dramatic successes of the UFW are inconceivable without the Movimiento in its emergent stages within the broader radicalized condition of U.S. society, especially among youth. For many non-Latino activists, the efforts of the UFW embodied a utopian project composed of diverse ethnic groups and classes. As one observer put it:

> Something remarkable has happened in the town of Delano, something that a scant few months ago no one foresaw. A pattern for a New America has emerged out of the chaos of a bitter labor dispute, the pattern of people of all races and backgrounds working and living together in perfect and unprecedented harmony. Idealistic people in other parts of America talk about this ideal; in Delano today it is working. When the strike began last September "Huelga" meant only that: "Strike." But something has happened along the way; "Huelga" has come to mean something more than "Strike"; it has come to mean cooperation, brotherhood, Love. (Nelson 1966, 122)

The distance between this statement, written in 1965, and the subsequent Summer of Love in 1967, the youth counter-culture, and the antiwar and Third World people's movements is not terribly great. The connection between César Chávez and the revolutionary period of the 1960s was perhaps best captured in the title of Peter Matthiessen's classic book first published in 1969: *Sal Si Puedes (Escape If You Can): Cesar Chavez and the New American Revolution*. According to Matthiessen's ambivalent characterization, this new "American Revolution" was an "American renaissance" led by young radicals whose "philosophical poverty and abrasive attitudes should not obscure the fact that these people are forming the front line in a *necessary* revolution" (2000, 113; emphasis in original).[6]

But how exactly did César Chávez fit into the panorama of 1960s radicalism? As we shall see, Chávez's unconventional leadership, drawing on religious and pacifist traditions, placed some Chicanos in the movement in the uncomfortable position of balancing the admiration they held for him with a preference many of them also held for warrior models of manhood. One of the more militant Chicano writers unfavorably compared Chávez to Che Guevara. Nephtalí de León's play, *¡Chicanos! The Living and the Dead!*, places Che in direct confrontation with Chávez's philosophy (represented by the character Manuel) and argues that nonviolence is of no use to Chicanos:

> Manuel: Yet there are many of us who had and still have faith. César Chávez has faith and look how far he has advanced.

> Che (somewhat exasperated): And how far is that hermano? Don't our people still do stoop labor? Only it's by contract now. Now they are really true slaves, for they have told the yankee farmers: "We will sell our bodies and our souls to you, but only if you promise us you'll buy them!" He should have asked not for contracts to pick grapes or lettuce, but for contracts for an education and a preparation to cope with the technical-industrial age that now governs the world—an age that still enslaves him and his people. How different are California's farm laborers from the Chinese peasants who sweat their lives away stuck in their rice paddies? No, Manuel, my heart has bled for Cesar, a giant of a man, stuck by his children into that earth that enslaves him and his people. While America basks in plenty, our dear brown Saint starves with his brothers and sweats his life out for a contract that has chained them. (de León 1972a, 61–62)

The criticism voiced by el Che, one of the more powerful symbols of the Movimiento, is harsh but captures some of the tensions that existed in left-leaning activist circles with regard to the objectives of the UFW. Elsewhere in his writings, however, de León praises Chávez (without sarcasm) as a "modern prince of peace," "a very human man," and "one of those rare happenings that occur every time a people are oppressed and every time the universe and man join hands to yield us such a being" (1972b, 43). The contradiction in de León's writing underscores the dilemma Chávez presented to movement militants. What many of them did not understand well were the origins of Chávez's spiritual praxis and its function in a time of revolutionary rhetoric, police brutality in the barrios, and massive military aggression in Southeast Asia.

In a curious column that appeared in an issue of the UFW newspaper *El Malcriado* (52: 22), it was announced that the papers official logo would be Don

Don Quijote

and

his

creator

Don Quijote

Figure 1: Don Quixote with UFW Eagle (1966). Drawing by unknown artist. Used by permission of United Farm Workers of America, AFL-CIO.

Quixote (see fig. 1). Wearing a UFW button on his lapel and with the union eagle on his shield, this farmworker version of Cervantes's *caballero andante* would be "a Quixote who represents accurately the spirit of our struggle, always in good humor in spite of the risk." According to the unnamed author:

> Quixote symbolizes the spirit of man which always believes in human strength; in defense of the weak; in protection of women and children; in sacrifice for one's fellow-men; in the struggle against evil; in the light against the powerful in favor of the disinherited; he represents these and many similar things, in the spirit of battle even when there are not enough resources for it, in the great causes in which man has involved himself.

What is interesting about this attempt to link the traditional image of Quixote to the farmworker movement is that it invokes both idealism and militancy at the same time.[7] Although Cervantes's character never killed anyone, his actions were at times quite violent, and at one point in the 1605 novel he is denounced by another character whose leg he has broken. The column in *El Mal-*

criado develops the theme of militancy by devoting some space to Cervantes himself. It specifically emphasizes his career as a soldier and participant in the battle of Lepanto, the 1571 naval conflict in which Catholic forces defeated the Muslim Ottoman Turks. According to the UFW author, Lepanto was "the first act in the establishment of what we now call 'Western Civilization.'"

Cervantes and Don Quixote, then, represented both the defense of traditional Catholic/Western values and the idealistic struggle to defend the disenfranchised. Whatever the traces of Eurocentrism that informed this interpretation of Don Quixote, the emphasis for the UFW writer fell primarily upon the call to service and social activism. The key ideological link, therefore, was to be found in the idea of "militancy," a concept Chávez himself had written about in reference to Dr. Martin Luther King Jr.: "His nonviolence was that of action—not that of one contemplating action" (1968a, 5). Chávez's distinction is between the "philosopher of nonviolence" and the active practitioner of nonviolence in the pursuit of justice. It was this latter idea that would inform Chávez's entire career.

HYBRID AND HYPER-MASCULINITIES

We must respect all human life, in the cities and in the fields and in Vietnam. Nonviolence is the only weapon that is compassionate and recognizes each man's value.

—César Estrada Chávez

In terms of his political persona, Chávez presented urban Chicanas and Chicanos with a form of masculinity virtually unknown outside the Catholicism of their *abuelitas*.[8] At its very core was the principle of "militant nonviolence." Seemingly an oxymoron, the phrase retains a commitment to social change but disassociates that commitment from aggression against other individuals or groups by incorporating a strong Christian-based empathy for the oppressor. Nonviolent change, therefore, is to be sought not only on the level of institutions but in the very attitudes of the antagonist. In their practical effects, Chávez's actions constructed a hybrid form of masculinity that combined "passive" elements most often linked by Western patriarchal structures to "feminine" subjectivities with a fearless determination that traditional gendered representations have reserved exclusively for "masculine" practices.

At the core of this hybrid agency is the belief that by resorting to physical violence the political activist is actually admitting his or her own weakness. A nonviolent approach requires a deeper and more sustained engagement. According to Chávez, "In some instances nonviolence requires more militancy than violence. Nonviolence forces you to abandon the shortcut in trying to make a change in the social order" (1969, 27). This is essentially what Martin Luther King Jr. advocated consistently throughout his career. Shortly before his death, Dr. King told an interviewer: "To be militant merely means to be demanding and to be persistent, and in this sense I think the nonviolent movement has demonstrated great militancy. It is possible to be militantly nonviolent" (Washington 1986, 661). In one of his most succinct definitions of nonviolence as he practiced it, Chávez articulated a similar view: "Our conviction is that human life and limb are a very special possession given by God to man and that no one has the right to take that away, in any cause, however just. . . . Also we are convinced that nonviolence is more powerful than violence. . . . We operate on the theory that men who are involved and truly concerned about people are not by nature violent. If they were violent they couldn't have that love and that concern for people" (1970, 1). As he would many times during his public life, Chávez argued that those who resort to violence do so because of their inability to organize their constituencies in an effective way.

Although neither Chávez's nor King's concept of nonviolence was as deeply wed to an elaborate religious and philosophical framework as was Mahatma Gandhi's method of *satyagraha* ("holding to truth"), in which the spiritual soul-force of existence triumphs over material reality, both men drew freely from Gandhi's practical methods.[9] Chávez's use of the fast, for example, combined Catholic practices with Gandhian ideas about self-purification. According to Gandhi's reading of the *Gita* and *Upanisads*, fasting ought not be used to produce direct political effects but rather to cleanse the sensory perceptions and strengthen the moral resolve of the subject and potentially facilitate a spiritual change of heart in the adversary.

In the Gandhian view, fasting as coercion designed to force specific political concessions was itself a form, albeit a lesser form, of violence, and ultimately could only produce a violent reaction (Borman 1986, 107).[10] Upon ending one of his more famous fasts on March 10, 1968, Chávez explained his use of the fast: "Some of you still wonder about its meaning and importance. It was not intended as a pressure against any growers. For that reason we have suspended negotiations and arbitration proceedings and relaxed the militant picketing and boycotting of the strike during this period. I undertook the fast because my heart was filled with grief and pain for the sufferings of farmworkers. The fast was first for me and then for all of us in this Union. It was a fast for nonviolence and a call to sacrifice" (1968c).[11] Three years later in an informal talk in which he elaborated on the negative consequences produced by the combination of large financial contributions and unions, he argued that the fast was an organizing tool of greater value than traditional fundraising. The fast modeled the sacrifice demanded of all supporters: "When you sacrifice, you force others to sacrifice. It's an extremely powerful weapon. When somebody finally stops eating for a week or ten days, people come and want to be part of that experience. Someone goes to jail and people want to help him. You don't buy that with money. That doesn't have any price in terms of dollars" (1971).

While Chávez modeled a Mexican American variation on Christian asceticism and studied the works of Gandhi, Aquinas, and St. Paul, young Chicano militants were reading Fanon and Che Guevara (Yinger 1975, 25).[12] Nonetheless, Chávez's rhetoric at times intersected with that of leaders elsewhere in the movement. In what seems an unlikely pairing, two photographs that shared the wall of Chávez's office at UFW headquarters were those of the pacifist Gandhi and of the armed revolutionary Emiliano Zapata. The word "revolution" had appeared in UFW documents as early as 1966, in Chávez's letter written before the march to Sacramento. With the Mexican Revolution as its primary inspiration, the letter portrayed Mexican Americans as the heirs to a tradition of insurgency, and invoked the historical fact that the Southwest was a conquered land whose original inhabitants had been colonized by foreigners: "Delano is [the farmworkers] 'cause,' his great demand for justice, freedom, and respect from a predominantly foreign cultural community in a land where he was first. The revolutions of Mexico were primarily uprisings of the poor, fighting for bread and for dignity. The Mexican American is also a child of the revolution. Pilgrimage, penance, and revolution. The pilgrimage from Delano to Sacramento has strong religio-cultural overtones. But it is also the pilgrimage of a cultural minority who have suffered from a hostile environment, and a minority who means business" (Yinger 1975, 106).[13] Chávez would claim that the religious underpinnings of his beliefs did not diminish the radical nature of his political objectives. The phrase "means business" invokes a more traditional form of masculinity premised upon the threat of physical action, but links it to religious practices associated with saintliness. The hybrid nature of Chávez's masculinity maintained these tensions in a precarious balance throughout the various stages of his public life.[14]

To "mean business" nonviolently was precisely what Dr. King had proposed in his use of the term "nonviolent gadflies" to describe militant activists. Taking the "gadfly" image associated with Socrates, King argued that to mean business, at least in the initial stages of a social movement, was to demand the attention of the powerful in order to shine light on the problems of the disempowered. According to the 1963 "Letter from the Birmingham Jail," nonviolent militancy, far from being a passive stance, was designed to create a crisis of consciousness within the ranks of the ruling majority: "Nonviolent direct action seeks to create such a crisis and establish such creative tension that a community that has constantly refused to negotiate is forced to confront the issue. It seeks so to dramatize the issue that it can no longer be ignored" (Washington 1986, 291). Less than two years later, he elaborated on the pedagogical goals of mass mobilization: "Our nonviolent direct action program has as its objective not the creation of tensions, but the surfacing of tensions already present. We set out to precipitate a crisis situation that must open the door to negotiation. I am not afraid of the words 'crisis' and 'tension.' I deeply oppose violence, but constructive crisis and tension are necessary for growth. . . . To cure injustices, you must expose them before the light of human conscience and the bar of public opinion, regardless of whatever tensions that exposure generates" (350).

César Chávez understood that the strategy of nonviolent militancy would expose to the light of day not only the plight of the invisible farmworker but the conditions of the vast majority of ethnic Mexicans in the United States. In the 1969 "Good Friday Letter" addressed to a California grower who had accused the UFW of using violent tactics, Chávez presented a brilliant analysis not only of the farmworkers' situation but also of the demands and aspirations of Chicanos and Chicanas in urban centers across the Southwest. Three sections in particular suggest the ways in which Chávez's analysis participated in the discursive field I have called the "critique of liberalism." In light of these correspondences, Chávez's occasional reluctance to refer to himself as a Chicano movement leader can be seen as unfortunate; they reveal his profound understanding of what the Movimiento, in all of its diverse sectors, took to be its principal issues and political objectives:

> The color of our skins, the languages of our cultural and native origins, the lack of formal education, the exclusion from the democratic process, the numbers of our slain in recent wars—all these burdens generation after generation have sought to demoralize us, to break our human spirit. But God knows that we are not beasts of burden, we are not agricultural implements or rented slaves, we are men. . . .

> While we do not belittle or underestimate our adversaries, for they are the rich and the powerful and possess the land, we are not afraid nor do we cringe from the confrontation. We welcome it! We have planned for it. We know that our cause is just, that history is a story of social revolutions, and that the poor shall inherit the land. . . .

> We advocate militant nonviolence as our means for social revolution and to achieve justice for our people, but we are not blind or deaf to the desperate and moody winds of human frustration, impatience and rage that blow among us. Gandhi himself admitted that if his only choices were cowardice or violence, he would choose violence. Men are not angels and the time and tides wait for no man. Precisely because of these powerful human emotions, we have tried to involve masses of people in their own struggle. Participation and self-determination remain the best experience of freedom; and free men instinctively prefer democratic change and even protect the rights guaranteed to seek it. Only the enslaved in despair have need of violent overthrow. (quoted in Yinger 1975, 112)

If Che Guevara had dreamed of a society in which "new men and women" would fundamentally transform the nature of capitalist social relations, Chávez saw the union as a means to decolonize the farmworkers' subjectivity and sufficiently transform surrounding conditions, albeit without addressing the farmworkers' place in the relations of production. Chávez argued that farmworkers, with their "natural dignity" restored, would no longer be at the mercy of the corporate bosses: "Workers whom they previously had treated as dumb members of a forgotten minority suddenly are blooming as capable, intelligent persons using initiative and showing leadership" (1968b, 9). But the newfound agency of the farmworker would not necessarily be shaped by the dominant ethic of capitalist individualism, which led necessarily to self-interest and personal rivalries, but rather by the idea of community solidarity and service. Speaking on the occasion of the historic contract signings in the summer of 1970, Chávez said of his union members: "They found that only through dedication to serving mankind—and in this case to serving the poor and those who are struggling for justice—only in that way could they find themselves" (Yinger 1975, 87).

The religious underpinnings of Chávez's message resonated with the tenets of liberation theology as they had been formulated in the 1960s in

Latin America and elsewhere. Pope John XXIII and Vatican Council II had attempted to shift the role of the Church toward service of the poor, and liberation theologians drew upon thinkers in both the Christian and Marxist traditions in order to formulate a powerful concept of religious activism or "orthopraxis" as opposed to abstract orthodoxy (G. Gutiérrez 1971). In fundamental ways, both the Vatican II reforms and Chavez's project embodied the earliest forms of Mexican Catholicism in which the role of the indigenous poor took precedence over institutionalized religion. One of the earliest treatises on la Virgen de Guadalupe, for example, depicts a scene in which Juan Diego, the indigenous man who had seen the Virgin on the hill at Tepeyac, complains that because he is a commoner (*macehual*) he is ill suited to carry the Virgins message to the bishop. The Virgin replies: "Do listen, my youngest child. Be assured that my servants and messengers to whom I entrust it to carry my message and realize my wishes are not high-ranking people. Rather it is highly necessary that you yourself be involved and take care of it. It is very much by your hand that my will and wish are to be carried out and accomplished" (Sousa, Poole, and Lockhart 1998, 71). The idea that it is the poor who carry out God's work was at the core of Chávez's public style and it resonated with the foundational working-class membership and principles of the vast majority of Chicano/a movement organizations.

Because of his conscious decision to draw upon Mexican Catholic iconography and rituals, Chávez would soon find himself in a position he had not anticipated and certainly did not seek. For some of his followers, Chávez became less a Don Quixote than a Christ figure who incarnated the saintly virtues of humility and service to the poor in a corrupt and immoral world. The beatification of Chávez coincided with the elevation of the murdered Kennedy brothers as figures in the Mexican American imaginary. Chávez's association with Robert Kennedy, martyred in June 1968, served to increase each man's stature, and indeed Bobby Kennedy's role in the development of Chávez's national reputation cannot be underestimated. His ties to the UFW leader were captured perhaps most dramatically in the widely circulated account and photographs of Kennedy feeding Chávez a piece of bread and conversing with him as he ended his fast on March 10, 1968 (see fig. 2).[15] Although Chávez met Kennedy for the first time in 1960, the two men actually spent very little time together over the ensuing years. Once Robert Kennedy was assassinated, however, the symbolism linking the two leaders took on an enhanced power.

THE ELABORATION OF THE LEADER

Instrumental in the earliest representations of Chávez as the leader for whom La Raza had been waiting was playwright and Teatro Campesino founder Luis Valdez. In 1970 he told the Berkeley, California, newspaper *La Voz del Pueblo*: "Pero allí teníamos al líder esperando y no nos dábamas cuenta. Era César Chávez, y estaba allí consumiéndose a fuego lento, pobre como nosotros y hablándonos, sugiriéndonos lo que debíamos hacer—nunca ordenando—y poco a poco nos fuimos reuniendo en torno suyo . . . un hombre, en fin, que había sufrido en carne propia las vicisitudes de toda la Raza

Figure 2: César Chávez and Robert Kennedy (1968). Photo by George Ballis. Used by permission of Take Stock Photos.

en los Estados Unidos" (La Voz del Pueblo 1970, 5). By this time, as the Delano Grape Strike was coming to a successful conclusion, the identification of Chávez with earlier holy figures was so great that California poet Ricardo C. Pérez (1970) could compose the following:

> Con un libru de Gandhi en la mano
> Cual héroe en un mundo putrefacto
> Buscando la justicia en un pacto
> Anda con alta frente el chicano.
>
> Sufre como un hereje el desprecio
> Sufre como un Cristo el martirio
> Sufre por sufrir que es el precio
> Del que ama la llama de amor, el lirio.
>
> Pero grande en su humilde aspecto es
> Y por todo lo que sinceramente cree
> Porque es suya la única vía que
>
> Es tocada por la redentora fe
> Que hará todo humilde a la vez
> Tan grande en heroísmo cual los Andes!

At once a Chicano "Everyman" and Christ himself, Pérez's Chávez is linked in the final stanza to all of Latin America and by implication to the struggles of Spanish-speaking communities throughout the hemisphere. The religious language of the poem ("la llama de amor, el lirio") taken from the Catholic mystic tradition, together with the reference to Gandhi, produce a tone of holiness, and establish Chávez as less a union organizer than a twentieth-century saint.

Other movement writers contributed to the canonization process. San Francisco poet Elías Hruska-Cortés (1973), for example, wrote:

Delano the strategy and César
César and Cristo and Victory
César and filipino hall and victory
Delano and Solidarity and People
Delano the boycott and victory
Delano the strike and César
            the strike and victory
                    huel-ga huel-ga huel-ga

Shortly after he ended his career as a movement attorney, candidate for sheriff of Los Angeles County, and all-around *vato loco*, Oscar Zeta Acosta solidified for the Chicano/a imaginary the image of Chávez the saint. Early in the 1973 novel *Revolt of the Cockroach People*, Acosta's literary alter ego makes a pilgrimage to Delano. As the character of the Brown Buffalo approaches the room in which Chávez has been fasting for twenty-five days, an air of other-worldliness permeates the scene: "I enter and close the door behind me. It is very dark. There is a tiny candle burning over a bed, illuminating dimly a wooden cross and a figure of La Virgen on the wall. My ears are buzzing. There is a heavy smell of incense and kerosene. I don't move. I hear nothing. I no longer have any idea of why I have come or what I will say. 'Is that you, Buffalo?' The voice is soft, barely audible" (Acosta 1989, 44). Seeking spiritual and political guidance, Buffalo is surprised to learn that Chávez is aware of his activities in Los Angeles: "In the darkness, I think again of his words. The Father of Chicanos, César Chávez, has heard of me" (45). For Acosta, then, the figure of Chávez functions as a powerful touchstone against which all other agendas and practices will be measured. Not only a saint, Chávez in Acosta's hands becomes the moral and ethical core of the Movimiento in stark contrast to the depravities of the Brown Buffalo and his associates. By giving his blessing to Acosta and "the Militants" in L.A., César Chávez assumes his role at the symbolic center of movement history.[16]

In a concluding section of the novel the figure of Chávez reappears as a character witness for Corky Gonzales, who had been detained after the Chicano Moratorium antiwar demonstration that took place on August 29, 1970. Chávez's stature is intact, according to the narrator, who tells us: "They [Chávez and Gonzales] are number one and two in the Nation of Aztlán" (Acosta 1989, 249). But the Brown Buffalo himself has moved away from the ideal of nonviolence: "I have not seen Cesar since I first began in L.A. He is still my leader, but I no longer worship him. I am pushing for Corky because when things go political, I will push for the more militant of the two. Corky laughs at me. He tells me that Cesar's work is more important than both of us combined. Speak for yourself, I tell him" (250). Given Acosta's real-life role as a movement participant, we must read this statement as more than a mere declaration made by a fictionalized character. The passage captures well the tension between Chávez's militant nonviolence and alternative Movimiento practices that viewed insurgency as necessarily linked to hyper-masculine acts of physical aggression.

Even as militant nationalist and leftist groups in the movement mounted critiques of the strategies preferred by the UFW, right-wing attacks on Chávez proliferated as the union continued to achieve moderate success. Ironically, what bothered conservatives more than anything else was Chávez's public image as a Gandhi-like pacifist. In a vitriolic book aimed at discrediting Chávez, conservative writer Ralph de Toledano wrote: "A small man with an oversize messianic complex has put his mark on Delano. He has been able to do so by mobilizing in this small town the raw power of organized labor, the hysteria and psychosis of the New Left, and the pressure apparatus of the clergy" (1971, 16–17). Toledano, the son of Spanish immigrants to the United States, had made a career in Republican Party circles by writing laudatory biographies of J. Edgar Hoover and Richard Nixon. As an early incarnation of a "Hispanic intellectual" in the service of corporate and law enforcement interests, Toledano made it his business to represent the growers as the victims of the UFW's evil intentions.[17]

Other writers inclined to follow Toledano's lead sought to portray Chávez as just another corrupt union boss: "Chávez has been depicted as an almost Gandhiesque character, loving his fellow man, eschewing violence, calling for peaceful resolution of human problems. His detractors view him as a conniving labor czar who deliberately defrauded the grape pickers in order to aggrandize his labor union. Generally, this latter view seems more accurate and to the point, for it dwells on the ability of one man to manipulate others and to use what can best be described as shady tactics to achieve his ends" (Machado 1978, 99).[18] Such attempts to cast Chávez as a thug were doomed to fail despite backing from a well-funded public relations campaign sponsored by the growers. The right-wing and anti-Mexican John Birch Society ran a small cottage industry throughout the Vietnam war period whose sole objective was to produce attacks against Chávez and the UFW in books such as *Little Cesar and His Phony Strike* (Huck 1974) and *The Grapes: Communist Wrath in Delano* (Allen 1966).[19] One of the more hysterical efforts to link the UFW to a communist conspiracy was produced by Orange County, California, reporter John Steinbacher: "The young who follow a Chavez are not unlike the Narodniks, those bearded beatnik young of the Czarist regime, who helped to bring on the blood bath that led to the Red takeover of Russia. . . . The young follow a Hitler or a Stalin or a Kennedy—or a Chavez—in a mad lust for power through the darkling bye-ways of America" (1970, 128–29). Rhetorical flourishes such as this, the product of an almost irrational hatred of liberalism, remained on the margins of public discourse in the 1970s.[20] Even conservatives could only view the implication that Chávez was somehow equivalent to Hitler and Stalin as extreme.

But not only conservative Birchers, Republicans, and their hired "Hispanic" writers criticized Chávez. As I have demonstrated, activists within the various sectors of the Movimiento itself were at times at odds with Chávez's political stances. In the early years of the movement, the most contentious point had to do with the UFW's public statements regarding undocumented labor. Advocating strict immigration controls and a closed-border policy, Chávez, Dolores Huerta, and other union leaders hoped to deprive growers of a vast pool of potential strikebreakers. In his 1969 testimony before the congressional subcommittee on labor, Chávez referred to "illegals" and "green carders" as "natural economic rivals of those who become American citizens or who otherwise decide to stake out their future in this country" (Jensen and Hammerback 2002, 43). From the union's perspective, the logic of this position made sense but many movement activists viewed it as misguided and complicit with reactionary and anti-immigrant rhetoric and legislation. By the early 1970s the critique of the UFW on this issue reached a breaking point, primarily on account of threats by the Department of Justice to begin deporting undocumented workers. Chávez, sensing the growing discontent among many of his supporters, published a defense of "illegal aliens" in a 1974 letter to the *San Francisco Examiner.* But tensions on the issue continued unresolved, and Chávez himself angrily told an interviewer in *El Malcriado* that "most of the left attacking us has no experience in labor matters. They don't know what a strike is. . . . And they don't know because really they haven't talked to the workers" (quoted in D. Gutiérrez 1995, 199).[21] Beyond the specific issue of immigration, however, other differences of opinion emerged from within a movement that increasingly encompassed diverse ideologies and agendas.

As early as 1965, members of Tijerina's Alianza Federal de Mercedes had declared the philosophy of nonviolence to be less desirable than the actions taken by the Black community in Los Angeles during the Watts riots. Alianza member Felix Martinez had visited both Watts and Delano in 1965, and upon his return to New Mexico he reported: "revolution speeds up evolution" (Navarro 1995, 24). In this view, Chávez's reformist agenda lacked the necessary urgency that drove alternative Chicano political programs. In his 1970 poem titled "Los caudillos," therefore, Tejano poet raúlrsalinas (1971, 74) could write:

> In rich Delano vineyards
> Chavez does his pacifist thing
> "lift that crate
> and pick them grapes"
> stoop labor's awright—with God on your side.
>
> Small wonder David Sanchez
> impatient and enraged in L.A., dons a beret . . .
>
> Tijerina, Indo-Hispano
> you're out man.

From a more strictly leftist position, activist Froben Lozada complained: "And the pacifists want us to preach morality to them who have none!" (1968, 6). One labor and antiwar activist took a more pragmatic position with regard to Chávez's perceived pacifism: "They [UFW] have been able to win broad public support by demonstrating that it is their enemies who are violent. But in elevating nonviolence to an absolute principle, the union's leadership has unfortunately given up the right of the union to physically defend itself in any circumstances" (J. Pérez 1973, 13). For many Chicanos, self-determination would never be realized without the right to self-defense, given the high degree of racialized violence and economic exploitation that characterized institutional practices in the United States.

Other sectors of the movement found themselves in disagreement with UFW strategies. Chicano organizers struggling to create a third political party were particularly critical of Chávez for his unwavering allegiance to the Democratic Party. The union newspaper *El Malcriado* had stated repeatedly that John F. Kennedy would "always be our president," and as we have seen Robert Kennedy had given the union his support in public statements and appearances. For some of the founders of La Raza Unida Party (LRUP), therefore, Chávez's efforts to keep Chicanos in the Democrat camp were counterproductive if not outright "treason":

> [Chávez] would he doing a disservice to people about the crying need to break with the Democratic Party. He would be miseducating people, and it's a lot harder to educate people after they've been miseducated about what is necessary. . . . It would make it harder for us to talk about a Chicano party if Chavez was at the same time campaigning and registering people in the Democratic Party. And the truth of the matter is that this has already been tried again and again and nothing has come from it. Malcolm X made a very strong statement on this. He said, "Anyone who supports the Democratic Party after its record of oppression, and what it has done to our people, is not only a fool, but a traitor to his race." (Camejo 1970, 346)

The exaggerated rhetoric of the attack was certainly divisive and the use of Malcolm X's remark misleading and out of context. In practical terms, the tensions between LRUP and Chávez produced serious signs of disunity. Filmmaker Jesús Treviño reports that Chávez turned down an invitation to attend the LRUP convention in 1972 because both José Angel Gutiérrez and Corky Gonzales had made clear to him that they were displeased with the union's endorsement of Democratic candidate George McGovern (2001, 281). According to one account, several LRUP officials in the Texas delegation saw the break with Chávez as a necessary step in the eventual displacement of older organizers considered to be too accepting of the status quo and their replacement by younger, more radical leaders (Castro 1974, 96–111).

The criticisms of Chávez by some members of LRUP precluded potential alliances that could have furthered the movement's agenda. Historian Juan Gómez Quiñones has summarized these unfortunate developments:

For all his visibility and connections, La Raza Unida viewed Chavez negatively; absurdly, they felt he was negligent in pursuing broader Chicano issues or in demanding political concessions for Chicanos. To LRUP, Chavez was simply an arm of the Anglo political establishment; and allegedly he represented the traditional negotiating posture in politics, one that clashed with La Raza Unida's rhetorical emphasis on Chicano "self-determination." LRUP, however, overlooked UFW strength in California and the fact that they were seeking electoral office in the system for themselves. La Raza Unida was weakened by the inability to incorporate support from a prominent Chicano organization. (1990, 138)[22]

The question of whether or not the UFW was a "Chicano organization," however, depended on how the latter term was defined. On various occasions Chávez himself had declared that he was a union leader, not a leader in the Chicano movement. Some activists noted early on that Chávez was conspicuously absent from important movement events such as the Poor People's Campaign in 1968 or the 1970 Chicano Moratorium antiwar demonstration in Los Angeles.[23] Had they been readers of the *New Yorker*, young Chicano and Chicana activists would have been surprised by Chávez's comments in Peter Matthiessen's 1969 essays. Stressing the need to avoid narrow race-based nationalism, Chávez seemed to attack some of the basic principles of emergent Chicana/o identities:

"I hear more and more Mexicans talking about la raza—to build up their pride, you know," Chavez told me. "Some people don't look at it as racism, but when you say 'la raza,' you are saying an anti-gringo thing, and it won't stop there. Today it's anti-gringo, tomorrow it will be anti-Negro, and the day after it will be anti-Filipino, anti-Puerto Rican. And then it will be anti-poor-Mexican, and anti-darker-skinned Mexican. . . . La raza is a very dangerous concept. I speak very strongly against it among the Chicanos. At this point in the struggle, they respect me enough so that they don't emphasize la raza, but as soon as this is over they'll be against me, because I make fun of it, and I knock down machismo, too." (Matthiessen 1969b, 66; 2000, 178–79)[24]

Matthiessen's conversation with long-time UFW organizer LeRoy Chatfield about Chávez's attitude toward the movement might have added fuel to the fire. Chatfield remarked: "Everyone should be proud of what he is, of course, but race is only skin-deep. It's phony, and it comes out of frustration—the *la raza* people are not secure. The want to use Cesar as a symbol of their nationalism. But he doesn't want any part of it. He said to me just the other day, 'Can't they understand that that's just the way Hitler started?' A few months ago, a big foundation gave some money to a *la raza* group—they liked the outfits sense of pride, or something—and Cesar really told them off" (Matthiessen 1969b, 69; 2000, 179).

It was moments like these that had the potential to strain the otherwise strong links between Chávez and younger Chicano/a radicals. Reflecting more than just a "generation gap" or even ideological differences, tensions arose around issues of leadership style and organizational structures. Veteran organizer Bert Corona, for example, recalled an argument between student militants at the University of California, Santa Barbara, and Chávez, in which the students complained about a lack of consultation despite the fact that they had provided the manpower for recent union pickets (1994, 261). When asked whether or not the organizing strategies of the Crusade for Justice were in conflict with those of the UFW, in particular with regard to coalition building, Corky Gonzales replied that there was no disagreement between the two but insisted that Chicanos ought not to enter into alliances as "junior partners." He said: "There's a difference between that [Chávez's] and my philosophy. He feels that maybe it's the only way he could do it, that is, to get this outside help and make this outside alliance in order to remain autonomous. That's quite a contradiction, but it's an irony that's true. In order to have autonomy he had to have financial support. We work differently. We feel that no matter how long it takes, we have to develop our own leadership. We don't want those alliances. We'll take their support, but they can't make any decisions for us. They can't influence us" (1971, 4). Differences of opinion continued to separate the organizing strategies of major movement leaders, despite their joint appearances and public pronouncements as to shared objectives.[25]

In the end, however, the most astute commentators of the period understood that the activities of the UFW and Chávez himself served as crucial points of reference for the Movimiento as a whole. At its core the movement was a working-class project and who, after all, was more exploited than the farmworker? As the poet Abelardo Delgado put it: "Many movement people charge that Chavez may be one hell of an organizer, but not a leader in the Chicano movement in that he fails to embrace many other areas of concern affecting millions of other deprived Chicanos. Whether the charge is a valid one or not, the fact remains that we can rally behind our national leaders, and whether movement Chicanos claim Chavez owes them something or whether Chavez himself acknowledges the movement, the fact remains that he is a Chicano whose immense contribution cannot be ignored or belittled" (1971, 17).[26] Delgado's sentiments were widely shared by movement activists. At the same time, some activists argued that the UFW's successes themselves were inconceivable without the mass mobilizations organized by various movement organizations. In a period in which the trade union movement was not particularly strong and the number of farmworkers relatively small, Chávez's efforts, they believed, depended on the popular base created by the Movimiento.[27] Even *chavistas* like author Peter Matthiessen—who in his book had constructed a subtle division between Chávez and what he called "la raza Mexicans," that is, movement activists—understood the strong ties that bound the various groups together. For Matthiessen, however, the source of "Brown Power" identities could be traced directly to the founder of the UFW. "The newborn pride in being chicano, in the opinion of most people, is due largely to Chavez himself" (2000, 109).

By the 1970s, with the exception of revolutionary groups like the August 29th Movement, which accused Chávez of reformism and class collaborationism, the artificial division between "movement people" and Chavez to a large extent had been repaired. After the arrest of Corky Gonzales on a fabricated concealed-weapons charge at the Chicano Moratorium, Chávez agreed to serve as a character witness for Gonzales at the Los Angeles trial. In response to questions from attorney Oscar Zeta Acosta, Chávez testified that Gonzales's "general reputation for truth, honesty, and integrity is excellent" (Villaseñor 1970, 3). Even Chicano socialists were rethinking the role of the UFW within the overall Movimiento. Writer and activist José G. Pérez, for example, who had covered Chávez for the Young Socialist newspaper, argued in 1971: "Because the UFW is part of both the Chicano Movement and the labor movement, both must rally to its defense—otherwise both will be weakened and the way will be cleared for further assaults by the employers and their racist government" (1973, 14).[28] As the American war in Southeast Asia came to an end, UFW publications became less critical of the concepts of "Aztlán" and "La Raza" although they always subordinated them to the discourses of trade unionism.

EL LEGADO DE CÉSAR

Attempts to organize farmworkers in California had met with failure in every decade of the first half of the twentieth century. The relative success of the UFW was the product of a historical conjuncture in which grassroots mobilizations around a variety of issues affecting Mexican Americans, the ascendancy of the liberal wing of the Democratic Party, Pope John XXIII's shifting of the Catholic Church's agenda toward the poor, the elimination of the Bracero program in 1964, the general politicization of U.S. society caused by the Vietnam war, and an emerging Chicana/o consciousness created a context in which it was possible to extract long-sought concessions from political and economic elites. At the end of this extraordinary historical moment, capital continued to treat labor as a commodity but at least working conditions had improved and the discourse of the worker's inherent dignity had achieved a temporary prominence. The Chicano/a critique of liberalism had forced capitalist democracy in the United States to deliver on some but not all of its promises.

At once a union movement and an ethnic Mexican movement, La Causa was thus a result of the more generalized social transformation known as the 1960s. As one astute student of farmworkers' movements wrote: "The United Farm Workers story is significant for three reasons. In general terms, the UFW exemplified the basic goals and strategies of the social movements of the stormy 1960s. The major social movements of the period were insurgencies, that is, organized attempts to bring the interests of previously unorganized and excluded groups into the centers of economic and political power. By organizing farmworkers, the UFW took up the interests of one of the more disorganized and marginal segments of American society" (Jenkins 1985, x). As I have argued in the present essay, a unique characteristic of the UFW was the fact that its most recognizable leader deployed a nontraditional form of leadership that was often at odds with other forms typical of the period.[29]

By the mid-1980s, the conservative counterattack against progressive social movements was winning on many fronts. In California, Governor George

Deukmejian, backed by affluent corporate growers, brought the "Reagan Rev-olution" to the farmworkers by gutting the Agricultural Labor Relations Act that had been passed in 1975. Chávez reacted to these rollbacks with anger: "There is a shadow falling over the land, brothers and sisters, and the dark forces of reaction threaten us now as never before. The enemies of the poor and the working classes hold power in the White House and the governors office. . . . They have created a whole new class of millionaires while forcing millions of ordinary people into poverty" (1984a). At this moment perhaps more than previous ones, Chávez understood that the early activities of the UFW had been inextricably linked to a broader movement having to do with the construction of new and contestatory ethnic identities that challenged the racial and economic status quo. In a speech to the Commonwealth Club of California, he said: "Our union will forever exist as an empowering force among Chicanos in the Southwest. And that means our power and our influ-ence will grow and not diminish. . . . The consciousness and pride that were raised by our union are alive and thriving inside millions of young Hispan-ics who will never work on a farm" (1984b). Whereas Chávez had criticized the "Brown Power" agenda in his 1969 *New Yorker* interviews, his recognition that the UFW had been an integral part of el Movimiento now tempered his concerns.[30]

As the decade of the 1990s began, Chávez reflected upon the legacy of Dr. King. In a speech delivered in January 1990, his critical analysis of the current state of affairs wove together the language of the movement with fundamen-tal messages about coalition building and nonviolence:

> My friends, as we enter a new decade, it should be clear to all of us that there is an unfinished agenda, that we have miles to go before we reach the promised land. The men who rule this country today never learned the lessons of Dr. King, they never learned that nonviolence is the only way to peace and jus-tice. Our nation continues to wage war upon its neighbors, and upon itself. The powers-that-be rule over a racist society, tilled with hatred and ignorance. Our nation continues to be segregated along racial and economic lines. The powers-that-be make themselves richer by exploiting the poor. Our nation continues to allow children to go hungry, and will not even house its own people. The time is now for people, of all races and backgrounds, to sound the trumpets of change. As Dr. King proclaimed, "There comes a time when people get tired of being trampled over by the iron feet of oppression." (1990, 2)

Throughout the years of the Bush Sr. and Clinton administrations, the conser-vative reaction Chávez had warned about during Reagan's presidency gained momentum. This was particularly so in California, where ballot initiatives attempted to destroy the social safety net for undocumented workers, elimi-nated affirmative action, and gutted bilingual education programs. Although the UFW grew in membership in the 1990s and carried out large organizing campaigns such as the one in the California strawberry industry, victories were few and far between. On the more than 400 farms where the union had won elections since 1975, less than half the growers agreed to sign contracts.

The problem of unsafe transportation for farmworkers, an issue captured in Tomás Rivera's classic novel set in the 1950s, *Y no se lo tragó la tierra*, had been responsible for numerous deaths over the previous thirty years. Despite Chávez's personal efforts to win reforms on this issue, it was not until 2002 that the California state legislature finally passed a law mandating that growers provide safe vehicles (Chávez 1974; Ingram 2002). Also in 2002, after a well-publicized march on Sacramento to force the hand of Governor Gray Davis, the union won the right to have outside mediators and the Agricultural Labor Relations Board decide disputes between workers and growers (Maxwell 2002). Not unlike his disembodied voice that speaks from beyond to all those who visit the UFW's official website, the image of Chávez hovers over these victories and all contemporary acts of Chicano/a activism.

Today, Chávez enjoys widespread admiration throughout Mexican American and Latino communities and even within Hispanic corporate culture. For progressive Chicanas and Chicanos, of course, he continues to be the major historical icon, and it would be difficult to imagine a contemporary Chicano/a rejection of Chávez's legacy like the backlash Michael Dyson records in his book on Martin Luther King Jr. Dyson reconstructs a conversation in which a thirty-something African American scholar vehemently denounces King for being upper-middle-class, accommodationist, and an Uncle Tom (and implicitly not "man enough") (2000, 101).[31] Unlike earlier critiques of Chávez from within some movement sectors that raised doubts about his political alliances and tactics, contemporary Chicano/a intellectual projects have refrained from such a harsh reinterpretation, perhaps because many ethnic Mexican professionals have rejected outright the more contestatory aspects of the Movimiento. In the context of a generalized dispersion and fragmentation of progressive forces in the United States, the image of Chávez has become one of the safer ones associated with a revolutionary period, a period that still frightens many in both the corporate art world and the corporate university.

The death of César Chávez in 1993 solidified his position as a historic Mexican American leader and by 2001 the state of California had instituted an official holiday in his honor. Although neoconservatives in their attempts to block the holiday continued to represent Chávez as a union mafioso, for the majority of Americans Chávez had become a somewhat romanticized and non-threatening figure that was less associated with unions and social movements than with nonviolence or religion or dot-com "creativity." The commodification of Chávez's image proceeded along the lines of that of King. Featured in the Apple Computers "Think Different" series, Chávez joined his ally Robert Kennedy as one more pitchman for corporate gain. Even as the depoliticization of Chávez moved forward, the general public's understanding of the plight of contemporary farmworkers in the United States improved only slightly, if at all, from what it had been in 1962 when Chávez, Dolores Huerta, Larry Itliong, and others created the UFW (see fig. 3). At the turn of the century, conditions in the fields were still deplorable, with Mexican farmworkers reporting significantly higher rates of cancer than other Latinos in California and a higher risk of contracting HIV/AIDS; 63 percent had only six years of school or less and 75 percent lacked health insurance.[32]

Figure 3: *Farmworkers* **(2002). Cartoon by Lalo Alcaraz. Used by permission of artist. See cartoonista.com.**

In contemporary Chicano/a culture, Chávez continues to fulfill a number of functions, not the least of which is that of a spiritual force at one with the powers of nature. Recently, novelist Rodolfo Anaya (2000, 26) has written:

> Our César has not died!
> He is the light of the new day.
> He is the rain that renews parched fields.
> He is the hope that builds the House of Justice.
> He is with us! Here! Today!
> Listen to his voice in the wind.
> He is the spirit of Hope,
> A Movement building to sweep away oppression!
> His spirit guides us in the struggle
> Let us join his spirit to ours!

In a process not unlike the one that transformed Che Guevara into a revolutionary saint, the mythologizing of Chávez removes him from the historical reality in which he lived and worked, and effaces his militant critique of economic inequality in order to construct a figure for the ages. In its weakest form, then, the image of Chávez becomes one more petrified icon deployed to demonstrate the virtues of American pluralism and liberal democracy—an aestheticized sign on a postage stamp. Poet César Cruz (2002) brilliantly captured the contradiction between this assimilated figure and the radical pursuit of social justice to which Chávez devoted his life:

I am wearing a
César Chávez t-shirt
driving a car with
César Chávez stickers
on César Chávez Boulevard
passing by
César Chávez school
on César Chávez Day
hearing
César Chávez commercials
on the local radio
and seeing
César Chávez billboards
announcing a
César Chávez march
sponsored by multinational
corporations
wondering
if
we praise you
or curse you
when farmworkers are still underpaid
under-appreciated
when immigrants
are scapegoated
when nothing you stood for
is respected. . . .

And yet even as the historical reality of Chávez recedes into the distant pantheon of "American" heroes there can be no doubt that his name may still be deployed as a catalyst for ongoing struggles to end exploitation and win full political rights for working-class people. In 2001, recently organized janitors and service workers made up overwhelmingly of Latina/o immigrants marched through the streets of San Diego, California, chanting "Sí se puede" as they locked arms behind the image of César Estrada Chávez.

NOTES

1. Based on Chávez's own comments in which he insisted that he was a labor leader and not a Chicano movement leader, several historians have argued that his connection to the Movimiento was tentative. Carlos Muñoz Jr., for example, writes: "Chavez was a union organizer and lent his increasing prestige and astute leadership abilities only to farmworkers" (1989, 60). It is my contention that on account of the immeasurable impact

that Chávez and the United Farm Workers (UFW) had on Chicano/a activism throughout the movement period, as well as his direct or indirect support of movement sectors such as the anti–Vietnam War National Chicano Moratorium Committee, it would be misleading to isolate his efforts—regardless of his own declarations. Historian Ignacio García argues similarly that both Tijerina's Alianza Federal de Mercedes and the UFW were essential to the broader Movimiento: "Some scholars argue that César Chávez's farmworkers' union and the Alianza were not part of the Movement because they never emphasized their *chicanismo*. I counter by saying that these two organizations were fundamental to the development of the militancy of the period" (1998, 14). Manuel G. Gonzales artificially separates the Movimiento into "radical and moderate wings" and situates the UFW to the latter (2000, 196).

2. Tijerina's rhetoric in particular was dependant upon traditional forms of masculinity and on homophobia. Referring to government agents who had threatened him and his family, he said: "Most of them are homosexuals now and very few men are found among them" (1969, 4). Tijerina's use of homosexuality as a "charge" with which to dismiss his political enemies is reminiscent of the novels of Oscar Zeta Acosta.

3. I take for granted that scholars of the Chicano movement agree that far from being a "monolithic" social movement (has there ever been such a creature?), the Movimiento was made up of diverse organizations with regional and ideological differences. In my opinion, attempts to totalize the movement under any one political language are reductive and therefore distort what was a complex tapestry of agendas and rhetorical strategies. I take up many of these issues in my forthcoming *Brown-Eyed Children of the Sun: Lessons from the Chicano Movement*.

4. A reviewer for *Aztlán* charged me with "mythologizing Chavez once again." Let me say at the outset that by recontextualizng both Chávez and cultural representations of Chávez, my intention is not to demythologize his legacy but to clarify its origins so that current and future generations of students and activists can comprehend its complexity and thus refashion it for use in their own struggles for social justice.

5. In 1971 Carlos Blanco astutely pointed out that few if any of the farmworkers (approximately half of them Mexican nationals in the early 1970s) felt compelled to "construct" a new ethnic identity, since they understood themselves to be Mexicano/as and workers: "They know exactly where they stand in terms of their Mexicanidad and of their working-class condition and, therefore, of their relationship to the ever-present and clearly definable bosses. . . . The Chicano aspect of the struggle, the Mexican 'identity' of the 'causa' did not even have to be alluded to for the simple reason that the talk [by César Chávez] was given in Spanish" (1971, 2). Indeed, in the earliest days of the UFW, Chávez often appealed not only to the workers' *mexicandad* but also to each one's specific regional identity within the Mexican context. One participant in a rally during the grape strike in 1965 reputed: "Speaker follows speaker as the enthusiasm of the crowd grows. 'Who is here from Jalisco?' César Chávez asks. 'Who is here from Michoacan?' A man from Tanguancícuaro rises: 'What have we to lose by going on strike?' . . . Men from state after Mexican state rise to pledge the aid of those from their part of the homeland, followed by cries of 'Viva Chihuahua! Viva Nuevo Leon! Viva Tamaulipas!'" (Nelson 1966, 27).

6. A new edition of Matthiessen's book was published in 2000, containing versions of some but not all of the materials in Matthiessen's original *New Yorker* articles. I have chosen to quote from the original articles because of their more properly *testimonio* style but I have included page references to both sources in those instances where material was either revised or reprinted.

7. Early in his activist career, Reies López Tijerina was referred to as "Don Quixote." After the June 5, 1967, courthouse raid on Tierra Amarilla, however, one media outlet declared: "Don Quixote has become El Cid" (Tijerina 2000, 102). On Chicano literary appropriations of the Don Quixote figure, see Childers 2002.

8. That Chávez's masculinity signified an implicit critique of traditional forms of leadership was noted early on by perceptive observers. In their book on farmworker organizing in California, Henry Anderson and Joan London (daughter of Jack London) wrote: "He is challenging the long-standing, deeply embedded folkways which equate aggressiveness with manliness in the cultures of Mexico, the Philippines, the United States—and in the culture of labor organizing itself. It is a breathtaking challenge" (1970, 184).

9. Chávez told Peter Matthiessen in 1969: "I didn't know much about Gandhi, so I read everything I could get my hands on about him, and I read some of the things that he had read, and I read Thoreau, which I liked very much. But I couldn't really understand Gandhi until I was actually in the fast. Then the books became much more clear" (Matthiessen 1969a, 64; 2000, 187). Central to Chávez's understanding of the activist Catholic tradition were the figures of Father Thomas McCullough and Father Donald McDonnell who founded a migrant ministry in the 1950s associated with the Spanish Mission Band and later the Missionary Apostolate. Father McDonnell exerted a direct influence over Chávez during his time in east San Jose. See London and Anderson 1970.

10. Chávez himself seemed to have practiced the fast according to this strict Gandhian interpretation, although many subsequent Chicano/a political actions have misunderstood the function of the fast and employed it as coercion. In their recent cartoon history, Lalo Alcaraz and Ilan Stavans perpetuate this misunderstanding by depicting Chávez on a fast saying: "I will not eat again until the grape growers concede" (2000, 121). During the Movimiento period, not all youth activists were convinced that the fast was an important strategy. In 1970 Ysidro Macias advised: "hunger strikes may be effective because of their sentimental value" (1969, 47). According to Peter Matthiessen, some UFW members left the union specifically because of Chávez's use of the fast: "One dismissed the entire fast as a 'cheap publicity stunt.' The other, who had once been a priest, accused Chávez of having a Messiah complex. Both soon quit the United Farm Workers for good" (1969b, 56).

11. Many years later, upon ending a fast in August 1988, Chávez explained: "The fast was first and foremost a personal act. It was something I felt compelled to do—to purify my own body, mind, and soul. The fast was also an act of penance for those in positions of moral authority and for all men and women who know what is right and just. It is for those who know that they could or should do more" (Jensen and Hammerback 2002, 169).

12. In his autobiography, African American leader Andrew Young recalls Chávez as "a small man with a soothing, spiritual presence" and "eyes that expressed the kind of loving determination with which the apostle Paul spread the Gospel" (1996, 445).

13. This quotation is from the so-called "Sacramento March Letter." In documents such as these it is difficult to determine authorship since Chávez, Luis Valdez, Eliezer Risco, and others may have written the text collectively. On the practice of multiple authorship in the UFW and El Teatro Campesino, see Broyles González 1994.

14. Questions have been raised about the ways in which Chávez's hybrid masculinity, in a sense "feminized" by its indebtedness to religious traditions, might have worked to "hail" or attract women activists during the movement period. This is an important issue that, in my opinion, deserves separate and multiple studies. Espinoza (2001) offers a possible model for such research. Equally needed are studies of the real-life ways in which farmworker women experience gender relations.

15. According to Peter Matthiessen's eyewitness account, a photographer staged the now famous 1968 tableau with RFK feeding Chávez (1969a, 68; 2000, 195). In his biography of Kennedy, Evan Thomas claims that meeting with Chávez initially did not appeal to Kennedy: "His involvement followed a familiar pattern: at first, he grumbled, he didn't want to fly to California to meet with some striking Mexicans . . .

But reluctantly, as a favor to his liberal activist friends in the United Auto Workers, he flew out to Delano, California, in mid-March" (2000, 320). Once he met Chávez, however, Kennedy became a staunch supporter.

16. Acosta's scene captured the tone of actual events in which movement leaders made the journey to Delano to consult with Chávez. In my personal conversations with Rosalío Muñoz, one of the founders of the National Chicano Moratorium Committee, he described a similar visit he made before deciding to refuse induction into military service.

17. Toledano's writings bear many of the marks of COINTELPRO disinformation and so there is some reason to believe they were subsidized by government agencies. The FBI had begun to construct a file on Chávez as early as 1965 on the premise that "communists" had infiltrated the UFW. In October 1969, the Nixon White House requested a "name check" on Chávez. J. Edgar Hoover relayed the Bureau's information to Nixon aide John Erlichman. Some of Chávez's FBI files are available online at http://foia.fbi.gov/chavez.htm.

18. Machado's attacks on Chávez's character would be repeated twenty years later by opponents of a César Chávez state holiday in California. Despite a well-funded opposition, the holiday was officially established in 2000 and celebrated for the first time in 2001.

19. Another example is *Cesar Chavez* by W. E. Dunham (1970).

20. Steinbacher was a reporter for the local Anaheim, California, *Bulletin*. His writings predated by a decade the reactionary "family values" project of the Reagan–Bush Sr. era. The hero of Steinbacher's book on the UFW is a certain Alfred Ramirez, founder of a group called "Mothers Against Chavez" and California chairman of the Spanish Surname Citizens for Wallace (George Wallace, the former Alabama segregationist governor, ran for president as a third-party candidate in 1968). By the 1990s an even more virulent strain of anti-liberalism was common currency. Right-wing hatred for centrist President Bill Clinton, for example, produced in Southern California bumper stickers that read "Clinton = Socialism" or juxtaposed "Clinton" with a hammer and sickle.

21. Although he disagreed with the UFW on the undocumented worker issue, Bert Corona later recalled: "Despite our differences with the United Farm Workers, we never had a major confrontation, even though on our side some people on the extreme left tried to provoke it (Corona and Garcia 1994, 249).

22. Elsewhere, Gómez Quiñones further criticizes LRUP's position: "La mesquina exclusión de César Chávez y de su sindicato fue espuria y ejemplo de la falta de visión de largo plazo. Se dejó fuera a una organización de estructura nacional, con una base de más de 70 mil trabajadores, con equipos organizados, considerable apoyo público y una fuerza que podía set reconocida en elecciones tanto estatales como nacionales. Viniendo de donde venían, los cargos en contra de Chávez eran hipócritas: trabajar con el Partido Demócrata y aceptar el apoyo de grupos no mexicanos" (1996, 247). The troubled relations between the UFW leadership and leftists within the union itself have yet to be chronicled. See remarks by union co-founder Philip Vera Cruz in Scharlin and Villanueva 2000, 120.

23. In a speech at a Los Angeles antiwar rally in May 1971, Chávez said: "It is hard for me because we in the farmworkers' movement have been so absorbed in our own struggle that we have not participated actively in the battle against the war" (Jensen and Hammerback 2002, 63). When asked why he did not attend the 1968 Poor People's Campaign, Chávez answered that he could not abandon his responsibilities in California in order to travel to Washington, D.C. (Matthiessen 2000, 242).

24. Many movement activists, for whom indigenous histories and traditions had become a central part of their new identity, would have been disappointed by Chávez's

favorable remarks in the same interview about the California mission system (Matthiessen 1969b, 65–66; 2000, 300).

25. To the degree that radical organizations adopted in increasingly strident rhetoric threatening the use of violence, the mainstream media cast Chávez as a safe alternative and someone who could be reasoned with. In the April 1, 1969 issue of *Look* magazine, for example, readers were told: "At a time when many American radicals are saying that nonviolence—as an instrument for social change—died with Martin Luther King, Jr., it is reassuring to meet a man of faith who preaches compassion rather than bloody confrontation, practices what he preaches, and gets results" (52). Throughout the interview, Chávez's religiosity is emphasized, he praises Bobby Kennedy for his "hechos de amor, deeds of love" and eloquently states: "It may be a long time before the growers see us as human beings. . . . But we will win, we are winning, because ours is a revolution of mind and heart, not only of economics" (57). What one writer called Chávez's "tenacious idealism" sat in uneasy juxtaposition to traditional images of the union leader (Daniel 1995, 401).

26. According to Ernesto Vigil, Corky Gonzales "admired Chavez and praised his dedication to the farmworkers, but he—like Chavez himself—saw the latter mainly as a labor leader" (1999, 10). Bert Corona, on the other hand, convincingly argued that the UFW deployed a form of Mexican nationalism that "complemented the stress on ethnic nationalism and ethnic revival in the sixties. . . . It was ethnic nationalism but it was interpreted through Cesar's earlier experience and consciousness which reflected a broader and more class-based approach" (1994, 248).

27. "It was the Chicano community that saw the struggle of the farm workers as its own struggle and formed the backbone of the [farmworkers'] movement" (Pendás 1976, 7).

28. Pérez argued further: "The UFW is the closest thing today to the militant, socially conscious unionism of the CIO in the late thirties. It supported the movement against the Vietnam War when few labor leaders would go near it. The struggle of these oppressed workers and their attempts to link up with broader concerns of the working masses point in the direction of a new labor radicalism" (8–9).

29. Chávez's spiritualized masculinity contradicts recent historiography and cultural criticism that casts the entire Chicano movement as a hyper-masculinist orgy, as if Oscar Zeta Acosta and not César Chávez were its primary inspiration. While there can be no doubt that the feminist critiques of the movement carried out in the 1980s were necessary correctives to the sexist practices that characterized all organizations, arguments about the "origins" of the Movimiento that posit "emasculation" as its primary cause are misleading. A sense of emasculation among working-class men (of any ethnicity), the product of racializing, capitalist formations, may produce a variety of pathologies ranging from alcoholism to domestic violence. In and of itself, however, emasculation cannot generate social movements. To argue that it can is to return to an older "pathological tradition" of social movement theory, a tradition for the most part rejected by contemporary scholars (Gamson 1992). For a rather hastily constructed analysis of the Chicano movement along these "pathological" lines, see R. Gutiérrez 1993.

30. As early as 1968, Chávez had spoken about the unavoidable links between labor organizing and other struggles in the Southwest: "People raise the question: Is this a strike or is it a civil-rights fight? In California, in Texas, or in the South, any time you strike, it becomes a civil-rights movement. It becomes a civil-rights fight" (Jensen and Hammerback 2002, 33).

31. Dyson's colleague who denounces King begins boldly enough: "Fuck Martin Luther King. The nigga was the worst thing to happen to black people in the twentieth century" (101).

32. On the situation for farmworkers in the 1980s and 1990s, see Acuña 2000 and Hanson 2002. In his groundbreaking study of farm labor in the late twentieth century, Daniel Rothenberg writes: "The basic statistics regarding agricultural labor reveal an ethical challenge that raises questions about our professed belief that honest labor should be justly rewarded" (1998, xiii).

WORKS CITED

Acosta, Oscar Zeta. 1989. *Revolt of the Cockroach People*. New York: Vintage.

Acuña, Rodolfo. 2000. *Occupied America: A History of Chicanos*. 4th ed. New York: Longman.

Alcaraz, Lalo, and Ilan Stavans. 2000. *Latino USA: A Cartoon History*. New York: Basic Books.

Allen, Gary. 1966. *The Grapes: Communist Wrath in Delano*. Belmont, Mass. and San Marino, Calif.: Review of the News.

Anaya, Rodolfo. 2000. *Elegy on the Death of César Chávez*. El Paso: Cinco Puntos Press.

Blanco Aguinaga, Carlos. 1971. "Unidad del trabajo y la vida—Cinco de mayo, 1971: *Aztlán* 2 (spring): 1–5.

Borman, William. 1986. *Gandhi and Non-violence*. Albany: State University of New York Press.

Broyles González, Yolanda. 1994. *El Teatro Campesino: Theater in the Chicano Movement*. Austin: University of Texas Press.

Camejo, Antonio. 1970. "A New Ideology for the Chicano Party." In *La Causa Política: A Chicano Politics Reader*, ed. F. Chris Garcia, 343–46. Notre Dame, Ill.: University of Notre Dame Press.

Castells, Manuel. 1997. *The Poem of Identity*. Vol. 2 of *The Information Age: Economy, Society and Culture*. Oxford: Blackwell.

Castro, Tony. 1974. *Chicano Power: The Emergence of Mexican America*. New York: Saturday Review Press/E.P. Dutton & Co.

Chávez, César E. 1990. "Lessons of Dr. Martin Luther King, Jr." Retrieved January 12, 1990, from the World Wide Web: http://www.sfsu.edu/~cecipp/cesar_chavez.

———. 1984a. Address to UFW's Seventh Constitutional Convention, September. Retrieved April 5, 2002, from the World Wide Web: http://chavez.scientech .com:8080/research.

———. 1984b. Address to the Commonwealth Club of California, November 9, in San Francisco. Retrieved August 13, 2003, from the World Wide Web: www.ufw.org/ commonwealth.htm.

———. 1974. "Chavez Blames Fatal Bus Accidents on Greed: 'Inhuman Treatment of Farmworkers Must End.'" *National Chicano Health Organization (NCHO) Newsletter* 3 (April): 7.

———. 1971. "On Money and Organizing." Speech delivered in Keene, California, October 4. Retrieved April 6, 2002, from the World Wide Web: http://chavez .scientech.com:8080/research.

———. 1970. "Cesar Chavez: Apostle of Non-Violence." Interview with the *Observer*, May. Retrieved August 13, 2003, from the World Wide Web: http://www.sfsu. edu/~cecipp/cesar_chavez/apostle.htm.

———. 1969. "Creative Non-Violence." *Center Magazine* (March).

———. 1968a. Telegram to Mrs. Martin Luther King, Jr. Reprinted in *El Malcriado* (15 April).

———. 1968b. "National Council Policy Statement." *Tempo* (summer–fall): 9–10.

———. 1968c. Speech ending fast, March 10. Retrieved April 7, 2002, from the World Wide Web: http://chavez.scientech.com:8080/research.

Childers, William. 2002. "Chicanoizing Don Quixote: For Luis Andres Murillo." *Aztlán* 27 (fall): 87–117.

Corona, Bert, and Mario T. Garcia, 1994. *Memories of Chicano History: The Life and Narrative of Bert Corona*. Berkeley and Los Angeles: University of California Press.

Cruz, César A. (Teolol). 2002. "Turning in Your Grave." Unpublished manuscript.

Daniel, Cletus E. 1995. "Cesar Chavez and the Unionization of California Farmworkers." In *Working People of California*, ed. Daniel Cornford, 371–404. Berkeley and Los Angeles: University of California Press.

de León, Nephtalí. 1972a. *Five Plays*. Denver: Totinem Publications.

———. 1972b. *Chicanos: Our Background and Our Pride*. Lubbock, Tex.: Trucha Publications,

Delgado, Abelardo. 1971. *The Chicano Movement: Some Not Too Objective Observations*. Denver: Totinem Publications.

Dunham, W. E. 1970. *Cesar Chavez*. Belmont, Mass. and San Marino, Calif.: Review of the News.

Dyson, Michael Eric. 2000. *I May Not Get There With You: The True Martin Luther King, Jr.* New York: Touchstone Press.

Espinoza, Dionne. 2001. "'Revolutionary Sisters'": Women's Solidarity and Collective Identification among Chicana Brown Berets in East Los Angeles, 1967–1970. *Aztlán* 26 (spring): 17–58.

Foucault, Michel. 1972. *The Archaeology of Knowledge and the Discourse on Language*. New York: Harper & Row.

Gamson, William A. 1992. "The Social Psychology of Collective Action." In *Frontiers in Social Movement Theory*, ed. Aldon D. Morris and Carol McClurg Mueller, 53–76. New Haven: Yale University Press.

García, Ignacio M. 1993. *Chicanismo: The Forging of a Militant Ethos among Mexican Americans*. Tucson: University of Arizona Press.

Gómez, David. 1982. "The Story of Ruben Salazar." In *Introduction to Chicano Studies*, ed. Livie Isauro Durán and H. Russell Bernard. New York: Macmillan, 499–505.

Gómez, Quiñones, Juan. 1996. "La era de los setenta." In *El México olvidado: La historia del pueblo chicano*, ed. David R. Maciel, 239–61. Colección Sin Fronteras, vol. 2. Ciudad Juárez, Mexico: Universidad Autónoma de Ciudad Juárez; El Paso, Tex.: University of Texas at El Paso.

———. 1990. *Chicano Politics: Reality and Promise 1940–1990*. Albuquerque: University of New Mexico Press.

Gonzales, Manuel G. 2000. *Mexicanos: A History of Mexicans in the United States*. Bloomington: Indiana University Press.

Gonzales, Rodolfo Corky. 1971. Interview in *La Voz del Pueblo* (June).

Gutiérrez, David G. 1995. *Walls and Mirrors: Mexican Americans, Mexican Immigrants, and the Politics of Ethnicity*. Berkeley and Los Angeles: University of California Press.

Gutiérrez, Gustavo. 1971. *Teología de la liberación. Perspectivas*. Lima: CEP.

Gutiérrez, Ramón A. 1993. "Community, Patriarchy and Individualism: The Politics of Chicano History and the Dream of Equality." *American Quarterly* 45 (March): 44–72.

Hanson, Pat. 2002. "Migrant Farmers Suffering in Silence: California Groups Look at Problems and Solutions." *Hispanic Outlook in Higher Education* (June 3): 28–32.

Hruska-Cortés, Elías. 1973. "Recuerdos." *La calavera chicana* (University of California, Berkeley) (September): 15.

Huck, Susan. 1974. *Little Cesar and His Phony Strike*. Belmont, Mass. and San Marino, Calif.: Review of the News.

Ingram, Carl. 2002. "Farm Workers Celebrate Safety Law, Chavez Holiday." *Los Angeles Times* online edition, April 2.

Jenkins, J. Craig. 1985. *The Politics of Insurgency: The Farm Worker Movement in the 1960s.* New York: Columbia University Press.

Jensen, Richard J., and John C. Hammerback. 2002. *The Words of César Chávez.* College Station: Texas A&M University Press.

La Voz del Pueblo. 1970. "El poder Chicano." December, 4–5.

London, Joan, and Henry Anderson. 1970. *So Shall Ye Reap: The Story of Cesar Chavez and the Farm Workers' Movement.* New York: Thomas Y. Crowell.

Look magazine. 1969. "Nonviolence Still Works." April 1, 52–57.

Lozada, Froben. 1968. Speech delivered at California State University, Hayward, November 1. Typescript in author's possession.

Machado, Manuel A. Jr. 1978. *Listen Chicano!: An Informal History of the Mexican-American.* Chicago: Nelson Hall.

Macias, Ysidro Ramón. 1969. "Plan de Political Action for Chicano Campus Groups." Document produced at Political Action workshop at the University of California, Santa Barbara conference, April. Reprinted in *El Pocho Che* 1 (April 1970).

Matthiessen, Peter. 2000. *Sal Si Puedes (Escape If You Can): Cesar Chavez and the New American Revolution.* Berkeley and Los Angeles: University of California Press.

———. 1969a. "Profile: Organizer-1." *New Yorker,* June 21, 42–85.

———. 1969b. "Profile: Organizer II." *New Yorker,* June 28, 43–76.

Maxwell, Lesli A. 2002. "Davis Gives UFW Major Victory." *Sacramento Bee* online edition, October 1.

Muñoz, Carlos Jr. 1989. *Youth, Identity, Power: The Chicano Movement.* London and New York: Venus.

Navarro, Armando. 1995. *Mexican American Youth Organization: Avant-Garde of the Chicano Movement in Texas.* Austin: University of Texas Press.

Nelson, Eugene. 1966. *Huelga: The First Hundred Days of the Great Delano Grape Strike.* Delano: Farm Worker Press.

Pendás, Miguel. 1976. *Chicano Liberation and Socialism.* New York: Pathfinder Press.

Pérez, José G. 1973. *Vivo la Huelga! The Struggle of the Farm Workers.* New York: Pathfinder Press.

Pérez, Ricardo C. 1970. "César." *El Chicano* (San Bernardino, California), January 12.

Rosales, F. Arturo. 1997. *Chicano! The History of the Mexican American Civil Rights Movement.* Houston: Arte Público.

Rothenberg, Daniel. 1998. *With These Hands: The Hidden World of Migrant Farmworkers Today.* Berkeley and Los Angeles: University of California Press.

salinas, raúl r. 1971. "Los caudillos." *La Raza* 1 (January): 74.

Scharlin, Craig, and Lilia V. Villanueva, eds. 2000. *Philip Vera Cruz: A Personal History of Filipino Immigrants and the Farmworkers Movement.* Seattle: University of Washington Press.

Sousa, Lisa, Stafford Poole, and James Lockhart, eds. 1998. *The Story of Guadalupe: Luis Laso de la Vega's Huei tlamahuiçoltica of 1649.* Palo Alto, Calif.: Stanford University Press; Los Angeles: UCLA Latin American Publications.

Steinbacher, John. 1970. *Bitter Harvest.* Whittier, Calif.: Orange Tree Press.

Thomas, Evan. 2000. *Robert Kennedy: His Life.* New York: Simon & Schuster.

Tijerina, Reies López. 2000. *They Called Me "King Tiger": My Struggle for the Land and Our Rights.* Trans. José Angel Gutiérrez. Houston: Arte Público.

———. 1969. Interview in the *Indicator* (University of California, San Diego), January 29, 2.

Toledano, Ralph de. 1971. *Little Cesar.* Washington, D.C.: Anthem.

Treviño, Jesús Salvador. 2001. *Eyewitness: A Filmmaker's Memoir of the Chicano Movement.* Houston: Arte Público.

Vigil, Ernesto. 1999. *The Crusade for Justice: Chicano Militancy and the Government's War on Dissent.* Madison: University of Wisconsin Press.

Villaseñor, Rudy. 1970. "Chavez Gives Testimony for Gun Suspect." *Los Angeles Times*, November 26: section II, 3.

Washington, James Melvin, ed. 1986. *A Testament of Hope: The Essential Writings and Speeches of Martin Luther King, Jr.* San Francisco: HarperSanFrancisco.

Williams, Raymond. 1989. *Resources of Hope*. London and New York: Verso.

Yinger, Winthrop. 1975. *Cesar Chavez: The Rhetoric of Nonviolence*. Hicksville, N.Y.: Exposition Press.

Young, Andrew. 1996. *An Easy Burden: The Civil Rights Movement and the Transformation of America*. New York: HarperCollins.

Teacher of Truth

John C. Hammerback

César Chávez was a farm worker, and leader of farm workers, and it seems right that his funeral took place in Keene, California, the heart of our state's farm region.[1] But it is also appropriate that a memorial for him take place in a university. And, it is fitting that a professor of speech communication, like myself, might be part of a memorial to Chávez.

The university is a center for teaching and learning spoken and written persuasion, or public address, and the study of it. I believe that these two topics interlock in ways central to Chávez's life. For a few moments I'd like to look at Chávez from the point of view of a teacher and student of rhetoric, of persuasion, of words.

César Chávez grew up the child of farmers who lost their ranch near Yuma, Arizona, during the Great Depression of the 1930s, and became migrant workers—and young César too became a crop-picker. Here he learned first-hand of the injustices to farm workers, of the wretched aspects of their life, of their suffering. From his family he also learned and believed the Christian doctrines taught by the Roman Catholic Church: that Christ loves the poor and hates injustice, that the Church must stand up for and care for the oppressed, and that a supernatural God loves us all and can control human events. From this beginning he took his religious views, his love of family, his hatred of the injustices done to farm workers.

In the 1940s César moved to San José and for a time worked in various jobs. Soon he met Father Donald McDonnell, a Catholic priest who influenced him to dedicate himself to fighting for legal and social rights for the poor, especially for farm workers. After he discovered that churchmen, for all their wonderful ideals, did not understand how to organize underprivileged people into effective pressure groups, he joined the Community Services Organization. Operating on the assumption that American institutions would respond to pressure, the CSO concentrated on organizing poor and working-class Mexican Americans to obtain their rights. It would be a perfect training ground for Chávez to develop his rhetorical skills.

John C. Hammerback: "Teacher of Truth," first published in *San José Studies*, vol. 20, num. 2 (1994): 101–4.

For ten years in the 1950s and early 1960s Chávez worked for the CSO as an organizer; and organizers, he soon discovered, must talk to people, must convince them to join with others to seek their rights. But Chávez was by nature a quiet and modest man. At first he was very awkward and nervous when speaking to groups. Yet he also realized that persuasive public address was essential in organizing. He began speaking frequently at homes and in other places, often agonizing over his words. By his own description, here is what happened after his speeches: "I often lay awake at night, going over the whole thing, playing the tape back, trying to see why people laugh at one point, or why they are for one thing and against another." He also learned that clear and concrete examples and illustrations are more effective than philosophizing. As he said: "You have to draw a simple picture and color it in."

César Chávez was mastering the art of spoken persuasion; it was on-the-job training. He would soon need all of his rhetorical skills.

In the spring of 1962 the thirty-five-year-old Chávez moved to Delano, to begin organizing farm laborers into an effective union. Few people believed he would succeed. California farm workers had typically been illiterate, penniless, and migratory; and growers had easily broken all unions since the first one in 1903. Moreover, Chávez initially lacked coworkers, personal wealth, and political power. He appeared to be no match for California agribusiness.

To even the odds a bit, Chávez launched an intensive rhetorical campaign. It was to last his lifetime. During his first eleven months in Delano he worked in the fields all day and then drove to farm workers' camps and homes almost every night, attending hundreds of house meetings while canvassing for members in eighty-seven communities within a hundred-mile radius.

His talking and efforts at organizing quickly produced results. By 1965 he had established a union with more than two thousand dues-paying members. His union soon offered precedent-setting services, such as a credit union, health clinics, and old age benefits. By 1972, the United Farm Workers passed thirty thousand in membership and was affiliated with the powerful AFL-CIO. The UFW's victories would include agreements regarding growers use of pesticides; contracts with many major wineries and other growers; and the nation's first collective-bargaining legislation for farm workers.

Although Chávez suffered many setbacks—his problems with the rival Teamsters' Union; boycotts that failed; political winds which shifted against him—he never lost his deep faith in words. He continued to speak and write extensively, and to engage in other dramatic symbolic events which captured public attention: strikes, marches, fasts, pilgrimages, boycotts—all of which established his reputation as a charismatic leader and the most persuasive union spokesperson in a generation, and won his UFW union support from many prominent political figures and organizations. His audiences expanded far past the homes of farm workers in and around Delano, and by the early 1970s included congressional committees, college students, political gatherings, viewers of television, and even Pope Paul VI. By then his written message was carried in national news magazines through his interviews.

César Chávez's persistence, which had typified his initial campaign in Delano, always remained a striking feature of his career. During a lengthy speaking tour in 1965, for example, he addressed a college audience which had members who threw eggs and tomatoes at him. Although he was nearly exhausted on this tour, a weary Chávez scarcely seemed to notice the flying food and continued calmly to present his case—and the audience applauded him for his apparent coolness. In 1969 he made a three-month speaking tour of some ninety cities in the US and Canada. That's an average of a speech each day, for three months. Throughout the 1970s and 1980s he continued to make intermittent speaking tours.

Why did Chávez have so much faith in words? Why did he say what he said, and in the way he said it? And what accounts for his effectiveness as a speaker? I believe that a key to answering these questions, and thus a vital element in any understanding of his success and influence as a leader, lies in his interconnected views of God, reform, public address, and contemporary history.

Chávez believed in God, and believed that God had a plan for the world. But it was not just any plan. It was a millennial plan, a plan to improve conditions, to end injustice. Thus he told audiences that the protests and reforms of the turbulent 1960s were evidence that the poor were on the march in a revolution to change the nation. To him, the UFW was a unique union, because it represented the poor and downtrodden who were part of the revolutionary movement to change social conditions. And because history was moving toward this millennial future, history was on the side of farm workers. As he said as the 1960s ended: "People are not going to turn back now. The poor are on the march: black, brown, red, everyone, whites included. We are in the midst of the biggest revolution this country has ever known." Or, to another audience: "Our cause is just, history is a story of social revolution, and the poor shall inherit the land. We will win, we are winning, because ours is a revolution of mind and heart, not only of economics."

Thus Chávez saw his goals as divinely sanctioned. But he also believed that success required human agents. God used human spokespersons to spread the facts and arguments and explanations to a public which, when properly informed, would inevitably end injustices. If he presented his case clearly and with ample facts and thoughtful arguments, then listeners and readers would inevitably recognize its truthfulness and respond to his persuasive appeals.

So César Chávez was a very different kind of labor leader. His conviction that God guided him and other human agents led him to select a characteristic content and form for his major speeches and also explains how he spoke and worded those speeches—and why he was so persistent. His ideology shaped his rhetoric.

What did his formal speeches look like? Well, they were very clearly organized, with many transitions, previews, other clarifying devices, all to make sure the message was easily understood. They bulged with evidence—statistics, examples, quotations—to support his well developed arguments which demonstrated the legal, economic, and social justice of the farm workers' cause. He spoke calmly, gently and quietly at times, unusual for a militant and charismatic leader; and he worded his ideas clearly, sometimes with painstaking efforts to be sure he was understandable—often employing repetition and restatement to make sure points were clear.

The picture or image audiences received of him, or what we in rhetorical studies call his persona, was created both by Chávez's conscious design in his speeches and writings and by providence through his life and appearance. Audiences saw a modest man who avoided taking any personal credit for his accomplishments, who sought to place all attention on his ideas and evidence and none on himself.

These and other of Chávez's rhetorical qualities reflected his unshakable trust that his facts and arguments would be persuasive, because God's plan would bring certain success if only he informed the public. It was as if the truth would speak for itself; he only needed to present it.

Of course, as a skilled and sensitive communicator, he also adapted his ideas to particular audiences. Thus he employed dichos and anecdotes, and formality, especially early in his speeches, all qualities common to Mexican and Mexican American public address and presumably expected by many of his listeners.

If we look at it broadly, Chávez combined his thought and character in his discourse. The man, his ideology, and his persuasion all merged. For students of discourse, this merger helps to explain his rhetorical power. He achieved a double-barreled identification with his listeners in a way which a rhetorical theory developed by Frederick Antczak says can reformulate audiences, can allow them to discover latent qualities in themselves and carry out acts they otherwise would not undertake.

César Chávez, then, was a teacher of truth as well as a labor organizer and union activist. His belief in God's plan for the world led him to his distinctive rhetorical profile, a profile which audiences found appealing and persuasive; and his unusual interpretation of the role of rhetorical discourse motivated him to persuade incessantly, whatever the odds—to speak, write, fast, lead pilgrimages, and engage in other rhetorical actions.

Thus the man, his words, and his teaching all come together. Because he was at his base a teacher of truth, it's fitting that we memorialize him in this university, and that we examine what he said. Now he is no longer among us, and I certainly lack the words to capture our loss. But his own words cannot be unsaid, and their influence cannot be undone—they remain in all of us. I only hope, and, like Chávez, I pray to God, that others will duplicate his commitment to speak the truth incessantly, to carry forth the cause of justice. If such leaders continue this tradition of speaking and writing, this war of words, we will all be better for it—and I can think of no better way to honor the legacy of César Chávez.

NOTES

1. This eulogy was delivered at a memorial ceremony honoring the life of César Chávez, at California State University, Hayward, California, May 10, 1993.

The Final Struggle

Richard Griswold del Castillo

We want radical change. Nothing short of radical change is going to have any impact on our lives or our problems. We want sufficient power to control our own destinies. This is our struggle. It's a life-time job. The work for social change and against social injustice is never ended.

César Chávez quoted in
Labor Leaders in America, p. 380.

A union organizer once compared César Chávez's life work to that of Sisyphus, the Corinthian king, who was condemned by the gods to spend eternity pushing a huge stone to the top of a hill only to have it roll down again when he neared the top. When reflecting on the history of the UFW during the 1980s, many might have considered it a form of Greek tragedy. The tremendous efforts that Chávez and the other UFW organizers put forth to build their union during the 1960s and early 1970s produced victories at the top of the hill. Within a short time, however, they had to start all over again, organizing and struggling to build the rebuilt union, over and over again. The battle into the 1980s and 1990s was led by the inspiring example of the UFW's founding president. Other UFW organizers and activists left the seemingly endless work of union building to pursue other occupations, but César remained. He persevered believing in the same principles that he had first brought to farm labor organizing as a young man.

A thorough and well-documented history of the last decade of the life story of César Chávez is yet to be written. The documents necessary to tell this story remain unavailable to researchers and the political sensibilities of the actors involved in this story are still rather sensitive, perhaps even more so since César Chávez's unexpected death. But even without access to primary documents, we know that the final years of his life, from middle 1970s to the time of his death in 1993 was one of decline in the fortunes of the union he loved so much—a fact that Chávez himself recognized and sought to re-

Richard Griswold del Castillo: "Cesar Estrada Chavez: The Final Struggle," first published in *Southern California Quarterly,* vol. 78, issue 2 (1996): 199–214.

verse. Why at the height of its power as a farm labor organization did the union decline in membership and political influence? What degree of responsibility did Chávez feel for the deteriorating strength of the union? Were the decisions that he made the correct ones? The answers to these questions are highly controversial and some UFW supporters may regard their being raised as a form of criticism of Chávez's leadership.

Certainly César Chávez's place as a major figure in American history is assured. While he was alive he was the subject of more written and published attention than any other Latino leader, past or present. His inspiring leadership of El Movimiento changed the way a whole generation thought about farm workers. It would not be too much to say that Chávez's leadership of the UFW was responsible for changing the nation's consciousness about the social and economic problems of Mexican Americans. Chávez has been justly eulogized in speech and print as an American hero.[1] World leaders have recognized Chávez's moral stature. In April 1993, the President of the United States urged all Americans to "reflect on and honor the life of this distinguished leader, veteran and American." The President of Mexico praised Chávez for his work for all the Mexican workers and held him as an example of a courageous leader. Pope John Paul II lauded Chávez's spirituality, courage, and untiring efforts for the workers and the poor. Working class men and women spoke, quite seriously, of canonizing Chávez as an American saint.

At this point in time we would do well to remember that César Chávez was a person whose life was a mixture of personal achievements as well as failures. What made him truly great were not necessarily his successes in labor organizing but rather his spirit—his ability to persist despite many adversities. That so few have focused on the final period in Chávez's life may reflect a very American bias of wanting a success story with a happy ending.

The theme of César's first ten years as president of the UFW, 1965 to 1975, was one of triumph over tremendous odds. In only five years César took a handful of friends and relatives along with some of the poorest workers in America and built an organization that triumphed over some of the most powerful multinational corporations in America.[2] The UFW succeeded in gaining protections for farm labor organizing in 1975 with the passage of the California Farm Labor Relations Act. This legislative victory marked the high point of the union's organizational strength. Thereafter there was definite deterioration in the union's membership and bargaining successes. By 1980 differences over the correct strategies to follow led to the defections of many long-time supporters. The number of union contracts dwindled and the media, which previously had been supportive of the UFW and Chávez began to criticize his leadership.

During the fall of 1989 I was privileged to have a lengthy interview with César Chávez at La Paz in the Tehachapi Mountains. For almost three hours he told me of his bitter disappointment with the press and his former allies and how they had hurt the union.[3] He believed that he had made a mistake in foregoing the boycott strategy during the late 1970s. He remained convinced that the grape boycott, begun in 1984, was the only way to rebuild support for the union and get new contracts. His total dedication to farm workers and to the UFW was evident in every word he spoke. He was optimistic about ultimate success but, at the same time it was evident, even then, that he was tired, worn down by years of personal sacrifice and frustration.

An appreciation of the last decade of Chávez's leadership gives a more complete picture of the man and his life. Recently a full-length biography of Chávez co-authored by myself and Professor Richard A. Garcia was published by the University of Oklahoma Press. This essay draws from several chapters in that book and also adds some new information and perspectives that were not included in the book. Enough partisan ink has been spilled both for and against the UFW to make us aware that there will always be controversy surrounding Chávez's life, and perhaps this is as it should be.

REACHING THE TOP OF THE HIIL

The high point of the UFW's strength and Chávez's leadership was in 1974–75 with the passage of the California Farm Labor Relations Act. This legislative victory gave the California farm workers the right to have government supervised union elections and juridical means of settling disputes with growers. In the years just prior to the passage of this law, the UFW had won several other battles that strengthened its hand as a political force within California. There had been a long struggle against the Teamsters Union. Four years earlier, in 1970, the UFW had won a tremendous victory when scores of corporate grape growers signed contracts recognizing the union. Almost immediately after this success, the Teamsters began a jurisdictional war with the UFW. The Teamsters signed sweetheart contracts giving the growers what they wanted without even negotiating wage rates for the workers. For the next several years Chávez fasted, marched, picketed, and boycotted along with thousands of supporters, forcing the Teamsters to gradually withdraw from the fields. Simultaneously he led a successful fight against several legislative attempts to hamstring the farm labor movement. In 1971 the growers sponsored Proposition 22, an initiative to outlaw boycotting and to limit secret ballot elections to full-time nonseasonal employees. On November 7, 1972, California voters, listening to Chávez and the UFW supporters, soundly defeated Proposition 22 by a margin of 58 to 42 percent.[4] Chávez led an effort to define worker rights. At the union's constitutional convention in late September 1973, UFW delegates drafted a constitution that did not distinguish between the rights of citizen and noncitizen members. The purpose of the union was defined "to unite under its banner all individuals employed as agricultural laborers, regardless of race, creed, sex or nationality." The constitution provided for a Bill of Rights for all members, regardless of legal status in the United States. All members had the right to participate equally in union affairs and to receive their legal entitlement as provided in the constitution.[5]

Following Chávez's life-long belief in providing social services for farm workers, the UFW developed more than thirty service centers scattered around California where members could receive help with all sorts of problems from rent disputes to immigration advice. The centers were places where farm workers could go to learn how to claim the various state and federal benefits for which they might be eligible. In addition to the use of these service centers, union members had a pension plan to which the employers contributed, a credit union for low interest loans, a number of UFW clinics with low-cost medical treatment including dentistry, a low-cost retirement home, and prepaid legal services.[6]

The capstone victory for the UFW was the passage of the Farm Labor Act in 1975. For years the growers had proposed various versions of a law that would regulate labor strife in the fields, especially since farm workers were exempt from national legislation under the National Labor Relations Act. This exemption had both positive and negative results. On the negative side, the government avoided taking responsibility for enforcing fair elections and representation; the result had been years of fighting between the Teamsters and the UFW. On the positive side, exclusion from the NLRA meant that the UFW was also exempt from the anti-secondary boycott provisions of that law and its successors. César had rejected and fought against attempts to include farm workers under the NLRA or any of the state sponsored labor laws, precisely because they outlawed what he considered his most powerful organizing tactic, the boycott.

Late in 1974 César began to think that a state agricultural law might work but only if the law had certain provisions. First, it had to allow for boycotts. Second, it had to allow seasonal workers to vote in elections. Third, a UFW-supported farm labor law had to allow for legitimate strikes. Initially, the growers opposed all these conditions for a farm labor law, but by 1975, after the years of strikes, jurisdictional violence, and boycotts, they were willing to negotiate.

The result was the passage of the California Agricultural Labor Relations Act in May 1975, the first such law in the continental United States governing farm labor organizing (farm workers in Hawaii had a similar law). The law gave César what he wanted, secret ballot elections, the right to boycott, voting rights for migrant seasonal workers, and control over the timing of elections. The growers, for their part, were convinced that the law would end boycotts and labor disruptions that had cost them millions of dollars in profits.

Within a month after the passage of the law, César decided to intensify both the boycott and organizing efforts so that they could have quicker recognition elections. He led a 59-day, 1,000-mile march from Calexico on the Mexican border through the Imperial and San Joaquin valleys. Each night along the way he spoke at rallies to advertise the coming union elections.

Meanwhile the struggle continued with the Teamsters who reemerged and were organizing farm workers and opposing the UFW. The first elections took place on August 28, 1975, amidst charges of voter fraud and intimidation by the growers. By the end of 1975 the UFW had signed 198 contracts representing 27,000 workers and the Teamsters had 115 contracts representing 12,000 workers.

The continued strength of the Teamsters largely resulted from the growers' tactics of allowing the Teamsters special access, threatening workers, firing UFW members, and calling the Immigration Service to get rid of UFW voters among the undocumented workers. The UFW challenged and filed more than 1,000 complaints alleging violation of the new law's election provisions.[7]

A controversy arose over the access rules for the union. The UFW wanted unlimited right to enter ranches and farms to talk to workers about the union, whereas growers wanted control over access, giving preference to the Teamsters. They posted armed guards at the entrances to their farms to prevent UFW organizers from entering. Threats and intimidation against union members continued.

Another problem was funding. The ALRB ran out of money for its daily operation at the beginning of 1976 and suspended operations for five months until the legislature could vote for a regular appropriation. The legislature lacked the necessary majority to pass an emergency appropriation, so the ALRB stopped reviewing and certifying elections.

César decided to attack the issues of funding and access by appealing to the voters. In a massive initiative campaign the UFW sent out its workers and gathered more than 700,000 signatures in only twenty-nine days. The initiative, known as Proposition 14, was to be voted on in November 1976. It would guarantee adequate funding for the ALRB and free access for union organizers. César directed the campaign to pass Proposition 14. He put all the union's spare volunteers on the campaign to secure its passage. Opposing him was a media campaign funded by oil companies and land corporations who spent $1.8 million to tell the voters that the initiative was a threat to everyone's property rights. But despite endorsements by Jerry Brown and the successful presidential candidate, Jimmy Carter, Proposition 14 lost by a two to one margin. The public seemed convinced that the funding of the Farm Labor Board was already a moot point and that the access provision was a threat to property rights.[8]

ROLLING DOWN, AGAIN

Some regard the defeat of Proposition 14 in 1976 as a turning point in Chávez's ability to mobilize the public's support for the farm workers and their union. Without adequate access to the workers, the promise of the ALRB as a means of helping organize farm workers rapidly disappeared. Republican pro-grower interests increasingly controlled the Farm Labor Board. They consistently ruled against the many grievances that were brought before it by the union. Moreover, the labor law did not require that the growers sign contracts, only that they had to bargain with the election winners. The UFW might win an election and then be tied up in interminable negotiations over the contract. The only weapon the union had to bring about contracts was to strike. But the nation had entered a conservative mood under the Republican administrations of Ronald Reagan. This meant a decline in public support for labor unions in general as well as a lessening of concern for the plight of the farm workers.

There were some victories, however. One was the result of years of lobbying and complex legal maneuvers, the abolition of *el cortito*, or the short-handled hoe, in 1975. For decades the growers had required field workers to use this tool that forced the workers to bend over while working. Thousands of farm workers permanently damaged their backs and spent the rest of their lives in disabling pain. Chávez and the UFW had opposed the use of el cortito because of its damaging effect on the workers' health. Together with attorneys for California Rural Legal Aid (CRLA), they began a campaign to outlaw its usage. After lengthy government hearings, a Supreme Court ruling (*Sebastian Carmona et al. v. Division of Industrial Safety*, 1975), and following a 1975 California administrative ruling, the short-handled hoe was outlawed.

As for union building, the period following the passage of the California Farm Labor Act was one of growth in membership and in number of contracts. The UFW had won almost two thirds of the elections after 1975, and the Teamsters admitted in March of 1977 that they were beaten and that they would not contest future elections. The dues paying membership of the UFW soared to more than 100,000 by 1978, and effective strikes resulted in contracts in the Santa Maria Valley and in the Imperial Valley. Also Chávez continued the union's policy of forging alliances with other unions. For instance, the UFW joined with a Puerto Rican farm worker's union and with the Farm Labor Organizing Committee in the midwest. Dolores Huerta and César continued to have a great deal of influence within the California legislature. Some of their proposals became laws. By 1978, Chávez announced that the grape and lettuce boycotts were over and that henceforth the union would boycott only selective labels.

After the defeat of Proposition 14, César decided to reorganize the union. In late 1975 he called for a conference to discuss ideas for modernizing the union. Later he invited Kenneth Blanchard, author of *The One Minute Manager*, to come to La Paz to give a management seminar. Blanchard accepted and did the session for free. César invited other consultants to the union headquarters, and the staff began discussing new ideas. As part of the modernization drive they began computerizing all the union records and purchased a microwave communications system so that they would not be dependent on public telephones. César even experimented with techniques of interpersonal communication borrowed from Synanon, a drug dependency/recovery program whose controversial director, Charles Diedrick, had known César since the 1950s.[9]

César wanted to decentralize the union. The plan was to create five groups within the UFW, each one responsible for its budgeting and programs. César's hope was to develop internal leadership that would not be so dependent on his decision making. These changes threatened some of the old guard, those who had been with César the longest, such as Gilbert Padilla, Jerry Cohen, and Marshall Ganz. Some departing UFW staff claimed that the Synanon "game" pitted them against each other and caused internal bad feelings. Newspaper editorials began leveling charges that César had given up traditional organizing activities in favor of electronic mass mailings. Others criticized the move from the Forty Acres in the San Joaquin Valley to La Paz in the Tehachapi Mountains as isolating the union from the membership. Critics said that César had centralized the leadership of the union too much and was acting like a dictator. César and the UFW leadership believed that maintaining loyalty to César's vision of the union was what had made the UFW a success, enabling it to respond rapidly to external threats. The union loyalists maintained that a strong leadership was necessary because there were many forces within and without that wanted to change and destroy the original vision that Chávez had developed of the UFW—an organization that was more than a union.[10]

There were other troubling signs of division. A number of longtime staff members quit the union, some expressing their unhappiness with César's leadership and others admitting to being burned out by the long hours at almost no pay. In 1977 Lair Chatfiled and Jim Drake, both among the first staff members of the UFW, quit and went on to other organizations. Gil Padilla, a cofounder of the union, had a disagreement over organizing issues and quit. Philip Vera Cruz, another cofounder of the UFW, resigned his post in protest over Chávez's meeting with President Marcos when he visited the Philippines. Other Filipino leaders then quit, leaving the UFW led mostly by Mexican Americans. In March 1979, Jerry Cohen, the UFW's chief attorney, quit after the executive board defeated his proposal to allow his staff to be paid salaries rather than in-kind benefits. In 1981 Marshall Ganz, who helped organize the lettuce strike, left the union, along with a number of other union leaders from the Salinas area, over a dispute having to do with the selection of union representatives.[11] Chávez contended that the dissidents were attempting to undermine his leadership by opposing his choices to the union board. When Chávez fired them, the Salinas dissidents went on a hunger strike in protest. Subsequently Chávez and the union filed a twenty-five million dollar libel suit against them. The newspaper and journal reactions to these resignations and rebellions were to magnify them as signaling the end of the Chávez-led union. For example, *The Village Voice* ran a two-part series entitled "César Chávez's Fall from Grace" supposedly exposing internal dissension within the union.[12] The conflict with Marshall Ganz was a bitter one that caused César a great deal of anguish. He felt betrayed by one of his closest confidants and was positive that Marshall had gone over to the other side and was trying to destroy the union. After this affair César would no longer place his trust in professional staffers. The union leadership would be more and more restricted to those members of his extended family that he could trust.

In addition to internal division, César got involved on the losing end of a political battle over the selection of the speaker of the Assembly in the California Legislature. In 1979 a long-time UFW supporter from Los Angeles, Howard Berman, was running for the speaker position against Willie Brown, also a Democrat from San Francisco. At issue was the UFW's political influence in the Assembly since Berman could influence key appointments to the Farm Labor Board. César had the promise of two Chicano assemblymen, Art Torres and Richard Alatorre, to initially support Berman during the voting, but both Torres and Alatorre switched on the final vote when Brown appeared victorious. This apparent betrayal enraged César.[13] Eventually, Richard Alatorre appeared before a UFW convention to apologize for his actions but Torres remained unrepentant. When Torres ran for reelection, César supported his opponent Alex Garcia, who nevertheless lost. Torres in turn retaliated by rejecting UFW supported candidates for the Farm Labor Board. The result was that Governor George Deukmejian was able to appoint to the board people hostile to the UFW. This struggle seemed to diminish the political capital of the UFW.[14]

By the 1980s the UFW had lost its earlier momentum. In 1984 only fifteen of the seventy grape growers in the Delano area were under a UFW contract. The union was winning fewer and fewer elections; in 1976 it had won 276, but in the years since it had won only 56. Union membership dropped to less than 12,000 active members from a high of more than 105,000. Fewer and fewer strikes occurred, and the UFW reduced the number of organizers in the fields hoping to encourage local leadership and initiative.

The answer to the decline, César thought, was the Farm Labor Board's prejudicial management in favor of grower interests. The board now was being used to stifle unionization. The ALRB took on the average of 348 days to settle disputes over contested elections and about half as long to render a decision whether to litigate an unfair labor practice. By 1984, after almost ten years of existence, the ALRB had not rendered a single award for violation of the labor law. The decline in organizing power in the fields was due to the tremendous economic and political power of the giant multinationals in California compounded by internal divisions within the UFW.[15]

The stalemate promoted by the grower influenced ALRB and dwindling union strength forced César to the conclusion that the only tactic left was to renew the boycott to pressure the growers to sign contracts. So on June 12, 1984, he announced that the union would embark on a new grape boycott. He said, "We put too much reliance on the laws. Now we are going back to the only thing that ever worked for us."[16] Since the UFW had sponsored more than fifty boycotts over the years, however, the public was confused as to what was and was not boycotted. The union needed to undertake a tremendous educational campaign; Chávez called for a modern strategy. This would be a high-tech boycott, relying on computer-enervated mailings, slick advertising copy, and media packets. César believed the most sensitive issue appealing to consumers was that of pesticide residues on the fruit.[17] The UFW produced a movie entitled *The Wrath of Grapes* where graphic footage showed the birth defects and high rates of cancer that pesticide poisoning produced among farm workers and consumers. In 1987 and again in 1988, César traveled on speaking tours to midwestern and eastern cities where grape consumption was viewed as a luxury item and where union support had always been the strongest. As the boycott effort grew some critics began to question the allocation of scarce resources away from organizing in the fields. Said one UFW worker, quoted in the press, "You don't see any organizers anymore. I would ask César: What are you doing? What I see is that the whole movement seems to have stopped."[18]

In 1988, to dramatize the boycott's purpose, César decided to go on a fast. He began on midnight July 16. The fast went largely unnoticed by the public until the children of Robert Kennedy visited César in La Paz to lend their support. As in the past the fast became a rallying point for union supporters. Daily bulletins on César's health were issued on the union's radio station KUFW, and nightly masses were held with thousands in attendance. Dolores Huerta noted that "This is a spiritual thing with him. This is not a publicity stunt."[19] Consequently, the fast, more than any other action by César, drew new attention to the boycott and the pesticide issue. Finally, on Sunday, August 22, César gave up his water-only fast. As an expression of support, Jesse Jackson, a presidential candidate, and actors Martin Sheen and Robert Blake vowed to continue the fast for three days to keep alive the "chain of suffering." Thereafter, for several months, individuals joined three-day mini-fasts to demonstrate their support for the union.

During the thirty-six day fast, César issued a statement that summarized his commitment to the union and the boycott:

> As I look back at this past year, I can see many events that precipitated the fast, including the terrible suffering of farm workers and their children, the crushing of farm worker rights, the denial of fair and free elections and the death of good-faith bargaining in California agriculture. All of these events are connected with the great cause of justice for farm worker families.[20]

Later, in the 1990s Chávez exhibited the same qualities of character that brought him success in the earlier boycott. Most of all he was tenacious in his leadership, despite an apparent change in the activist mood of the country. He believed that a modern boycott could be won with an alliance among Latinos, blacks, and other minorities, plus allies in labor and the Church. He also had faith that for the generation of activists from the 1960s and 1970s the boycott would become "a social habit." By 1991 statistics seemed to bear out his optimism. During the crucial period from May to August 1990, grapes delivered for sale declined in 12 major cities. In New York City grape consumption was down 74 percent; in Los Angeles it declined by 37 percent, and 36 percent in San Francisco. The UFW could cite official statistics showing that the growers were selling grapes at a loss. Chávez was confident about the ultimate success of the boycott.

In the early 1990s César Chávez continued his fight for the farm workers, although it was period of tremendous struggle and sacrifice. Journalists and op-ed writers occasionally devoted their columns to the problems the union faced, but their mood was largely pessimistic. In 1991, for example, the newspapers reported that the UFW had been dealt a significant financial setback when the 4th District Court in California upheld an earlier judgment against the union by Daggio Inc., an Imperial Valley grower, for 1.7 million dollars. Including interest, the ultimate cost to the union could exceed 2.4 million dollars. The damages sought by the grower arose out of a 1979 vegetable strike that resulted in property damage as well as the death of a UFW striker, Rufino Contreras. To pay the fine, the UFW mounted a nationwide direct mail campaign. But almost immediately another lawsuit threatened the UFW's existence, this one by Bruce Church Inc. who won a 5.4 million dollar judgment for alleged damages incurred during the boycott. The union appealed.

Chávez remained hopeful. He continued to appear at fund raising rallies at college and university campuses and traveled to promote the grape boycott. He also has stepped up organizing in the fields. Ranch by ranch and week by week during the summer and fall of 1992, César and the UFW staff sought to advance the union's issues. He continued organizing the grape boycott to force growers to sign contracts to control pesticide use. In 1992, he and the union helped organize large-scale walk-outs in the Coachella Valley during the summer grape harvest to protest the lack of drinking water and sanitary facilities. They won concessions from the grower to organize a Worker's Committee to watch-dog the situation. Chávez had been active in organizing other walk-outs and protests in the San Joaquin Valley. Led by Chávez, in the summer of 1992 more than 10,000 farm workers in the Salinas Valley staged a protest march in support of better conditions in the fields.

Chávez was confident about the ultimate success of the UFW struggle. In late April 1993, he traveled to San Luis, Arizona, near his birthplace to give testimony in the union's appeal of a judgment against them for 5.4 million dollars won by Bruce Church Inc. Chávez stayed with a farm worker family and began a fast to gain moral strength. On Thursday his friends convinced him to break his fast and he went to sleep apparently exhausted. That night César Chávez died in his sleep.[21]

His unexpected death on April 23, 1993, was a shock to his supporters throughout the world. The tremendous outpouring of condolences and support that followed his death was a testimony to his importance as a leader who touched the conscience of America. On the day of his funeral, more than 35,000 people followed his casket for three miles from downtown Delano to the union's old headquarters at the Forty Acres. They came from all over, Toronto, Miami, Mexico but mostly from California where Chávez had worked most of his life. Parents took their children out of school and drove all night to give them the experience of participating in the funeral of a great leader of the poor. Middle class Chicanos took off work to march, perhaps for the first time, with a UFW flag led by César Chávez's son. Cardinal Roger M. Mahony, who had worked as a mediator for the UFW more than twenty years earlier, led a huge outdoor mass where he offered a personal condolence from the Pope. César's twenty-seven grandchildren went up to the altar to lay a carving of a UFW eagle and a short-handled hoe. Dolores Huerta delivered the eulogy for the man she had worked with for more than forty years. Luis Valdez and the Teatro Campesino paid the final tribute. "You shall never die," said Valdez, "The seed of your heart will keep on singing, keep on flowering, for the cause."[22]

The historian's evaluation of the legacy of César Chávez must ultimately take into account the power of his appeal to the common man. He was a symbol of everyman's struggle against the big corporations and impersonal uncaring government. The final decade of his life was quite different than that of the activist years, 1965–1975 when Chávez created a union that succeeded in gaining recognition, contracts and legislation to help the farm worker. After 1975, due to the resurgence of conservative political mood in the country at large and within California in particular, Chávez saw the mythical boulder roll back down the hill. Union membership declined, longtime supporters departed in bitterness, the number of contracts with growers dwindled. By 1983 César was starting slowly to push the boulder up the mountain, this time with a different group of supporters and staff. That he died before he could see the top again was a tragedy. For many, especially the farm workers whom he loved, his life mirrored theirs. For them and for thousands of others, his perseverance and courage despite tremendous difficulties made him an authentic American hero.

What is the legacy of César Chávez? He would probably most want to be remembered for having improved the lives of farm workers. In the 1980s, the UFW farm worker wage was twice the minimum wage; UFW workers had a pension plan, health insurance, free legal services, and access to service centers that provided a wide variety of assistance. Most of all the UFW undercut the power of the labor contractors through the use of the union hiring hall. Chávez led the fight to abolish the use of the short-handled hoe, an agricultural tool that created hundreds of disabled farm workers. He was largely responsible for the passage of the first farm labor law regulating grower-worker relations in California

Ultimately, however, César Chávez's most lasting legacy is a moral and spiritual one. In an age when we are increasingly cynical and made aware of the lack of values within American society, César Chávez stands out as one of the bright lights in our nation's development; proof that America can produce men and women of rare courage and conviction who struggle for social justice. César Chávez's life was one built on basic moral values. To a large extent these principles have also been part of the Mexican American heritage: self sacrifice for others, tenacious struggle despite overwhelming odds, respect for other races and religions, nonviolence, belief in a divine soul and moral order, a rejection of materialism, and a faith in the moral superiority of the poor, as well as a central belief in justice. These values César Estrada Chávez championed. As a person, Chávez represented the struggles of all peoples to achieve a better life. Perhaps he represented a moral code that can point a way out of the dilemmas we all face as we enter the twenty-first century.

NOTES

1. A small sample of the obituaries: Nicholas Mills, "Remembering Cesar Chavez," *Dissent*, 40 (fall, 1993), 552–55; "Cesar Chavez: Champion of Migrant Farm Workers," *Migration World Magazine*, 21 (March–June, 1993), 53; "Remembering Cesar Chavez," *Multinational Monitor*, 14 (May, 1993), 2; "Cesar Chavez: A Symbol of Hispanic Rights," *Crisis*, 100 (April–May, 1993), 28; Proclamation 6552-Death of Cesar Chavez (President Bill Clinton), *Weekly Compilation of Presidential Documents*, 29 (May 3, 1993), 709; "A Great & Good Man," *Commonweal*, 120 (June 4, 1993), 4; Peter Matthiessen, "Cesar Chavez," *New Yorker*, 69 (May 17, 1993), 82–84; "Champion of Farm Workers Dies," *Christian Century*, 110 (May 12, 1993), 513–15; David Gates, "A Secular Saint of the '60s: Cesar Chavez, Farm Workers' Champion, 1927–1993," *Newsweek*, 121 (May 3, 1993, 68; "Died, Cesar Chavez, 66" *Time*, 141 (May 3, 1993), 25.

2. The story of the UFW struggles in the early years is told by a number of authors. Some of the best are Eugene Nelson, *Huelga: The First Hundred Days of the Great Delano Grape Strike* (Delano: Farm Workers Press, 1966); John Dunne, *Delano, Story of the California Grape Strike* (New York: Farrar, Straus and Giroux, 1967); Peter Matthissen, *Sal Si Puedes: Cesar Chavez and the New American Revolution* (New York: Random House, 1969); Joan London and Henry Anderson, *So Shall Ye Reap: The Story of Cesar Chavez and the Farm Workers Movement* (New York: Thomas Crowell, 1970); Mark Day, *Forty*

Acres: Cesar Chavez and the Farm Workers (New York: Praeger Publishers, 1971); Jacques E. Levy, *Cesar Chavez Autobiography of La Causa* (New York: W. W. Norton, 1975); Sam Kushner, *The Long Road to Delano: A Century of Farm Worker Struggle* (New York: International Publishers, 1975); Ronald Taylor, *Chavez and the Farm Workers* (Boston: Beacon Press, 1975); Dick Meister and Anne Loftis, *A Long Time Coming: The Struggle to Unionize America's Farm Workers* (New York: Macmillan, 1977).

3. Interview with César Chávez, October 20, 1989. Unfortunately I was not given permission to quote directly from the interview.

4. For an analysis of this period see Dick Meister and Anne Loftis, *A Long Time Coming: The Struggle to Unionize America's Farm Workers* (New York and London: Collier Macmillan Publishers, 1977), p. 182.

5. E. M. Colbert, *The United Farm Workers of America: The United States of America* (Geneva: International Labour Office, n.d.), p. 40. Chávez emphasized the fact that undocumented immigrants was an important constituency within the UFW in one of his last interviews. See *César Chávez una entrevista* (Mexico, D.F.: Instituto Matias Romero de Estudios Diplomáticos, 1993), pp. 25–26.

6. Ibid., p. 21.

7. See J. Craig Jenkins, *The Politics of Insurgency: The Farm Worker Movement the 1960s* (New York: Columbia University Press, 1985), pp. 195–199.

8. Ibid., pp. 226–27.

9. Los Angeles *Times* 29 December 1978, A1.

10. San Jose *Mercury* 20 May 1982, p. 1; *New York Times* 5 December 1982, p. 22; 3 January 1983, A8; Los Angeles *Times*, 25 October 1981, A1, 19; 6 September 1981, B1; 13 November 1981, A1, 14.

11. *The Wall Street Journal*, 17 May 1982, p. 2; Los Angeles *Times*, 6 December 1982, Pt. IV, p. 1; 6 September 1981, A3.

12. Jeff Coplon, "César Chávez's Fall from Grace," *The Village Voice*, August 14, and August 21, 1984. The UFW initiated a libel suit as a result of this article. Other articles written in a similar vein appeared in regional journals and newspapers, such as John Hubner's "The God of the Movement," in *West*, August 19, 1984.

13. Los Angeles *Times*, 29 November 1990, A1, 20.

14. See *Wall Street Journal*, 9 September 1986, p. 1, 20; Los Angeles *Herald Examiner* 31 January 1982, p. 1.

15. Another reason for decline may have been the growers sophistication in offering benefits to counter those offered by the union. See Cletus E. Daniel, "Cesar Chavez and the Unionization of California Farm Workers," in *Labor Leaders in American*, Melvyn Dubofsky and Warren Van Tine, eds. (Urbana and Chicago: University of Illinois Press, 1987), p. 380.

16. *The Wall Street Journal*, 9 September 1986, p. 29. See also "Why Growers Want Cesar Chavez to Do More Organizing," Los Angeles *Times*, 3 November 1991, p. 6.

17. "Cesar Chavez Goes High-Tech," *California Journal*, 16 (April 1985), 167–69.

18. Los Angeles *Times*, 30 October 1988, p. 41.

19. Ibid., 5 August 1985, A1.

20. Ibid., 19 August 1988, A1.

21. Ibid., 24 April 1993, A23.

22. Ibid., 30 April 1993, A1, 29, 30.

THE FIRST AND LAST
OF THE CHICANO LEADERS

José Angel Gutiérrez

In this article, I hope to describe and analyze the leadership qualities of Cesar Chavez Estrada during the time he spent organizing the farm-worker union that he led until his untimely death. This piece is neither a eulogy nor a biographical update. Rather, it is intended to shed light on the various and significant contributions Chavez made to leadership and community organization among Mexican Americans in the United States. The fact that Chavez was a Chicano and rose to leadership during the Chicano Movement era made his contributions even more valuable to this ethnic group.

Cesar Chavez was the first Chicano leader to be introduced in English to the United States reading public.[1] The publicity generated and sustained by him and by the union of farmworkers via their public information and communications operations, the regional publications of Chicano Press Association members, and those of the mainstream press, made Chavez a household word not only for Chicanos but also for significant numbers of Americans, some Europeans, and governmental leaders in Mexico. Chavez was the best known of the various Chicano leaders of the era from the mid-1960s into the 1980s. "Cesar," as he was known to Chicanos and his supporters, was the first Chicano leader to emerge from the Movimiento Chicano generation. He also was the last to remain active in the organization he founded.

Though initially only one of the "Four Horsemen" of the Chicano Movement, Chavez's only significant competitor in the media was Reies Lopez Tijerina.[2] Tijerina was the leader of the land recovery movement based in New Mexico. During the late 1960s and into the 1970s Tijerina was most active in taking national forest park land by force. And, during the Poor People's Campaign in Washington D.C. he was the Chicano spokesman for the contingent of Raza involved with that event. Because of his activity, Tijerina was tried, convicted, and jailed for burning a forest park sign, a federal offense. Today, Reies Lopez Tijerina is in self-imposed seclusion near Coyote, New Mexico, and without an organizational base or political program. He does engage in public activity from

José Angel Gutiérrez: "The First and Last of the Chicano Leaders," first published in *San José Studies*, vol. 20, Num. 2 (1994): 32–44.

time to time In November, 1993, his home, warehouse, and adjoining buildings, three in all, were mysteriously firebombed. No charges have been made against anyone and the crime remains unsolved. Rodolfo "Corky" Gonzales founded the Crusade for Justice in the mid-1960s. The purpose was to militate against police brutality and educate La Raza about its heritage. Annually for the past 24 years, the Crusade has held a youth conference in Denver. The 1968 Chicano Youth Liberation Conference issued "El Plan Espiritual de Aztlan." The plan was a revolutionary call to radical social change. Corky became well known for his epic poem *Yo Soy Joaquin*.[3] Together with La Raza Unida Party activists from Texas under the direction of myself, Jose Angel Gutierrez, the Crusade promoted the formation of an independent political party for Chicanos during the decade of the 1970s.[4] Later, in the mid-1980s the Crusade declined and Corky sold the Crusade for Justice building in Denver. The sale ended what was left of the organization and *escuelita* "Tlatelolco." He is currently suffering severe health problems related to personal injuries sustained during an automobile accident combined with a stroke. I, myself, remain only minimally active as member, no longer a leader, in a number of Mexican-American and professional organizations in Texas and in immigrant defense work.

CHAVEZ: THE BEGINNINGS OF A LEADER

Cesar Chavez was recruited and joined the Community Services Organization (CSO). It was in CSO that Chavez learned community organizing, direct action tactics, urban electoral politics, and voter registration campaigns. In the early 1960s he left CSO to organize Chicano migrant farm workers in rural California. He first organized the National Farm Workers Association (NFWA). In 1965, Chavez's NFWA merged with the Agricultural Workers Organizing Committee (AWOC), comprised largely of Filipino farm workers affiliated with the AFL-CIO, into the United Farm Workers Organizing Committee (UFWOC). They now call themselves the United Farm Workers Union of America, AFL-CIO. His unionization efforts beyond California into Arizona and Texas made *la causa* of the farm workers a Chicano issue. The overwhelming numbers of farm workers west of the Mississippi were seasonal, migrant agricultural workers of Mexican ancestry. His example spawned other unionization efforts among Mexican-American farm workers in Washington, Wisconsin, and Ohio, for example. The Farm Labor Organizing Committee (FLOC) in the Midwest under the leadership of Baldemar Velasquez continues to this day.[5] The organizing efforts of a network of support groups nationally and internationally made the name "Cesar," *la causa*, his *persona*, and *el Movimiento Chicano*, household words, particularly to Chicanos. Chavez was not the first to seek to organize Mexican labor,[6] nor will he be the last.[7] Chavez did not reach his goal of a national union of farm workers, in spite of his lifelong efforts. Over his life span his union lost elections and organizing campaigns more often than they won. Chavez and the United Farm Workers Union of America, AFL-CIO, did gain regional influence in the Southwest, particularly California, Arizona, and Texas.

The goal of a national farm worker union probably is impossible to reach. Persons of Mexican ancestry in the United States are entering the United States labor market at unprecedented rates in blue-collar and white-collar occupations, not agriculture. Chavez, however, will probably be remembered in history as among the last to organize Mexicano migrant farm workers. The need for agricultural labor in the United States is rapidly declining. What little demand continues to exist for labor-intensive agriculture work is being adversely impacted by advanced technology and mechanization; by chemistry with improved pesticides and herbicides; and, by biogenetic engineering of stronger, bigger, better cloned crops.

The real contribution of Cesar Chavez lies not only in his total and exclusive dedication to *la causa* of farm-worker unionization but also to his transcendental leadership qualities.

CHAVEZ: THE FIRST VOICE OF CHICANOS

Cesar Chavez was able through his organizing work among farm workers to give Chicanos their "first voice." Cultural anthropologists use this term to identify the first articulation by a leader of an ethnic group interpreting its culture, expressing itself on its terms, and presenting its views on pressing issues of importance to the ethnic group. "Other voices" of ethnic groups and cultures traditionally have been the anthropologists and other social scientists who study the ethnic group. These social scientists interpret, analyze, and comment upon the ethnic group. Social scientists introduce members of the ethnic group under study via quotations and anecdotal reference. The ethnic group subjects are permitted to speak much in the fashion of a ventriloquist's dummy.[8] Cesar Chavez and the *campesinos* ended the age of ventriloquism for Chicanos. The farm-worker movement and other social protest movements by other Chicanos in the 1960s began the evidentiary contradiction for the academy of "social science fiction." In decades past, social scientists utilized faulty conceptual models and paradigms to study Chicanos.[9]

Cesar, while the leader of the farm-worker union, also became a spokesman for the Chicano Movement generation. Even though Cesar primarily addressed only farm-worker issues such as collective bargaining, working conditions, health and safety, product boycotts, and farm-labor contracts, he was nevertheless seen by many non-farm-worker Chicanos as speaking for them. Occasionally, he would accept appearances at other Chicano-related events such as bilingual education conferences, Chicano Studies student programs, and voter registration colloquia. Public speaking at non-farm-worker union gatherings was an instrument for fund raising.

Chavez was also instrumental in interceding for Chicano students at Mt. Angel College, Oregon.[10] Chavez also campaigned for the Raza Unida Party slate of candidates in Crystal City, Texas, during 1972. He traveled the United States widely and often, logging more miles than any other Chicano leader of his time in the furtherance of his message.

CHAVEZ: LA PERSONA

Chavez used the term "Chicano" as a self-identifier, he referred to himself as a Chicano. He dressed as a working man. He wore khaki pants, most often, with sport shirts, *guayaveras*, or flannel long sleeved shirts. He did not use name-brand toiletries such as underarm deodorants, hair grooming liquids or sprays, aftershave, colognes, or eau de toilette; nor did he dye, color, highlight, or tint his jet-black hair. The scant gray by his temples began to emerge in the last few years. He was natural, at ease, almost stoic but was betrayed frequently by his impish smile. He was comfortable with himself. He usually spoke in Spanish. He spoke in English to staff non-Mexican audiences and reporters, and on college campuses. He was bilingual and bi-cultural. He didn't have an eloquent, grandiose or verbose speaking style. He was plain speaking and monotonal. Rarely did he raise his voice to make a point or command attention. He was tireless in all his roles as father, husband, Catholic, leader, Chicano, organizer, staff manager, and man. In his personal simplicity he was poignant. The simplicity of his message—justice for farm workers—made him eloquent. He had a firm belief in the righteousness of *la causa*. He was tenacious, aggressive, and militant. This commitment to *los campesinos* was total and complete. He looked *mestizo*. He was dark skinned, short, with high check bones, piercing black eyes, and sparse facial hair. He was the embodiment of a Chicano. Chicanos could see themselves in Cesar: clothes, personal style, demeanor and commitment. Chavez inspired himself. And, his inspiration moved Chicanos.

CHAVEZ: EL LIDER

As a Chicano leader of farm workers, he introduced a new and fresh leadership style. His rhetoric, slogans, symbols, tactics, strategies, demeanor, appearance, and management and organizational methods were new. Some of his contributions were new to students of community organizing; most were just new to the farm-worker population and to Chicanos, in general. For example, he used both la Virgen de Guadalupe's image and the religious song of the *cursillo* movement, "De Colores," borrowed from the Mexican Catholic church, as an umbrella of symbolic protection. He recruited and used Catholic priests and nuns, Protestant clergy, and Jewish rabbis as his advocates, another umbrella for sheltered opportunity to expand his network of support and blunt criticism of the Catholic hierarchy in California. He borrowed from Gandhi the notions and rhetoric of non-violence and peaceful civil disobedience. And all the while, his principal leadership cadre, many followers, supporters, his family, and he suffered extreme violence at the hands of many enemies such as growers and Teamsters. Many farm workers have died from violence inflicted on them by those who opposed unionization efforts. Like Ghandi, Chavez fasted, too many times and for too long. He hurt his body. But he made the important politicians come to him during these fasts and even made enemies pray he would end his fasts and the boycotts. Chavez did craft a successful model of organizing the poor, migrant, seasonal, agricultural workers into a union. Chavez modified and re-invented the Black Thunderbird icon of the Hopi peoples as the union symbol—a Chicano phoenix. He made propaganda through political buttons, bumper stickers, lapel pins, posters, newspapers, and videos. He used and promoted el Teatro Campesino to carry the farm-worker message via guerilla theater. He initiated strikes, picket lines, and boycotts. He made many learn to shout "Huelga" while at picket lines and rallies and he made a generation of Chicanos and other supporters stop eating grapes. Chavez even exported his attack strategies and tactics internationally, following the farm products he was boycotting. His brother, Ricardo Chavez, traveled to Great Britain, Scandinavia, and elsewhere in Europe, building a boycott support network. With the international boycott of grapes, Cesar Chavez mastered the Third Party boycott strategy. Chavez built both a national and international support network for his union.

Chavez was the first Chicano leader to bring organized, poor Mexicanos into the political arena. He brought the *Chicanada* out from the campos into hotels, urban grocery stores, cathedrals, national conventions, and election precincts to make their presence known, felt, listened to, and dealt with by middle class Mexican Americans, white politicians at all levels, national union bosses, agribusiness interests, and other minority groups. In so doing, he made Chicanos present and active and gave them their first voice of power.

CHAVEZ: TRANSCENDENTAL AND TRANSACTIONAL LEADER

We know that Cesar Chavez became a master organizer of people. The union is living proof of his success. We know and witnessed his leadership. In achieving organizational status, official affiliation with the AFL-CIO, and official contract representation for the membership, Chavez also became a manager. This dimension of Cesar Chavez is not well known. With each union/grower contract victory, Chavez had to make good on the promise of the union as a good thing. Chavez had to grow into a great transactional leader. The transactional leader is one who works on behalf of constituents on difficult problems and who seeks practical, negotiated solutions. Usually, the arena for this type of problem-solving or service delivery is found in institutions and bureaucracies. Chavez however, was a transcendental leader more often than a transactional leader. The difference between the two is vast. A transactional leader is a broker. A transactional leader can arrange a deal; broker an opportunity; negotiate an impasse; effect a compromise; and fix a problem. Examples of such persons are elected officials, political party workers, labor union job stewards, organizational volunteers and members, public relations personnel, maîtres d'hôtel, concierges, and attorneys.

Transactional leaders deal with issues of narrow scope and stay the course on tangible, realizable short-term goals. Their words are practical, simple, and clear. On the other hand, a transcendental leader is one who has a big picture in mind. Such a person has a vision beyond the proverbial trees and can see past the forest to the horizon. Such a leader is not bound or focused on the mundane or the detailed. Rather, this leader seeks out the grandiose and moves masses with articulation of a dream.[11] The focus of this leader is long-term and often abstract. Such a leader speaks in symbolic rhetoric that excites and incites. Chavez was such a man for Chicanos. He was one of the migrants. He spoke plainly but articulated larger than life goals for migrants, especially that of building their own union. He was effective because he organized and could mobilize his masses. He made others, both Chicanos and non-Chicanos, accept him as he was. He made being Chicano legitimate to middle-class Mexican Americans and non-Mexican supporters.

The nature of union representation is transactional in nature. The subject is the individual member. The focus often is on employee grievances, contract language, delayed or denied services, missed opportunities for advancement and higher pay, and even slights in recognition for union work done and not praised. Chavez not only organized the unorganized with appeals to higher levels of personal activity and commitment, but also delivered on the appeal. By his mastery of transactional work Chavez made real the promise of an improved quality of life and with union/grower contracts in hand, he made self-determination for individual members possible. But, Chavez was neither chained to detail nor enslaved by union management problems. He was able to transcend the transaction, regardless of the situation.

Chavez, for example, made connections for his audience, *campesino* and consumer alike, between health and safety issues for farmworkers and consumers of farm produce; between the use of pesticides and herbicides on fruits and vegetables and consumers' health; and between the condition of labor and the national economy. Because of this ability to move his audience rhetorically from the transaction at hand and transcend to the larger issue, Chavez made his name and cause among the most recognized of all Chicano leaders and movements of his time.

Chavez was able to lead and able to manage. He built a vertically integrated union. He developed many programs within the union to offer health care, housing, legal services, communications, credit unions, training, and education to the membership. He almost achieved a full-service union for its members at the headquarters, La Paz, near Keene, California. The union headquarters at La Paz is a nerve center of the organization and a retreat center. This location is a small city replete with its own telephone system, water supply, housing, health center, and office complex.

Chavez was able, at once, to deal with symbols, images, ideas, and the union agenda to the point that taken together as *la causa* the people supporting him and the union became galvanized. They made events happen and became a force in history. Chavez not only focused on the union tasks of tomorrow but also kept in view the goal of the day after tomorrow. With each transaction he worked on for his membership, he transcended them into the future.

THE LACK OF LEADERSHIP STUDIES

In the academic study of political activity among Mexican Americans, there has been a critical lack of academic interest by political scientists.[12] A few exceptions are the recent works of Mario T. Garcia (1989)[13] and Richard A. Garcia (1991),[14] in the area of leadership among Mexican Americans in the United States. But traditional research done by political scientists on Chicano leaders, community organizations, and politics among Mexican Americans in the United States has a distinct bias. The research focus has been primarily on European-American groups. The peculiar ethnic politics of Chicanos have been seldom studied for two major reasons: first, the historical evidence relied upon by social scientists confirmed very limited levels of participation in electoral and political affairs; and, second, this limited participation in politics was considered by these researchers to be insignificant, statistically and qualitatively. Until the late 1950s, recruitment into and membership in United States political parties, trade unions, Protestant church congregations, Chambers of Commerce, country clubs, and even public schools were denied the Mexican American because of race and class standing.[15] Within the Catholic Church there were segregated Mass services and rituals for Mexicanos. This exclusion of Mexican Americans was not taken into account by the social scientists as a proximate cause of their low level of public activity.[16] Ignoring this segregation and exclusion of Mexican Americans is a major flaw in their research methodology.

The lack of study of Chicano leadership and organizations is not due to the lack of leadership or organization.[17] This research focus is simply omitted by scholars. We know from research published beginning three decades past that Mexicano-based associations and mutual aid and benefit societies existed in the Southwest and Midwest since the turn of the century, as has trade unionism in occupational strata from *vaqueros* to factories.[18] And, during all these decades of this century leaders in the Mexican American community were striving for social change. Today, leaders such as Teresa Urrea, Ricardo and Enrique Flores Magon, Aniceto Pizana, Luis De La Rosa, Octaviano Larrazolo, Eluterio Escobar, Maria Hernandez, Dennis Chavez, Emma Tenayuca, Luisa Moreno, Raymond Telles, Eduardo Quevedo, Ignacio Lozano, Carlos Castaneda, Arthur Campa, Alonzo Perales, J. Luz Saenz, Hector Garcia, J. T. Canales, Manuel C. Gonzales, and Virgina Muzquiz, for example, today are still without major biographical study. Popular interest in the subject of Chicano biography has been sporadic. Some biographical material on post-World War I to World War II leaders was produced during the Chicano Movement era.[19] During the late 1960s to early 1970s, this type of material was published by beer and tobacco companies in the form of calendars, guides, and paperbacks. Recently, in this past decade, guides on community-based organizations and rosters of elected officials of the Mexican ancestry community have been published.[20] Major corporations such as Ford Motor Company's Dealers and Southland Corporation (7-Eleven Convenience Stores) have begun role-model projects.[21] The Ford dealers have an annual dinner—"Hispanic Salute"—to laud local Hispanic leaders in major metropolitan areas across the nation. In 1992 Southland Corporation began a national traveling exhibit entitled "Hispanic Role Models—Inspiring Young Minds To Dream," featuring twenty-six prominent Hispanic Americans. Brochures and posters of leaders in the exhibit are available to the viewing public. Politicians, as a type of leader, are frequently favored as subject-matter by the media and regularly are the focus of scholarly interest.[22]

Local public schools across the nation have always relied primarily, and continue to rely, on material designed and developed in-house on Mexican Americans and other Latinos for use in the classroom, especially during Hispanic Heritage Month (September). There is no college level text or compilation of articles on Mexican American leadership as there is, for example, for

African Americans.[23] Some biographies about the Mexican American people, the organizations of LULAC and American G.I Forum, on individuals exist in addition to autobiographies.[24]

During the Chicano Movement era, the leadership received the attention of documentary film producers. Such early documentaries as *Yo Soy Chicano* and its sequel *Yo Soy* were followed by feature films such as Jesus Trevino's *Raices de Sangre* and the Mexican government-produced *Chicano* on the exploits of Reies Lopez Tijerina. There are various biographical feature films still in circulation today such as *The Ballad of Gregorio Cortez*, *Zoot Suit*, and *Stand and Deliver* on specific historical figures and events. Yet, the inventory of material on leadership of the Mexican American people either in print or on film/video is severely limited. Perhaps the death of Cesar Chavez Estrada, the first and last of the Chicano Movement generation of leaders, will spark a greater and renewed interest concerning the leadership in the United States of people of Mexican ancestry.

CHAVEZ: HIS CHALLENGE

Biography of the Mexican American people, organizations, leaders, institutions, issues, and communities as well as studies of individual leadership are of critical importance. In *Hispanic Americans Today* Current Population Report, the Bureau of the Census, the U.S. Department of Commerce reports as of June, 1993, that Hispanic Americans have reached a critical mass of population in approximately nine states of the nation (23–183). The population of this ethnic community grew over seven times as fast as the rest of the nation's population during the 1980s. In 1990, one in every ten Americans were Hispanic. As we enter the next century, demographers predict Hispanics will be one of every five Americans. This ethnic community has the most children and fewer elderly than the rest of the nation's population. As a sizeable population and distinct ethnic group, Hispanics will figure centrally in the future of America.

The challenge of governance and leadership in the next century rests largely on the shoulders of Mexican Americans and other Hispanics. The road taken by Cesar Chavez and how he traveled that road are examples of ways in which such leadership must develop.

NOTES

1. Available biography on Cesar Chavez Estrada, somewhat dated, includes Day, Dunne, Kushner, Levy, Matthiessen, Meister and Loftis, and Taylor. These publications capture the character and personality of Cesar Chavez as well as chronicle the early union efforts. The value of these materials is three-fold: they were written about a Chicano leader at a time when few publications on Chicanos existed; they were published by national publishers; and, they are descriptive and journalistic in nature, not analytical.

2. See Meier and Rivera (1972). According to these authors, in a chapter entitled "Four Horsemen," four Chicano leaders have had considerable impact since 1965. They are Cesar Chavez of California, Rodolfo "Corky" Gonzales of Colorado, Jose Angel

Gutierrez of Texas, and Reies Lopez Tijerina of New Mexico. For the other works on Reies Lopez Tijerina see Nobokov, Gardner, Blawis, and Tijerina.

3. See Gonzales (1972).

4. See Igancio Garcia (1989), and Shockley (1974).

5. See Valdes (1984, 1989), and Escobar and Lane (1987).

6. See Galarza (1970). See also Reisler (1976)

7. See Zamora (1993).

8. The concept of "first voice" is best exemplified by recent Nobel Peace Prize winner, Rigoberta Menshu of Guatemala. Her work for peace and defense of the indigenous peoples of Guatemala garnered that award. She insisted that her culture be allowed to speak for itself, to describe its history; to express its art-forms through their mediums, and to stand as different, not deficient peoples among humanity. Recently, in San Antonio, Texas, during a national conference of the National Association of Latino Arts and Culture, Dr. Amalia Mesa-Bains, a MacArthur Foundation Fellow, speaking on the needs of Latino art said, "The age of the ventriloquist is over. We are here to speak for ourselves."

9. See Romano (1968). His three essays in *El Grito* (1968–70) are among the pioneering Works on "social science fiction."

10. Chavez personally sought an audience before federal officials of Housing and Urban Development (HUD) in Washington, D.C., to re-negotiate the terms of a loan for the students in order for them to build an alternative institution of higher education for Chicanos in the Pacific Northwest. The Chicano students had taken over the Mt. Angel campus administration building in the 1970s with a demand to make the liberal arts college a Chicano College rather than close the facility for lack of financial resources to maintain the institution. The property was owned by a local order of nuns. The nuns agreed to the demand provided the loan was re-negotiated and re-issued to another party, not their religious order. Chavez was successful in this refinancing arrangement with HUD. Mt. Angel College became a Chicano college and later changed its name to Colegio Cesar Chavez. It was headed by various Chicano academicians and students. They took the beginning steps toward accreditation. At a most critical and final time in 1981 for accreditation review, the Board of Directors selected one of its own, a nonacademic, support staffer and former secretary, Irma Gonzales as President. The Colegio Cesar Chavez was denied accredited status and folded. Assets of the campus were sold by Irma Gonzales. Eventually the remaining buildings were put up on the auction bloc as a foreclosure. Ironically, the minimal foreclosure balance on the note for the Colegio was successfully bid for in 1984 by the local Catholic archdiocese. Ms. Gonzales now serves on the Board of Directors of the National Council of La Raza and is a consultant to the Kellogg Foundation.

11. See Hammerback and Jensen (1980).

12. See Higham (1978). This author totally omitted mention of Mexican Americans and other Latinos in his analysis of ethnic leadership.

13. See Mario T. Garcia (1989). Garcia elaborates on the concept of a "political generation" in the context of Mexican American politics. A political generation is different from a biological generation, the favorite benchmark of anthropologists and different from a historical generation. A political generation not only is a group of heterogenous people engaged in action during a shared historical era but also group membership can span an age as broad as twenty-five years and share in making the political era. In this book, Garcia also discusses the Mexican American generation, a precursor group to the Chicano Movement generation.

14. See Richard A. Garcia (1991). This author discusses the "Mexican American generation" of leaders in San Antonio, Texas, during 1929 to 1941.

15. See Acuna (1988); McWilliams and Meier (1990); and Vigil (1977).

16. These articles have been reprinted in *Voices: Readings from El Grito* (1973). See also Vaca (1970).

17. See Martinez (1979).

18. See Meier and Rivera (1972); Rodolfo Acuna (1988); Escobar and Lane (1987); Montejano (1987); and Zamora (1993).

19. See Oscar Zeta Acosta (1972); Sloss-Vento (1977); and Salazar (n.d.).

20. Philip Morris U.S.A. *A Guide to Hispanic Organizations.* New York. 1985.

21. The Ford Motor Company Dealers is a local event promoted nationally. The Southland Corporation exhibit information is available at 7-Eleven, Urban Affairs, 2711 N. Haskell, Dallas, Texas 75204. Recently, three more individuals were added to the exhibit. These additions are being co-sponsored by Pepsi-Cola with 7-Eleven.

22. See Acosta and Mendosa (1990), Cardenas, (1990), Dwornik and Mendosa (1993), and Mendosa (1989), for recent articles on Hispanic political action committee (PAC) takers and givers, funding for political campaigns of Hispanic members of Congress in the House of Representatives, and Hispanic mayors in U.S. cities.

23. In an effort at Mexican-American leadership, see Larralde. This is the first and only such book treating eighteen Mexican American political leaders and Venustiano Carranza, former President of Mexico.

24. See Galarza (1971); Acosta (1972); Gonzales (1972); Sloss-Vento (1977); Tijerina (1978); Allsup (1982); Ramos (1982); Acura (1984); Matthews (1988); Shorris (1992); Skerry (1993); Marquez (1993); and Newlon (1972).

WORKS CITED

Acosta, Oscar Zeta. 1972. *The Autobiography of a Brown Buffalo.* San Francisco: Straight Arrow Books.

Acosta, Sarah and Rick Mendosa. 1993. "The D.C. Cash Flow." *Hispanic Business* October.

Acuna, Rodolfo. 1984. *A Community Under Siege: A Chronicle of Chicanos East of the Los Angeles River 1945–1975.* Chicano Studies Research Center Publications Monograph No. 11. Los Angeles: University of California Press.

———. 1988. *Occupied America.* 3rd edition. New York: Harper and Row.

Allsup, Carl. 1982. *The American G.I. Forum: Origins and Evolution.* Austin: University of Texas Press.

Blawis, Patricia Bell. 1971. *Tijerina and the Land Grants,* New York: International Publishers.

Cardenas, Francisco. 1993. "What's a Mayor to Do?" *Hispanic Business* October, 20–34.

Day, Mark. 1971. *Forty Acres: Cesar Chavez and the Farm Workers.* New York: Praeger.

Dunne, Gregory. 1967. *Delano.* New York: Farrar, Straus and Giroux.

Dwornik, Ardi and Rick Mendosa. 1993. "Washington's Big Givers." *Hispanic Business* November.

Escobar, Edward J. and James B. Lane. 1987. *Forging a Community: The Latino Experience in Northwest Indiana 1919–1975.* Chicago: Calumet Regional Archives and Cattails Press.

Frammolino, Ralph. 1993. "New Wave of Chicano Activists Shaking Up College Campuses." *The Dallas Morning News.* December 3, 34A.

Galarza, Ernesto. 1970. *Spiders in the House and Workers in the Field.* Notre Dame: University of Notre Dame Press.

———. 1971. *Barrio Boy.* Notre Dame: University of Notre Dame Press.

Garcia, Ignacio. 1989. *United We Win.* Tucson: University of Arizona Press.

Garcia, Mario T. 1989. *Mexican Americans Leadership, Ideology, and Identify, 1930–1960.* New Haven: Yale University Press.

Garcia, Richard A. 1991. *Rise of the Mexican American Middle Class.* College Station: Texas A & M University Press.

Gardner, Richard. 1970. *Grito!* Indianapolis: Bobbs-Merrill Company.

Gonzales, Rodolfo. 1972. *Yo Soy Joaquin.* New York: Bantam Books.

Hammerback, John C. and Richard Jensen. 1980. "The Rhetorical Worlds of Cesar Chavez and Reies Tijerina." *Western Journal of Speech Communication* Summer.

Higham, Paul. 1978. *Ethnic Leadership in America.* Baltimore: Johns Hopkins University Press.

Kushner, Sam. 1975. *Long Road to Delano.* New York: International Publishers.

Larralde, Carlos. 1976. *Mexican-American: Movements and Leaders.* Los Alamitos, California: Hwong Publishing.

Levy, Jacques. 1975. *Cesar Chavez: Autobiography of La Causa.* New York: Norton.

Loftis, Anne and Dick Meister. 1977. *A Long Time Coming: The Struggle to Unionize America's Farm Workers.* New York: MacMillan.

Marquez, Benjamin. 1993. *LULAC.* Austin: University of Texas Press.

Martinez, Julio A. 1979. *Chicano Scholars and Writers: A Bio-Bibliographical Directory.* Metuchen, N.J.: The Scarecrow Press.

Matthews, Jay. 1988. *Escalante.* New York: Henry Holt.

Matthiessen, Peter. 1969. *Sal Si Puedes: Cesar Chavez and the New American Revolution.* New York: Random House.

McWilliams, Carey and Matt Meier. 1990. *North from Mexico.* New York: Preager.

Meier, Matt S. and Feliciano Rivera. 1972. *The Chicanos.* New York: Hill and Wang.

Mendosa, Rick. 1989. "How Rich Is the Public Trough?" *Mexicans in the Midwest. Perspectives in Mexican American Studies.* Tucson: University of Arizona Press. 18–25.

Montejano, David. 1987. *Anglos and Mexicans in the Making of Texas, 1836–1986.* Austin: University of Texas Press.

National Roster of Latino Elected Officials. The National Association of Latino Elected and Appointed Officials (NALEO). Annual.

Newlon, Clarke. 1972. *Famous Mexican Americans.* New York: Dodd, Mead.

Nobokov, Peter. 1969. *Tijerina and the Courthouse Raid.* Albuquerque: University of New Mexico Press.

Philip Morris U.S.A. 1985. *A Guide To Hispanic Organizations.* New York.

Quinto Sol Publications. 1973. *Voices Readings from El Grito.* Berkeley: Quinto Sol Publications.

Ramos, Henry A. J. 1982. *A People Forgotten, A Dream Pursued: The History of the American G.I. Forum 1948–1972.* n.p.

Reisler, Mark. 1976. *By the Sweat of Their Brow.* Westport: Greenwood Press.

Romano, Octavio I. V. 1968. "The Anthropology and Sociology of the Mexican-Americans: The Distortions of Mexican American History." *El Grito* Fall.

———. 1968–69. "The Historical and Intellectual Presence of Mexican-Americans," *El Grito* Winter.

———. 1970. "Social Science, Objectivity, and the Chicanos," *El Grito* Fall.

Salazar, Veronica. n.d. *Dedication Rewarded.* San Antonio: Mexican American Cultural Center.

Shockley, John. 1974. *Chicano Revolt in a Texas Town.* Notre Dame: Notre Dame University Press.

Shorris, Earl. 1992. *Latinos: A Biography of a People.* New York: Norton.

Skerry, Peter. 1993. *Mexican Americans, The Ambivalent Minorities.* New York: The Free Press.

Sloss-Vento, Adela. 1977. *Alonso S. Perales: His Struggle for the Rights of the Mexican American.* San Antonio: Artes Graficas.

Taylor, Ronald B. 1975. *Chavez and the Farm Workers.* Boston: Beacon Press.

Tijerina, Reies Lopez. 1978. *Mi lucha por la tierra*. Mexico D.F.: Fondo De Cultura Economica.

Vaca, Nick C. 1970. "The Mexican American in the Social Sciences: 1912–1970; Part I: 1912–1935." *El Grito* Spring.

Valdes, Dennis Nodin. 1984. *From Following the Crops to Chasing the Corporations: The Farm Labor Organizing Committee, 1967–1983*. National Association for Chicano Studies.

———. 1989. *Mexicans in the Midwest*. Mexican American Studies and Research Center.

———. n.d. *Perspectives in Mexican American Studies*. Tucson. University of Arizona Press.

———. 1984. *The Chicano Struggle*. Binghampton, New York: Bilingual Press/Editorial Bilingue.

Vigil, Maurillo. 1977. *Chicano Politics*. Washington, D.C.: University of America Press.

Voices: Readings from El Grito. Berkeley: Quinto Sol Publications, 1973.

White, John. 1990. *Black Leadership in America: From Booker T. Washington to Jesse Jackson*. 2nd ed. New York. Longman.

Zamora, Emilio. 1993. *The World of the Mexican Worker in Texas*. College Station: Texas A & M University Press.

Mapping the New Global Spiritual Line

Luis D. León

It wasn't that saving my soul was more important than the strike. On the contrary. I said to myself, if I'm going to save my soul, it's going to be through the struggle for social justice.

—Cesar E. Chavez[1]

When Cesar Estrada Chavez (1927–1993) founded the United Farm Workers Union (UFW) in 1962, he concomitantly inspired the Chicano political movement and largely occasioned its attendant cultural renaissance. On July 4, 1969, he was featured on the cover of *Time* magazine. The accompanying article dubbed him the "mystical" and "earthy" leader of the Mexican American civil rights movement, and the Chicano Martin Luther King Jr. The symbolism of the date, Independence Day, bespeaks Chavez's psychosocial location: he had become a prophet of U.S. civil religiosity. Today he is unequivocally the most widely remembered Chicano public figure in the United States and globally.[2]

Chavez was broadly recognized for his social justice work during his life, but since his death in 1993, he has been multiply memorialized, awarded the Presidential Medal of Freedom, nominated for the Congressional Gold Medal, celebrated in an official California state holiday, and commemorated in an official U.S. stamp. In 2006, he was counted among the first group of inductees into the California Hall of Fame—the few posthumous awardees included naturalist John Muir, as well as Chavez nemesis Ronald Reagan. Should the movement to establish a national holiday on his birthday prove successful, this honor would be the equivalent of reaching full U.S. sainthood—trumping in significance even the ongoing efforts to canonize him as an official Catholic saint.[3]

At Chavez's funeral, Art Torres, California Democratic Party state chairman, spoke for millions of Latina/os when he declared: "[Cesar Chavez] is our Gandhi, our Martin Luther King."[4] Chavez's political leadership became,

Luis D. León: "Mapping the New Global Spiritual Line" first published in *American Quarterly* 59:3, 857–81.

even before his death, intimately linked to his larger status in the community as a charismatic leader who, as Richard Rodriguez put it, "wielded spiritual authority."[5]

This essay explores the nature of that "spiritual authority" and argues for its significance in any comprehensive understanding of Chavez and his importance as a leader for Chicanos. In his national ascendancy, ironically, a distinct but amorphous Christian identity became pivotal in his efficacious campaign for the hearts and minds of Americans. As devotee Gary Soto has professed, "In the course of this movement, Cesar became—whether he accepted this status or not—a spiritual leader for all Chicanos."[6] In what follows I argue that he indeed accepted this role, albeit with initial reluctance, and that his religious identity, complex and fluctuating, erudite and theological, was central to establishing what Los Angeles Catholic Archdiocese bishop Roger Mahoney described as his "prophetic" vocation.[7]

Chavez signified in various religions, though he identified broadly as "Christian," and he produced an unmistakably Christian ethics. However, his variegated theology has resulted in a religious identity that is ultimately irretrievable as, I argue, he intended it to be. Still, this essay seeks a clearer understanding of his sacred acts as they intersected his political practices.

Chavez did not separate religion and politics into two discrete personal and public dimensions that informed each other. Rather, he melded these two realms into prophetic narratives and practices, directly responding to and engaging the unlikely place of Christianity in American political discourse. Chavez was a prophetic agent in a broadly spiritual, ecumenical, and political sense. He is best understood as a prophet in the particular sense that Max Weber defined: a leader whose vision is not produced in a vacuum, but instead responds from within, outside, and on the boundaries of his inherited tradition.[8]

Yet biographers (especially those writing in Chavez's wake) neglect his unmistakably prophetic role within American religious and political history, grossly underestimating the level of his intellectual and spiritual engagements. Therefore, as a part of a larger revisionist project, this essay attends first to Chavez's religious identity, paying close attention to his own philosophies, through writings, interviews, and speeches. The secondary literature on Chavez and the UFW regularly presents conflicting dates and other details. Hence, I rely first on interviews and accounts with the Chavez family and on the documents produced by the Cesar E. Chavez Foundation.

I argue that Chavez's radical ecumenicalism positioned him beyond Catholicism, and that a closer scrutiny of this positioning allows a revised and enhanced perspective on the intersection of religions and politics in the United States. My conclusion expands on the social ethics of Chavez, proposing a critical model to understand the twenty-first century, waxing not "scientifically" but theologically—that is, as advancing an understanding of the transcendent within the limitations of the temporal and the terrestrial.

I have come to neither praise nor condemn Cesar, but to describe his role in American political religiosity, unpacking and expanding his program for social change, which is, as I see it, a model for social justice. This focus obviates the banal academic mandate to render criticism of the subject in order to prove "objectivity," as if perfectly neutral. Of course, human perfection is impossible—in my work on Chavez, and in Chavez's own life—and I simultaneously resist also the impulse to lionize him for certainly he was all too human. Efforts to both canonize Chavez and to condemn him are more interesting for what they reveal about the narrators, and the power of memory and forgetting, than for what they say about the man himself.

A PROPHET FROM THE DESERT

Chavez was a prophetic agent: a person, a *human*, who advocates for social change by critical discourses and acts based in religious and moral convictions vis-à-vis the status quo. Certainly he was not a perfect human, an "angel" (as he would say), nor a saint, but a charismatic leader—a leader with a powerful magnetic appeal, according to Weber. Chavez's authority was not conferred by virtue of an institutional office such as priest; according to many testimonies—including those printed in the *New York Times* and *Time* magazine—it adhered naturally. "Natural" charismatic endowment is Weber's key criteria for the prophetic designation. Additionally, the prophet speaks on behalf of the poor and the oppressed as if bringing a novel revelation from God, or by stressing existing doctrines that have gone overlooked—each resonating with (re)fresh(ed) narratives of salvation.[9]

Prophets typically emerge from out of crisis events that occasion the need for social criticism and change. Many undergo a life cycle punctuated by times of separation, trial, and return, known as the "hero's tale" or "song."[10] Like Gandhi and Martin Luther King Jr., Chavez's formation replicates in broad patterns classical training for his quasi-religious work. He was born and died in the same county. At the ground base of his struggle was a longing to return to his childhood home, a 160-acre ranch that his father and grandfather built from a parched space of neglected Arizona desert. In 1937, the Bruce Church Corporation engineered a foreclosure of the ranch so the property would be available for acquisition. In addition to the ranch, the Chavez family owned and operated a few small businesses in town that ultimately failed because of the many unpaid accountants they extended to the community, and drought years had cost the ranch a fortune. In spite of the family's relentless efforts to keep their property, the cards were stacked in favor of Bruce Church, who needed the land to straighten out his property line.

Chavez marks the exile from his homeland as fundamental to his own memory: "I bitterly missed the ranch. Maybe that is when the rebellion started. Some had been born into the migrant stream. But we had been born on the land, and I knew a different way of life. We were poor, but we had liberty. The migrant is poor, and he has no freedom."[11] His goal was to reoccupy the primal desert soil, which, in a sense, he achieved. He died in his homeland while in the midst of a court trial against the Bruce Church Corporation; his death was pivotal in gaining the jury's sympathy and favorable decision.[12] His formative childhood experiences of injustice led him down the path to working for social change; through the faith of his family he learned "heroic" and prophetic values.

But young Cesar learned also from stories and books, and the fictions of his life begin with a distortion of this fact. Orthodox narratives of his days start with the misnomer "common man from common origins." That is not exactly correct, for while poor, his family was never "common," "simple," or even "humble," as in uneducated. His grandmother, Dorotea Chavez, or "Mama Tella," was raised in a Mexican convent, where she learned Latin and Spanish. His grandfather, Cesario Chavez, or "Papa Chavo," fought in the agrarian reforms that boiled into the Mexican Revolution, catalyzed by the philosophies of "land" and "liberty." Cesar's mother, Juana Estrada, was a woman of uncommon faith. She was a *curandera*, skilled in the elaborate world of indigenous postcolonial curing. "My mother had a reputation in the valley for her skill in healing," Chavez notes, "a skill she put to constant use, for she couldn't bear to see anyone in pain, and there were no doctors in the valley. She was especially knowledgeable in the use of herbs, choosing some to cool a fever, others to cure colic, and mixing brews for specific illnesses. Her faith in her skill was as strong as her belief in the saints and the Virgin of Guadalupe."[13]

Chavez is careful to position his mother's indigenous faith as equal in importance to her Christian faith. He credits her for his initial adoption of a theology of peace. "When I look back I see her sermons had a tremendous impact on me. I didn't know it was nonviolence then, but after reading Gandhi, St. Francis, and other exponents of nonviolence, I began to clarify that in my mind. Now that I'm older I see she is nonviolent."[14] Cesar's father, Librado Chavez, taught him to abhor the behaviors associated with the macho racist stereotype, and also taught him to fight for social justice. Librado was uncommonly active in the earliest efforts to unionize farm workers.

Cesar left school at age fifteen, upon graduating from the eighth grade in 1942, in order to return to work the fields full time, thereby liberating his mother from the back-breaking work. This was also a rebellious period in his life, and his identity underwent a brief but conspicuous transformation during his "pachuco" or zootsuit period. He began to smoke, drink beer, and dance: the erotic choreography and uninhibited parties of the pachucos and pachucas gave Chicana/o youth a Dionysian idiom for expressing their alienation and rage. The adolescence of prophetic "heroes" is often characterized by rebellion, followed by a continually morphing personal identity.

In 1946 Chavez joined the U.S. Navy and served in the Pacific. "Those were the worst two years of my life: this regimentation, this super authority that somehow somebody has the right to move you around like a piece of equipment. It's worse than being in prison. And there was a lot of discrimination."[15] While in the navy he was exposed to racism and suffering on a global scale, crystallizing his resolve to advance universal justice, beginning at home. This episode marks a phase of total separation from a world in which he was familiar, and immersion into a hostile environment in which he was made to battle and endure an unjust and unrelenting force.

It was during Chavez's military service that an incident occurred at a local theater that would further impress upon him the urgency of working for democratic morality; this has been called his "Rosa Parks" moment. On shore leave, he was not in uniform.

> For a long time, movie theaters throughout the San Joaquin Valley were segregated. It was just accepted by the Mexicans then. In Delano, the quarter-section on the right was reserved for Mexicans, blacks, and Filipinos, while Anglos and Japanese sat elsewhere. . . .
>
> This time something told me I shouldn't accept such discrimination. It wasn't a question of sitting elsewhere because it was more comfortable. It was just a question that I wanted a free choice of where I wanted to be. I decided to challenge the rule, even though I was very frightened. Instead of sitting on the right. I sat down on the left. . . .
>
> It was the first time I had challenged rules so brazenly.[16]

He was forced from the cinema and detained in jail. He was not formally charged, and was released after a police officer threatened and degraded him. In the same way, the Chicano movement was ignited largely by veterans who became intolerant of racial discrimination, for such was inimical to democratic values that military indoctrination held sacred. As his response to segregation in a San Joaquin Valley theater suggests, Chavez's experience in the navy educated him in the religion of the nation-state, especially its transcendent promises of freedom, justice, and equality—until death.

In 1946 Chavez returned to California and married Helen Fabela. The couple settled in San Jose. There he began his role as husband, father of eight children, and a leader in the infamous barrio know as "sal si puedes," or "escape if you can." In 1952 he befriended a missionary priest from the San Francisco diocese, Father Donald McDonnell. McDonnell mentored Chavez in the church's teachings on farmworkers and social justice, involving Chavez in his labor camp ministry and recommending readings for him. Contrary to popular fiction, Chavez continued to educate himself after leaving school, but his apprenticeship with the missionary priest focused and increased his reading.

That same year Chavez met Fred Ross—a man whom Chavez claims "changed" his life. Ross was a forty-two-year-old organizer who worked with the Community Service Organization (CSO) directed by Saul Alinsky. Cesar soon became a disciple of Ross, who secured a position for his young apprentice also as a community organizer. But much of Chavez's first three years in the CSO were spent isolated in an office working through piles of Western and Eastern classics, accompanied by cigarettes, cans of Tab cola, and a giant, dog-eared dictionary. He read voraciously, including works on photography, art, philosophy, politics, economics, and religion. Typical of the biographers, Peter Matthiessen trivializes his intellect, but reports on his reading nonetheless: "He is a realist, not an intellectual, and his realism has been fortified by *extensive acquaintance* with political treatises, from St. Paul to Churchill, and from Jefferson to 'all the dictators': His self-education, in the CSO years, included readings in Goebbels and Machiavelli and Lord Acton."[17] His wife, Helen, once expressed her fear when she and her husband came across a bookstore: "I hope it isn't open. Books and camera stores—he'll be in there all night."[18] Today Chavez's personal library housed at La Paz reflects an impressive bibliographic mind. Indeed, much like Gramsci's organic intellectual, his erudition was occasioned and nurtured by and within a political movement.

Chavez credits Ross as his most influential mentor; he worked at the CSO under the tutelage of both Alinsky and Ross for ten years before leaving to organize farmworkers on his birthday, October 31, 1962. The date marks a rebirth for Chavez. Like Gandhi's return to India from South Africa, and King's return to his home church in Atlanta, Chavez returned to Delano to confront the master beast who had plagued his people for generations. The time had arrived for him to assume the prophetic role for which he had been training all his life.

At its apex, Chavez's prophecy revealed another of America's great sins to itself—the national abomination that was the treatment of the farmworkers, laying bare their mass suffering. He tore down the opaque veil that blinded Americans to the injustice in their own backyard—a condition tantamount to slavery in its offenses to the sacred orthodoxy the citizenry professed. In the course of his work, Chavez learned to transliterate racial and cultural politics into public Christianity: "Everywhere we went, to school, to church, to the movies, there was an attack on our culture and language, an attempt to make us conform to the 'American way,'" Chavez exclaimed. "What a sin!"[19] Chavez's movement, like American political theology more broadly, captures, reassembles, and synthesizes the confessional fragments of traditional dogmas, capitalizing on the ambiguities and overlaps in their lexicons of the sacred and the profane—all the while appealing to the Deity of reason and nature, revealed by the will of the majority.

Indeed, Chavez was all too human, and he knew that romantic notions of him could not he sustained and would inevitably give way to disillusionment and bitter criticism. Movements animated by the charismatic endowment of their founders are inextricably tied to a singularly ineffable quality. Intense personal charisma cannot be sustained and will inevitably suffer decline, or "routinization"; such was true of the UFW.

Rightly or not, aspects of Chavez's life and leadership have been publicly criticized: his imperial leadership style, the demands for utter loyalty, and the direction he took the UFW during the latter years of his life—especially the time he dedicated to fund-raising. Yet, early on Chavez described himself as a "practical" man, and recognized that organizations without money are powerless. As he saw it, there were two essential human ingredients for a successful movement, time and money: "An individual who is willing to give his time is more important than an individual who is willing to give his money. I think money would be number two."[20] In this he took cues from King, but especially Gandhi: "It's amazing how people lose track of basics. Gandhi was one of the best fund-raisers the world has ever seen! (*Laughter.*) But people don't look at it that way! They don't!"[21] Nonetheless, these fund-raising efforts have recently been condemned. Miriam Pawell of the *Los Angeles Times* discloses her bias in this regard. After all, why would a social movement need money in the United States? Pawell speaks for many, rushing her righteous indignation: Chavez, like other racialized public leaders, is not allowed to develop and change. Indeed, his image is most consumable when frozen as a striking farmworker holding picket signs, or as a fasting penitent. By contrast, his progression dispels

comfortable notions of an isolated problem easily fixed by national pater-
nal care.[22] Chavez cut an imposing figure as an American prophet on the
world stage decrying the ideology of capitalism that privileges the rich.

Chavez never claimed that he would remain forever in the fields, organizing workers, picketing, and fasting. In fact, as early as 1978 he publicly
declared that his role was more akin to that of a teacher: "I think my role has
changed from one of an organizer to possibly one of a teacher. . . . Mostly I
want to teach people to initiate and accept change within the movement because we can't live in the late '70s with the concepts we had in the mid '60s.
The things we did in 1965 are no longer necessary, valid, or even important."[23]
In 1981, the *Los Angeles Times* ran a story entitled "UFW Transforming Itself
from 'Cause' to 'Businesslike Union.'" It reported: "Even as a costly modernization program continues, the union stresses its role as a social cause, a near-
religion requiring vows of poverty from its top officers, attorneys, doctors,
nurses, and even the lowest level of file clerk."[24] By 1983 Chavez told the UFW
annual convention that he had formed a "Chicano lobby" to support Democratic candidates.[25] That same year he addressed a lesbian and gay coalition,
called Project Just Business, at Circus Disco in West Hollywood.[26] He was,
as has been noted, many things to many people, and he continued to evolve
throughout his life.

THE MYTH OF CESAR CHAVEZ

Chavez's public memory has emerged as a highly contested political field
of self-interest and (un)holy constructs. Some scholars and activists, anxious
to claim Chavez as "one of the people," insistently and publicly remember
Chavez as a simple, ignorant man with little in the way of self-reflection, religious or otherwise. Luis Valdez and other Chicano political leaders have
helped to script this fiction of simplicity and ignorance. "The essence of his
[Chavez's] greatness," claims Valdez,

> is his simple humanity. All who had the opportunity to know and work with
> him in his day-to-day struggle know this to be true: he was not a saint; he was
> not a miracle worker; he was just a man. That's why his impact on history is
> so remarkable. This is the common man, inspiring leader and unforgettable
> brother that lives.[27]

While most memories of Chavez misrepresent his complexity (especially
posthumously), cofounder of the UFW Dolores Huerta disagrees: "But in
truth, I find him a very complicated person."[28] Similarly, Stan Steiner wrote of
him in 1969: "Chavez is an enigma to many. He is a different man to different
people."[29]

Even inasmuch as Valdez and others remember Chavez singularly as an
ordinary man, they clash over the issue of canonization. Fred Dalton's treatment of Chavez follows the work of Chicano priest and scholar Virgil Eli-
zondo; it reads as a hagiography, professing Catholic identity for "Cesar."
In fact, professions of Catholic loyalty are rampant in the print on Chavez,

especially in the posthumous literature, which often popularizes the myth, already circulating in his life, declaring Chavez a "devout" Catholic believer. Dalton writes: "While César respected other religious and moral traditions, actively promoted an ecumenical spirit within the union, and incorporated meditation and yoga into his own spirituality, he was quite open about his commitment to the [Catholic] Church. Chavez *always* identified himself as a member of the *Catholic* faith community."[30]

In reality, such claims of an exclusive commitment never came from Chavez himself. Although he was baptized Catholic, his catechism was informal and he was schooled in a form of Mexican home-based Catholicism. Attitudes and values toward the church in Mexico stem largely from the anticolonial philosophy of the Mexican Revolution, which rejected the hierarchy as a feudal institution yet which privileged Catholic symbols that had been indigenized and therefore possessed the potential to mobilize masses of people for revolution.[31] Cesar's formation as a Catholic was informed by this history: he rarely attended mass as a child, but was prepared for confirmation by his grandmother, and was confirmed without formal church instruction. As an adult, Chavez attended mass, but he was also active in many faith congregations—including Pentecostal. Moreover, his Catholic subjectivity became decreasingly pronounced throughout the duration of his work. When asked about his religious identification in his later life, he responded: "For me, Christianity happens to be *a* natural *source* of *faith*. I have read what Christ said when he was here. He was very clear in what he meant and knew exactly what he was after. He was extremely radical, and he was for social change."[32] He bespeaks a savvy Christian identity with a hearty salute to his Pentecostal and otherwise Protestant followers in his claim to have studied the scriptures. Indeed, his earliest organizing efforts in Delano began in Pentecostal house churches in his neighborhood. He prayed with churchgoers, and there he developed the idea for singing in the union.[33]

Chavez's spiritual practices were diverse not only within Christianity, but beyond; he was fascinated by the study of and engagement in other religions. Around his neck he sported a Jewish mezuzah. "I'm sure Christ wore a mezuzah," he once quipped. "He certainly didn't wear a cross."[34] According to artist and curator of the Cesar Chavez museum in Phoenix, Jim Covorrubias, the labor leader returned periodically to the Arizona desert to fast privately and to consult with an indigenous healer or *curandera*.[35] Cesar's granddaughter, Julie Rodriguez, spokesperson for the Chavez family, explained that her grandfather's spirituality was manifest as a physical commitment: "His spiritual beliefs affected his diet as well; he was a vegetarian and . . . became a macrobiotic. Cesar understood embodying the way of nonviolence as centering himself and understanding himself as one with the universe, he was the optimal example of a lifelong learner. I have never come in touch with someone who was so self aware."[36] Later in his life, Chavez developed a commitment to the quasi-religious practices of Synanon, imposing the "Game" strategy on his union staff—much to the staff's dismay.[37]

It is, of course, impossible for anyone to judge Chavez's level of faithful commitment to Catholicism, but his strategic intentions are made clear in his writings. In a 1968 academic paper read at a Chicano studies conference, Chavez called upon the church to live out its teachings of social justice.

> The Church is *one* form of the presence of God on Earth, and so naturally it is powerful. It is powerful by definition. It is a powerful moral and spiritual force which cannot he ignored by any movement. Furthermore, it is an organization with tremendous wealth. Since the Church is to be servant to the poor, it is our fault if that wealth is not channeled to help the poor in our world.
>
> In a small way we have been able, in the Delano strike, to work together with the Church in such a way as to bring some of its moral and economic power to bear on those who want to maintain the status quo, keeping farmworkers in virtual enslavement.[38]

Chavez's reasoning here is logical and sound: the church must practice what it preaches, and because it is rich and globally influential, those resources could be wielded for tremendous advantage. However, these same words have been distorted, twisting the narrative into a magical incantation: "A devout Roman Catholic, he described the church as a 'powerful moral and spiritual force' in the world. God controls the earth's events and people, seeing to it that good causes triumph. . . . Chavez felt that he could be divinely guaranteed of eventual success if he persisted in presenting his righteous case."[39]

This paternalistic reading completely neglects the historical context for the statement. Three years into the grape strike and boycott, the Catholic Church remained officially "uncommitted," arguing that their endorsement would bias and thus invalidate their role as presumed mediators between the striking farmworkers and the growers—many of whom were Italian Catholics and major contributors to the church. Yet, Protestant denominations had served farmworkers well before the strike and thus became immediate supporters of the UFW. The earliest efforts began in 1928 with the National Council of Churches Migrant Ministry. In 1957, the California Migrant Ministry crystallized and advanced aid to farmworkers, bringing a newly endowed focus and a director whose activities included enlisting the support of mainline Protestant churches.[40] Many churches offered financial support as well as personnel, and the grape boycott was officially endorsed by the California Council of Churches, the National Council of Churches, and the International Council of Churches. One minister reflects: "In the 1960s and '70s virtually every major religious body in the United States and many in Europe and Canada gave attention to U.S. farm workers, took positions on what the workers were doing, and were a significant force in rallying 17 million Americans to participate in the common act of not buying grapes."[41]

Still, the Catholic Church resisted. Chavez formally petitioned the American bishops for their expressed support in 1968, and again in 1969; on both occasions his request was denied. In 1969 the church formed an ad hoc committee to deal with the farmworkers, but it remained officially neutral until the middle of the lettuce boycott in 1973.[42] During this time, however, individual priests and nuns worked for the strikes and boycotts—and to these efforts Chavez has attributed the initial victories of the union.[43] Though the church remained officially neutral, California bishops remained split, some supporting the UFW, others siding with the growers. Catholic groups helped to finance the strikes early on, and individual priests and nuns marched on picket lines in California, defying the church's position. Whereas many commentators represent Chavez's simple, almost naive devotion to the church, clearly his actual engagements with Catholic institutions combined religion and the practical exigencies of political struggle.

But Chavez eventually grew weary of the church's official neutrality. In 1971, Franciscan Mark Day recounted the following exchange.

> I asked Cesar about his feelings toward the church one evening. Day recounted, when he and his wife, Helen, had supper at Guadalupe Church rectory with me and some visiting priests.
>
> "Most farm workers are Chicanos," Cesar said, "and most Chicanos are Catholics. The church is the only institution which our people are closely associated with. When the church does not respond to us, we get offended, and we are tempted to lash out against it."
>
> "You know," he continued, "there are many changes in the church today. But many of these changes, like the new ritual of the mass, are merely external. What I like to see is a priest get up and speak about things like racism and poverty. But, even when you hear about these things from the pulpit, you get the feeling that they aren't doing anything significant to alleviate these evils. They are just talking about them.
>
> "Here in Delano, the church has been such a stranger to us that our own people tend to put it together with all the powers and institutions that oppose them."[44]

While Dalton and others evince Chavez's commitment to the Catholic Church with this very same passage, the practical union leader meant it as a criticism and careful mechanism for his own religious positionality; it nowhere represents a buttress for his own Catholicism; nor does his 1968 admonition to the church represent a fatalistic, primitive faith (as some have argued).

There was one occasion when Chavez clearly identified himself as specifically and emotionally Catholic—upon meeting Pope Paul VI, on September 25, 1974. Chavez did not request the audience, however; it was initiated by U.S. bishops as part of their new campaign supporting the farmworkers. Chavez had been planning a trip to Europe that fall to urge labor leaders there to enforce the lettuce boycott. The flight was paid for by the National Council of Churches. During the visit, Cesar followed standard procedure and kissed the pope's ring. He then dramatically unfolded a UFW flag and presented it to the Pontiff while photographers shot pictures. Of this meeting Chavez remarked: "I have difficulty expressing its meaning, except that being a Catholic, having a chance to see the Holy Father in person, to have a special audience, is like a small miracle." The Vatican later made a statement supporting the farmworkers, which Chavez said was the most important aspect of the meeting: "And what was really significant was the statement that he made about the farm workers and the Mexican-Americans in the United States."[45]

After the meeting, Chavez responded with an enthusiasm that was at once sentimental and pragmatic: he makes clear his emotional identification with the church and his feelings of awe, but he stops far short of claiming that his is a Catholic movement, or that he himself is solely committed to the church.

Chavez was pragmatic in developing a social ethics looking toward the church, especially liberation theology, but not allowing himself to be beholden to it. Efforts to canonize him as a Catholic evince his success in gaining the church as a base of support. At the same time, there are stakes involved in refusing to concede a specifically or singularly Catholic identity to Chavez. Every indication is that he saw himself as far more ecumenical than is often assumed. By contrast, connecting Chavez solely to the institutional church enables his co-optation in support of sundry church positions and projects that he reviled—especially those involving the church's misogyny, homophobia, and pedophilia.

THE SACRIFICIAL BODY: PERFORMING NONVIOLENCE

Chavez is best understood as a complex thinker and ecumenical believer, whose political work was deeply influenced by Gandhi, based in the spirituality and philosophy of nonviolent sacrificial struggle for social justice. And nothing exemplifies this commitment so much as his leadership in Delano, the central California town at the heart of the state's agribusiness. For more than a century, police and local sheriff departments had been deployed as militia forces by growers, who successfully thwarted efforts at unionization and workers' rights. Chavez's return to the Central Valley would mark the beginning of change. Intent on forming a union even at great personal cost, he called for a grape boycott in 1965, a battle that was bitterly fought for five years. In 1966 the first union contracts were signed, and the dream of a union was realized. However, negotiating new and lapsed contracts became a series of fierce battles involving endless picket lines and lawsuits.

The fledgling union was dwarfed by labor's Goliath. Agribusiness was California's economic giant: it enjoyed the favor of local and federal politicians. Moreover, the initial victory motivated the Teamsters'/Mafia union to compete for deals: they offered growers "sweetheart" contracts that decreased benefits and pay for labor; the Teamsters had previously ignored Chicano fieldworkers. Mafia goons savagely attacked striking women and children, brutalizing them under the gleeful gaze of police officers, who stood nearby idly, gawking. Inevitably, police arrested the bloodied strikers, even while they had been the victims rather than the perpetrators of a crime.

These events drew media attention, and as a result in 1960, the U.S. Senate Subcommittee in Migratory Labor held hearings in Sacramento. The arrest of strikers was a preemptive measure, pleaded the sheriff. This tortured reasoning occasioned Robert Kennedy's now famous quip: "Can I suggest that in the interim period of time, the luncheon period of time, that the sheriff and the district attorney read the Constitution of the United States?"[46] Kennedy's support of the union came partially as payback for Chavez's organizing efforts throughout the 1950s. During those years, Chavez, UFW's first vice president

Dolores Huerta, and activist Fred Ross registered and delivered nearly 300,000 new Latino Democrats in California, making it the most powerful Chicano group in the United States. This campaign coalesced around the "Viva Kennedy" slogan, which is thought to have tipped California's electoral votes for John F. Kennedy in 1960. Working with the Community Service Organization, Chavez learned the potentials and pitfalls of the democratic process; he never trusted it blindly as a panacea.

As the grape strike continued throughout the late 1960s, growers stubbornly refused to sign contracts and continued to attack strikers. Despite Chavez's best efforts, retaliatory violence erupted in the UFW, and some of the growers' properties were burned and goons assaulted. Chavez himself never abandoned his foundational principal, nonviolent sacrificial love: "Love is the most important ingredient in nonviolent work—love the opponent—but we really haven't learned yet how to love the growers," he explained.

> I think we've learned how not to hate them, and maybe love comes in stages. If we're full of hatred, we can't really do our work. Hatred saps all that strength and energy we need to plan. Of course, we can learn how to love the growers more easily after they sign contracts.[47]

Certainly he had many sacred models for this political philosophy of love, including Jesus Christ and Saint Francis of Assisi.

Most biographers assert that Chavez was introduced to Gandhi by Father Donald McDonnell in San Jose in 1948. However, Chavez's own version is more complicated, and also contradictory. In 1975 he claimed that McDonnell introduced him to many books, including Louis Fischer's *Life of Gandhi*; he further stated that his exposure to the Indian guru was limited to newsreels and newspapers. In 1990, however, three years prior to his death, he was quoted as follows:

> I was eleven or twelve years old, and I went to a movie. In those days, in between movies they had newsreels, and in one of the newsreels there was a report on Gandhi. It said that this half-naked man without a gun had conquered the might of the British empire. . . . It really impressed me because I couldn't conceive of how that had happened without guns. Even though I had never heard the name Gandhi before. . . . since then, I have made a life project of reading about Gandhi and his message.[48]

The long versions of the stories are reconcilable in all but one detail, and noteworthy especially inasmuch as Chavez was more inclined to cite Gandhi as his muse later in his life. Still, Gandhi's influence was central to his work from the start. It begins from the following maxim: "Nonviolence also has one big demand—the need to be creative, to develop strategy. Gandhi described it as 'moral jujitsu.' Always hit the opposition off balance, but keep your principles."[49] For Chavez, morality meant consistency in ethics, but moral values could also be deployed for political gain in the public marketplace of ideas.

In this, he also drew from the prophetic tradition of Martin Luther King Jr., whose acumen for narrating public morality revitalized and established fresh grammar for discourses of American civil religion. Chavez and King communicated with each other, spoke on the telephone, and announced their collaboration on King's Poor People's March and Campaign in 1968. After King's assassination, the Reverend Ralph Abernathy and Coretta Scott King were present at many of Chavez's public actions, including his subsequent fasts in 1972 and 1988. Chavez published an homage to King titled "Martin Luther King, Jr.: He Showed Us the Way."[50]

King founded the Southern Christian Leadership Conference (SCLC) in the 1950s with the messianic and prophetic mission to "redeem the soul of America."[51] The ideological power of this motivation illustrates the suasion of an American identity embedded in a Protestantism that continues to be reshaped and retold by its most recent professors. In the tradition of the Black Church, King rendered the meaning of Christian redemption from his own experience. Chavez followed suit.

A conception of social evil is possible within many traditions and appears as a formative trope in the politics of Gandhi, King, and Chavez. All three went beyond the boundaries of their inherited traditions and thrived in the spiritual borderlands: King's pilgrimage to India, Gandhi's multiple self-religious identities, and Chavez's radical Christian ecumenicalism combined with indigenous teachings and practices. They all intersected, however, in their commitment to nonviolent social change, coalescing with the organization of workers.

For Chavez, organizing workers required exposing the injustice in Delano to a national audience. To this end he engineered several key public events to transform the UFW from a Western farmworkers union into a (mostly) Latino/a civil rights movement with international fame. By November of 1968, the *New York Times* described his work as "a civil rights issue" and "a quasi-religious cause"; these events transformed the strike, into "The Cause," or "La Causa."[52]

The first event was a march from Delano to Sacramento that was modeled after King's "prayer pilgrimage" and Gandhi's Salt March. The march took place during holy week of 1966 and culminated in a massive interfaith ceremony on Easter Sunday. It was called "Pilgrimage, Penitence, and Revolution." Its charter, the "Plan of Delano," was penned by Luis Valdez and Chavez and expressly mimicked Emiliano Zapata's "Plan of Ayala"; it articulated the group's central articles of faith. Each marcher was literally sworn in, verbally declaring allegiance to the plan while resting one hand on it and holding a crucifix in the other. Dolores Huerta performed each initiation. The plan itself was recited each night of the procession, in "spirited" ceremonies. An avowed "Plan of Liberation," its religious professions were multiple:

> The Penance we accept symbolizes the suffering we shall have in order to bring justice to these same towns, to this same valley.... The Pilgrimage we make symbolizes the long historical road we have traveled in this valley alone, and

the long road we have yet to travel, with much penance, in order to bring about the Revolution we need.[53]

Theirs was a distinctly Mexican American civil religion: drawn from revolutionary traditions yet consonant with the major teachings of the Constitution, principally freedom and liberty, but also justice, equality, and progress. The UFW added to this creed a motherly femininity embodied by the Virgin of Guadalupe, while emphasizing dynamic human sacrifice.[54] Chavez stressed the sacrificial element: "The thing we have going for us is that people are willing to sacrifice themselves. When you have that spirit, then nonviolence is not very difficult to accomplish."[55]

Nonviolent sacrificial struggle was the heart of the movement; it was linked with religious symbols to increase its rhetorical appeal. The marchers claimed to "seek, and have, the support of the church in what we do." However, the "church" is not specifically identified, even while the plan quotes *Rerum Novarum*—the church's key statement on justice for workers. Still, the marchers were careful to qualify their relationship to the symbols and orthodoxy of Catholicism: "At the head of the pilgrimage we carry LA VIRGEN DE GUADALUPE because she is ours, all ours, Patroness of the Mexican people. We also carry the Sacred Cross and the Star of David because we are not sectarians, and because we ask the help and prayers of all religions. . . . GOD SHALL NOT ABANDON US." The plan is rife with God talk, and emerges de facto as its own theological statement. "We seek our basic, God-given rights as human beings. Because we have suffered—and are not afraid to suffer—in order to survive, we are ready to give up everything, even our lives, in our fight for social justice. We shall do it without violence because that is our destiny."[56] The ceremony ending the pilgrimage was celebrated on Easter Sunday, on the steps of the State Capital building. Governor Pat Brown was not counted among the ten thousand; his absence was conspicuous. He spent the holiday at the Palm Springs' home of Frank Sinatra.

Even more than the peregrination, Chavez's fasting impressed the hearts and minds of Americans with the plight of the farmworkers. Chavez embarked upon three public fasts, following Gandhi's example in number and duration. In 1972 he fasted for twenty-five days in Phoenix, for "social justice." In 1988, he fasted in Delano for thirty-six days, protesting the use of pesticides. But it was his first fast in 1968, the "love fast," that transformed his movement from a strike and boycott into a moral crusade and Chavez into its prophet. Again, the symbolism of time, free and accessible, was a central trope in the event: it began on February 14. Like the first fast of Gandhi, Chavez's actions were precipitated by violence erupting within his own movement: Chavez wanted to recommit the movement to its foundational principles. Ignoring the counsel of his advisors, he told his followers he was embarking upon the fast because he loved them.

During this initial starvation period, Chavez cloistered himself in a small "cell" at Forty Acres, which subsequently became a makeshift pilgrimage site. Chavez stressed the distinct yet broadly religious quality of his actions, preaching the favor of God. Each night an ecumenical "religious ceremony" was celebrated, involving rabbis; Catholic priests sporting bright red vestments adorned by a UFW black eagle; Presbyterian, Methodist, and Episcopalian ministers; and Pentecostal preachers.[57] Of these events Jerry Cohen observed:

> I visited the Forty Acres on several occasions during the fast. It was both a fascinating and awesome spectacle to view. By the second week of the fast a sprawling tent city had sprung up around the little service station at the forty acres. Farm workers from all over California came to live in the tents and to share in the event. . . . the deliberate pace, the quiet voices, the huddled figures, the sharing of food and drink—all these gave the impression of serious religious vigil. . . . I'm not religious at all, but I would go to those masses at the Forty Acres every night. No matter what their religious background, anyone interested in farm workers, or with any sense about people, could see that something was going on that was changing a lot of people. The feeling of the workers was obvious. They talked at those meetings about their own experiences, about what the fast meant in terms of what the Union was going to mean to them. That was a really deep feeling, but it wasn't religious in the sense that somebody like me couldn't relate to it.[58]

Like that of the nation-state, the religion of the UFW was open to all who professed even secular beliefs in the sanctity of freedom, liberty, equality, and justice—but a belief in a monotheistic God served best to elevate these principles above the earthly terrain into a cosmic arena. People from all backgrounds experienced spiritual conversions through their devotion to the Chicano guru.[59]

The fast was terminated in dramatic fashion, covered by media from around the globe. Senator Robert F. Kennedy returned for the event, and fed bread directly to the leader who had mortified his flesh to enhance reliance on his spirit. In fact, Chavez claims to have received a fresh revelation from God during his retreat that was read aloud during the mass:

> Our struggle is not easy. Those who oppose our cause are rich and powerful, and they have many allies in high places. We are poor. Our allies are few. But we have something the rich do not own. We have our own bodies and spirits and the justice of our cause as weapons. . . . We must admit that our lives are all that really belong to us. So it is my deepest belief that only by giving our lives do we find life. I am convinced that the truest act of courage, the strongest act of [humanity] is to sacrifice ourselves for others in a totally nonviolent struggle for justice. To be [human] is to suffer for others. God help us to be [human]![60]

On this same occasion, Martin Luther King Jr. sent a telegram to Chavez.

> As brothers in the fight for equality, I extend the hand of fellowship and goodwill and wish continuing success to you and your members. The fight for equality must be fought on many fronts—in the urban slums, in the sweatshops of the factories and fields. Our separate struggles are really one—a struggle for freedom, for dignity, and for humanity. You and your valiant fellow workers

have demonstrated your commitment to righting grievous wrongs forced upon exploited people. We are together with you in spirit and in determination that our dreams for a better tomorrow will be realized.[61]

During his famed initial "spiritual fast," Chavez received visitors while he meditated, reposing in a full lotus position. He was asked to explain the fast. In one characteristic response, he pointed to a blank wall. "See that white wall? Well, imagine ten different-colored balls, all jumping up and down. One ball is called religion, another propaganda, another organizing, another law, and so forth. When people look at that wall and see those balls, different people look at different balls; each person keeps his eye on his own ball. For each person the balls mean many different things, but for everyone they can mean something!"[62]

The meaning of the fast, like the movement itself, paralleled the religious dimension of the state in that it was broadly coded, enabling mass appeal. Prior to the fast, Chavez further clarified his motivations in a letter to the National Council of Churches: "My fast is informed by my religious faith and by my deep roots in the Church. It is not intended as a pressure on anyone but only as an expression of my own deep feelings and my own need to do penance and to be in prayer." "Penance" is a Catholic rite, but not exclusively. Again, Chavez deploys circumlocution, positioning, and deft border crossing while emphasizing the ritual's distinctly religious aspects. Orthodoxy in this case is belief itself, rather than a discrete faith.

CESAR CHAVEZ AND THE AMERICAN FAITHFUL: TRUE BELIEVERS WITHOUT TRUE BELIEF

As a social movement within a democratic republic, Chavez's campaign was for American hearts and minds. "America is comprised of groups," he once remarked. "So long as the smaller groups do not have the same rights and the same protection as others—I don't care what you call it, Capitalism or Communism—it is not going to work. Somehow, the guys in power have to be reached by counter power, or through change in their hearts and minds."[63] Thus, his appeal was not exclusively to any particular religious group—even while his base was predominantly Christian, and specifically Catholic. He appealed to those religious sentiments around which all like-minded believers congealed, while attaching those amorphous "moods and motivations" to his political cause. He once explained as follows: "See, everybody interprets our work in a different way. Some people interpret its as a union, some people interpret our work as an ethnic issue, some people interpret our work as a peace movement, some people see it as a religious movement. We can appeal to broad sectors because of these different interpretations."[64] Taking my cue from Chavez himself, I interpret his work as a *broadly* religious movement—one not distinctly Catholic.

Inasmuch as his description of his group is antithetical to a traditional church orthodoxy, it recalls President Eisenhower's famous one-liner: "America makes no sense unless it is founded on a deeply held religious faith—and I don't care what that faith is." Comparing King's SCLC to Chavez's UFW, one theorist writes: "Both agencies attempted to convince the larger public that the symbols of their respective movements were in keeping with the values of the nation as they had been inculcated into the metaphors of earlier historical situations and became part of the accepted civil religion by the majority."[65] The prophetic translation and iteration of the American story was central to Chavez's rhetorical appeal.

Chavez's vision began with the organization of farmworkers, but he always intended that union to catalyze a much larger social transformation. "And if this spirit grows within the farm labor movement, one day we can use the force that we have to help correct a lot of things that are wrong in this society. But that is for the future. Before you can run, you have to learn to walk."[66] Learning to walk involved deconstructing the codes that legitimized racism and the mass exploitation and suffering of the many for the benefit of the few; hence, he read, beginning with classical philosophy, economics, politics, and religion. From this he fathomed the moral and ethical foundation of U.S. democracy, and engaged it—a system that is marked by the advances and limitations of the European Enlightenment.

In the eighteenth century Rousseau addressed the ideological limits of a democratic republic voided of its divine right: mass secularization would strip social inequities of the sacred vestments that clothed the status quo in an aura of truth and legitimacy. The naked injustice of economic inequality threatened the peace of society. But rather than proposing broad reform, Rousseau first theorized a "civil religion," whereby sacred authority would become the manufactured domain of what he called the state's "spiritual dimension," through the continuing confluence of history and revelation. Though avowedly secular, the liberal republic could retain its sacred authority in what is perhaps modernity's greatest sleight of hand: a secular state whose sacred authority is reflexive, or self-generating. In the American democratic system, as De Tocqueville proposed, the authority that the masses once attributed to the Mind of God alone could now be found in the Will of the People, writ large and revealed by the democratic process.

Rather than a sui generis religious system, civil religion is perhaps best described as a national collection of myths, symbols, and rituals that express Judeo-Christian teaching along nonspecific religious lines within national narratives of transcendent significance. The symbols themselves are shadow representations of the majority traditions that can be reflected by minority faiths. Hence, Robert Bellah's 1965 liberal reprisal of Rousseau is a corruption of the original aristocratic intention. What the French modernist first described was not a self-supporting institution aligned with the state, but a "religious dimension" of the nation capturing and synthesizing mass religious sentiments supporting it. His "civil religion" would function as a mystifying agent of the state that would enable believers to reassemble and affirm the fragments of primitive beliefs, hopes, and fears shattered by enlightened thought within the certainty of their collective. For Rousseau, this spiritual dimension of the republic could free the rulers from devotion to medieval institutions in favor of populist tropes, all the while reproducing the ultimate stakes of heaven and hell as a psychic technique of social regulation. The religion of the democratic republic could suit modern demand for tangibility, efficacy, and participation.

Political discourse in the United States is a triumph of Rousseau's theories. On June 27, 2005, Supreme Court justice Antonin Scalia spoke for millions of faithful Americans when explaining his vote to allow the Ten Commandments to be displayed on public space: "It is a profound religious message, but it's a profound religious message believed in by the vast majority of the American people. . . . the minority has to be tolerant of the majority's ability to express its belief that government comes from God, which is what this is about."

For such believers, the state's divine legitimacy is implicit, allowing it to (re)produce its own discourses of the holy. Devotion to the state was described by Nietzsche's Zarathustra as the "New Idol." The modern death of God left a void filled by a generalized mysticism that surrounds, shapes, and inflects the democratic process so that it becomes a sacred system. Hence, the principle of majority rule is the process whereby God's will is revealed. Echoing Rousseau, Nietzsche's prophet declared that all nations invent and speak their "own tongues of good and evil." The history of the twentieth century has repeatedly proven the efficacy of this tool as a mechanism of mass political suasion—even while its parent abuses are obvious and repetitive. Bellah and other liberal twentieth-century theorists have promoted the deist rendering of modern national religion as a tongue for good, celebrating a consensus social spirituality and ethics indebted to Enlightened principles of justice and equality. In this way they overlook the great suffering and injustice legitimized by religious nationalism.

The danger of a nation-state dedicated to popular spiritual beliefs manifests in self-interested, myopic forces that concomitantly manipulate love, fear, and hatred into a Christian theocracy. As President Jimmy Carter warns: "Although considered to be desirable by some Americans, this melding of church and state is of deep concern to those who have always relished their separation as one of our moral values."[67] For better or worse, state constructs of the sacred fall short of tight control over effervescent moods and motivations, and therefore new and unorthodox spiritual energies are continually produced. Conversely, antihegemonic religious stories circulate throughout the population within, outside, and in direct opposition to churches and other institutions functioning as regulatory mechanisms.

Religious nationalists have invested in modern normative models of human subjectivity; at times, racial and erotic identities are attached as appendages to grand economic, political, and cultural narratives. Ironically, civil religion is also a democratic field of social relations, and the complicated truths of race, gender, and sexuality rupture the architecture of the state's version, opening new spaces to theorize the nation, beginning with the most primal element in statecraft—the human body and soul. Racism begins from a narration of a "natural" order to the world, delimiting a hierarchy of races crafted through Enlightenment discourses. Gandhi, King, and Chavez confronted these racializing narratives, demonstrating that people of color are equally children of God.

In this way, Chavez's fasts proposed his own corporality as the metonymic national body upon which to imprint a fresh template of virtuous being. His body was broken and suspended in a deathlike state before a resurrection to enliven a praxis of new life and national redemption. His explanation for the fast, "love," strengthens the allegorical tie to the sacrificial Christ—a signification not lost on most observers. Chavez redefined God and the national good for an American community of believers (and make-believers).

MAPPING THE SPIRITUAL LINE FOR THE TWENTY-FIRST CENTURY

There is no small irony in the coalescing of religion and politics into the civil rights movements of the second half of the twentieth century—a century ushered in by the "death of God." Religious authority emanating from church pulpits does not flow securely into the hands of government officials, no matter how successful the politician or party. Instead, democratic impulses continually disestablish religious boundaries, thereby establishing the conditions for spiritual dominance to circulate as so many individuals' and groups' will to power. America's most remembered leaders thrived from this reality, King and Chavez foremost. At best, they functioned as theologians of American civil religion who moved the national logos against racial intolerance, toward the promise of universal Christian grace. But the pendulum continues to swing.

On the current coalescence of religion and politics, President Carter warns: "It is the injection of these beliefs into America's government policies that is cause for concern. These believers are convinced that they have a personal responsibility to hasten this coming of the 'rapture' in order to fulfill biblical prophecy. Their agenda calls for a war in the Middle East against Islam. . . . At this time of rapture, all Jews will either be converted to Christianity or be burned."[68]

To this warning Sam Harris adds: "Many who claim to be transformed by Christ's love are deeply, even murderously intolerant of criticism. While we may want to ascribe this to human nature, it is clear that such hatred draws considerable support from the Bible. . . . most disturbed of my correspondents always cite chapter and verse."[69] For Harris, religious designations and their attendant oppositional identities are divisive and immoral beyond the faulty logic of other social cleavages: "Religion raises the stakes of human conflict much higher than tribalism, racism, or politics ever can, as it is the only form of in-group/out-group thinking that casts the differences between people in terms of eternal rewards and punishments."[70]

Chavez's work and the current religious state of emergency in the United States lead me to conclude that the problem of the twenty-first century is the problem of the spiritual line, an ideological border delineated by social constructs separating good from evil, saved from damned, straight from gay, Christian from Muslim, Muslim from Jew, and the religious from the secular. This is not to say that race is no longer a problem. Rather, racial hatred is now further complicated, receded, and recast in a drama starring saints and sinners. No government or individual legitimate in the eyes of the world can openly sanction racial hatred. Yet, they all respect religious difference. Chavez's religious politics were thus prescient regarding our current religious crisis. In narrating his own nuanced spiritual identity he mitigated the insistence on fundamentalist belief, rightly attributing to religious identity the randomness of birth: "To me, religion is a most beautiful thing. And over the years, I have come to realize that all religions are beautiful." Here he echoes the famous aphorism of Gandhi: "All religions are true, and all contain error." Hence Chavez advanced multiculturalism before it became an academic industry.

In contrast to religious leaders confident in their ability to judge the difference between sinners and saints, Chavez recognized the continuing fall of the human condition (including, of course, his own) and its need for redemption, a spiritual conversion: "We need a cultural revolution. And we need a cultural revolution among ourselves not only in art but also in the realm of the spirit."[71] Chavez knew that in the United States, democratic change arises from the soul of the majority and that that soul could be touched and informed—transformed—by religious discourse emerging from prophetic agency. Yet religiosity was only one tactic he deployed as a key dimension of his arsenal. The quintessential organic intellectual, he was armed with many discourses, including religious and constitutional, and tactics, including strikes and boycotts. He further recognized that strategies need to change and develop following the vicissitudes of history. In this regard, he cited Gandhi's rendering of "moral jujitsu. Always hit the opposition off balance, but keep your principles."[72]

NOTES

1. Cesar Chavez, quoted in Jacques Levy, *Cesar Chavez: Autobiography of La Causa* (New York: Norton, 1975), 276.

2. Throughout I refer to the late leader by his last name, Chavez, unless clarity requires a more familiar reference. This usage directly rejects the more common and, I argue, disrespectful first-name references to him in the literature by authors who never met him. Too often racist and sexist discursive practices allow women and minorities first-name references within academic grammar; regrettably, this is especially true in the literature on Chavez.

3. On civil religion, see especially Robert Bellah, "Civil Religion in America," *Daedulus* (Winter 1967); and *The Broken Covenant: Civil Religion in Time of Trial*, 2nd ed. (Chicago: University of Chicago Press, 1992).

4. Art Torres, quoted in Richard Griswold del Castillo and Richard A. Garcia, *César Chávez: A Triumph of Spirit* (Norman: University of Oklahoma Press, 1995), 154.

5. Richard Rodriguez, *Days of Obligation: An Argument with My Mexican Father* (New York: Penguin, 1992), 68.

6. Gary Soto, in *The Fight in the Fields: Cesar Chavez and the Farmworkers Movement*, edited by Susan Ferris and Ricardo Sandoval (New York: Harcourt Brace, 1997), xvi.

7. Ibid.

8. Max Weber, "The Prophet," in *The Sociology of Religion*, trans. Ephraim Fischoff (Boston: Beacon, 1963), 46–59.

9. Ibid., 9.

10. See Joseph Campbell, *The Hero with a Thousand Faces* (Princeton, N.J.: Princeton University Press, 1949).

11. Cesar Chavez, quoted in Ronald B. Taylor, *Chavez and the Farm Workers* (Boston: Beacon Press, 1975), 61.

12. See Griswold del Castillo and Garcia, "Conclusion: A Legacy of Struggle," in *Triumph of Spirit*, 172–78.

13. Chavez, quoted in Levy, *Cesar Chavez*, 11.

14. Ibid., 19.

15. Ibid., 84.

16. Ibid., 84–85.

17. Ibid., 280–81.

18. Helen Chavez, quoted in Peter Matthiessen, *Sal Si Puedes (Escape If You Can): Cesar Chavez and the New American Revolution*, 2nd ed. (Berkeley, University of California Press, 2000), 231.

19. Chavez, quoted in Levy, *Cesar Chavez*, 84.

20. Chavez, quoted in "A Conversation with Cesar Chavaz," in *Readings on La Raza: The Twentieth Century*, ed. Matt S. Maier and Feliciano Rivera (New York: Hill and Wang, 1974), 251.

21. Chavez, "People Are Willing to Sacrifice Themselves: An Interview with Cesar Chavez" in *Peace Is the Way: Writings on Nonviolence from the Fellowship of Reconciliation*, ed. Walter Wink (Maryknoll, N.Y.: Orbis, 2000), 228.

22. Miriam Pawell, *Los Angeles Times*, January 10–14, 2006. The Cesar E. Chavez Foundation has categorically answered her shrill charges on their Web site at www.cef.org.

23. Cesar Chavez quoted in William P. Colleman, "At 51, Cesar Chavez Emphasizes Teaching." *Los Angeles Times*, March 26, 1978, 3.

24. Harry Bernstein, "UFW Transforming Itself from 'Cause' to 'Businesslike Union,'" *Los Angeles Times*, October 25, 1981, 20.

25. Robert Lindsey, "Cesar Chavez Tries New Directions for United Farm Workers." *Los Angeles Times*, September 19, 1983, 16.

26. Doug Smith, "UFW Leader Addresses 100 at Buffet-Dance," *Los Angeles Times*, March 31, 1983, WS1.

27. Lois Valdez, quoted in Susan Drake, *Fields of Courage: Remembering Cesar Chavez and the People Whose Labor Feeds Us* (Santa Cruz, Calif.: Many Names Press, 1999).

28. Dolores Huerta, quoted in Matthiessen, *Sal Si Puedes*, 176.

29. Stan Steiner, *La Raza: The Mexican Americans* (New York: Harper and Row, 1970), 62.

30. Fred Dalton, *The Moral Vision of Cesar Chavez* (Maryknoll, N.Y.: Orbis, 2003), 46; emphasis added.

31. I have written at length on this issue in my book *La Llorona's Children: Religion, Life, and Death in the United States Mexican Borderlands* (Berkeley, University of California Press, 2004); see especially chap. 2, "Virtual Virgin Nation: Mexico City as Sacred Center of Memory," 59–90.

32. Chavez, quoted in Catherine Ingram, *In the Footsteps of Gandhi: Conversations with Spiritual Social Activists* (Berkeley: Parallax Press, 1990), 27; emphasis added.

33. See Levy, *Cesar Chavez*, 50.

34. Chavez, quoted in Matthiessen, *Sal Si Puedes*, 326.

35. Interview by the author with Jim Covarrubias, Phoenix, Arizona, December 8, 1999.

36. Julie Rodriguez, interview by the author, March 1, 2006.

37. See Pat Hoffman, *Ministry of the Dispossessed: Learning from the Farm Workers Movement* (Los Angeles: Wallace Press, 1987), 113.

38. Cesar Chavez, "The Mexican American and the Church," *El Grito* 4 (Summer 1968): 215–18, 215.

39. Richard J. Jensen and John C. Hammerbeck, "Introduction," in *The Words of Cesar Chavez*, ed. Richard J. Jensen and John C. Hammerbeck (College Station: Texas A&M University Press, 2002), xxii–xxiii.

40. For a history of the Migrant Ministry, see Sydney D. Smith, *Grapes of Conflict* (Pasadena, Calif.: Hope Publishing House, 1987).

41. Hoffman, *Ministry of the Dispossessed*, 6–7.

42. See Marco G. Prouty, *Cesar Chavez, the Catholic Bishops, and the Farmworkers Struggle for Social Justice* (Tucson: University of Arizona Press, 2006).

43. See especially George G. Higgins with William Boyle, *Organized Labor and the Church: Reflections of a Labor Priest* (New York: Paulist Press, 1993).

44. Mark Day, *Forty Acres: Cesar Chavez and the Farm Workers Movement* (New York: Praeger, 1971), 58.

45. Chavez, quoted in Levy, *Cesar Chavez*, 524–25.

46. Robert Kennedy, quoted in James Terzian and Kathryn Cramer, *Mighty Hard Road: The Story of Cesar Chavez* (New York: Doubleday, 1970), 107.

47. Chavez, quoted in Levy, *Cesar Chavez*, 196.

48. Chavez, quoted in Ingram, *In the Footsteps of Ghandi*, 119.

49. Chavez, quoted in Levy, *Cesar Chavez*, 270.

50. Chavez, "Martin Luther King, Jr.: He Showed Us the Way," *Maryknoll*, April 1978, 52–55.

51. Ibid.

52. Dick Meister, "'La Huelga' Becomes 'La Causa,'" *New York Times*, November 17, 1968.

53. From the "Plan of Delano," by Luis Valdez and Cesar Chavez (n.d., n.p.).

54. See Spencer Bennett, "Civil Religion in a New Context: The Mexican-American Faith of Cesar Chavez," in *Religion and Political Power*, edited by Gustavo Benavides and M. W. Daly (Albany: State University of New York Press, 1989).

55. Chavez, "People Are Willing to Sacrifice Themselves," 227.

56. From the "Plan of Delano"; capitalization in original.

57. Chavez noted the involvement of preachers in Matthiessen, *Sal Si Puedes*, 186.

58. Jerry Cohen, quoted in Levy, *Cesar Chavez*, 283.

59. See especially Hoffman, *Ministry of the Dispossessed*.

60. Chavez, quoted in Levy, *Cesar Chavez*, 286.

61. Martin Luther King Jr., telegram to Cesar Chavez, March 1968, reprinted in full in Levy, *Cesar Chavez*, 246.

62. Chavez, quoted in Matthiessen, *Sal Si Puedes*, 186.

63. Chavez, quoted in Griswold del Castillo and Garcia, *A Triumph of Spirit*, 150.

64. Chavez, quoted in Ingram, *In the Footsteps of Ghandi*, 114.

65. Bennett, "Civil Religion in a New Context," 4.

66. Cesar Chavez, "The Organizer's Tale," in *Chicano: The Evolution of a People*, ed. Renato Rosaldo et al. (Minneapolis: Winston Press, 1973).

67. Jimmy Carter, *Our Endangered Values: America's Moral Crisis* (New York: Simon and Schuster, 2005), 64.

68. Ibid., 114.

69. Sam Harris, *Letter to a Christian Nation* (New York: Knopf, 2006), vii.

70. Ibid., 80.

71. Cesar Chavez, "Introduction," in Day, *Forty Acres*, 12.

72. Chavez quoted in Levy, *Cesar Chavez*, 270.

PART II
VOICES

A Catalyst for Change

Josephine Méndez-Negrete

> *People remember when Kennedy died . . . its like that for us.*
> *We had to be here.*
> —Ruben Chávez[1]

When people speak about John F. Kennedy's assassination, they invariably ask where we were when we first heard the news of his killing. Most of us remember where we were, what we were doing, and the immense feelings of sadness and emotional turmoil we experienced upon hearing the news. If someone were to ask me where I was when I heard the news of César Chávez's death, I would recall vividly a drive over the Santa Cruz Mountains. I was going to San José to do another interview for the life history of one of the subjects for my research on Chicana/Latino leadership formation. I switched the radio from one station to another, hoping that what I was hearing had not happened. Yet, the news came over the airwaves again and again: "César Chávez is dead."

Who was César Chávez? What did he represent? How was he perceived? How did Chávez influence the leadership and activism of those he inspired to work toward social change? If one is to measure César Chávez's leadership, it can best be done through the reflections of other organizers, activists, and leaders who knew or worked with him. The following is a series of such reflections.

THE CHÁVEZ INTERVIEWS

As I asked those who were involved in the Chicano Movement or who have supported the farm workers' struggle about their loss, most expressed a sense of disbelief. This seems to be the common thread in responding to the loss. Some recalled where they were. Others spoke of experiencing a void, an emptiness and loss of direction upon hearing the news. Some expressed regret at not having been more recently active in the struggle and emphatically professed a recommitment to the struggle for social justice. *César no a muerto porque su espiritu continua en la lucha,*[2] emerges as a mantra for dealing with our loss.

Jenny Alejandrez, a UFW supporter and anti-violence activist, spoke of that day. She remembered being at home. "I felt a great loss. I felt saddened. I cried

Josephine Méndez-Negrete" "A Catalyst for Change," first published in *San José Studies*, vol. 20, num. 2 (1994): 71–83.

because we had lost a great leader. He was a great man, and he was somebody we could look up to, who showed us direction."[3] Immediately after having voiced these thoughts, almost as if to make her loss more palpable, she reminisced about the honor she felt upon meeting Chávez at a conference in Fresno.

Like Jenny, Celia Organista, director of Proyecto Adelante, spoke of feeling a sense of loss when she heard the news. However, she also identified her loss as different from that which she felt as a young idealist who worked in the 1960s Kennedy campaign. For her, JFK's death was more personal because it came with the loss of her idealism. She remembered hearing of Chávez's death in her Santa Cruz County office: "I felt more sad for the community than for myself personally. Losing César was different because I felt more sadness for the people who were going to be directly impacted by his loss than for myself."

Sofia Mendoza, an activist and community organizer, recalled being at home where she got a call from one of Chávez's family members in San José. When I asked her how she had felt, she said that she had felt an emotional void: "He was one of my mentors." For Sofia, Chávez's loss meant losing the reinforcement she got from her interactions with him and the other organizers who had recently left her life. She recalled being told by Chávez "With us organizers it's just different. It's like all our feelings come into play, when we do our work." As she reflected, Chávez's death was a great personal loss because other people who were touched by her connection to him were also going to feel the loss. Because of prior experience with farm labor struggles— her father was an organizer during the Lemon Grove Strike in Filmore—her affiliation with the UFW was the natural and unending organizing relationship that Sofia had maintained.

The unifying theme in these comments is loss. The sense of loss experienced at John Kennedy's death was imbued with the idealism of the 1960s and is etched in the national consciousness. Chávez's loss, despite his thirty years of tenacious involvement in the labor movement, has yet to be appreciated. However, Chávez's influence on the leaders he inspired, mentored, and motivated is embedded in their ideals and actions.

WHO WAS CÉSAR CHÁVEZ?

After losing their family ranch, the Chávez family survived as migrant farmworkers in the stream of field work "usually landing in San José for the fall and winter harvests,"[4] finally settling in San José in the early 1940s. Chávez established a special relationship with San José residents, activists, organizers, and leaders. In their recollection of Chávez, they remember him as a complex individual. Chávez began his march toward prominence in San José as an organizer for the Community Services Organization (CSO) from 1952 to 1962. In a *Mercury News* interview, Chávez recalled:

> I was working in apricot orchards near town and living with my family in the rough East San Jose Barrio called Sal Si Puedes (Get Out If You Can). . . . What

followed was a frenetic 40 days and nights as we registered 4,000 new voters—the first such drive in Sal Si Puedes.[5]

When reflecting on their leadership interactions with Chávez, leaders speak about the community organizer who understood the meaning of mobilizing from the bottom up, and the migrant urban Chicano who selflessly returned to the fields to organize farmworkers.

Remembering the emergence of Chávez as a leader, Eugene García, Professor of Education and Dean of Social Sciences at the University of California, Santa Cruz, presented an understanding of the man as influenced by his social surroundings. García accounted for Chávez's attributes, by placing these in a specific historical context. According to García, Chávez rose to the occasion aided by the circumstances that fanned an agricultural movement in California. Along the way, Chávez inspired others in different parts of the United States to organize. According to García

César Chávez was produced by a set of circumstances. Certainly he had a personality and a set of values and fire, and so forth, but clearly, if farm workers weren't being so badly dealt with, he wouldn't have been a leader.

García is not devaluing Chávez's presence and influence in the Chicano Movement, and the farm workers' struggle in particular; rather he is emphasizing the historical, social, and political conditions that contributed to identifying Chávez as a leader.

For those individuals who had an opportunity to work with Chávez directly, like Sofia Mendoza, another story emerged:

[He was] a common everyday person who loved people, regardless of color. He was fearless. He never stopped struggling. He was a person who always gave; he never took. He wore in the fields what he wore everyday—his plaid shirt and work clothes. He was a hard worker.

Her recollections of Chávez reflect an understanding of a working-class person who knew common working individuals, and accepted them regardless of their class, ethnicity, or politics. San José Vice Mayor Blanca Alvarado recalled a compassionately committed human being. While voicing her regret for not remaining as strong a supporter of the leader and his movement in their most recent struggles with the boycott of pesticides, Alvarado said:

César Chávez is somebody that I just adored. I mean, I idolized him so much, and I regret that I didn't do more for him and for his cause. . . . I remember the wonderful, wonderful model of humanity, dignity, and respect that this quiet man epitomized. He was a gentle giant who believed so very strongly in his cause, and, because he believed so strongly in his cause, he was able to get the rest of us, or so many, many more of us, to embrace his cause and to feel passionately about it like he did.

While Alvarado presented a complex image of a quiet, yet intensely committed organizer and leader, Ernestina García, a long-time activist, evaluated Chávez's commitment to others as a source of strength for the movement. For García, Chávez was the reflection of selflessness, emphasizing that concern for himself always came after concern for others. He believed in his cause so much that he would give himself to other causes looking to create unity. As García put it,

> *César Chávez siempre miraba for el projimo; el no estaba mirando por que tanto hay en esto para mi? Nunca se hizo rico. Y si miraba que habia injusticia alli te la decia;* if he saw that, there, *alli te lo decia,* "esto esta mal y correct it."[6]

Chávez's sense of justice was so great that he consciously made an effort to identify those injustices he witnessed. Then he would bring these issues to the attention of others, expecting them to correct these weaknesses on their own. García continued:

> [El no andaba buscando credito] y tampoco andaba echandole habladas o celos a la genie . . . y si habia una junta de alguien que no era de el, he would go, pero no iba to instigate o a quebrar la unidad que tenian, el se sentaba y oia; he would support. He would support whatever was going on, and that's what I call a leader.[7]

As García pointed out, for Chávez, confrontation was an aboveboard and open process. According to her, jealousy was not in his vocabulary; Chávez worked for unity. The theme of selflessness, unity, and commitment arose once again as Felix Alvarez, a cultural and community activist, elaborated on César's commitment to his people:

> [As a leader] César Chávez was committed to the whole group rather than to himself. Yes, in his life, he demonstrated commitment to fighting for farm workers, fighting for a union, fighting for a religiosity, even. César was multifaceted; he wasn't just one thing, even though people identified him with farm labor.

Thus, for Felix, César was more than a leader of farm workers; he influenced goals and policies in other arenas. While working with the union

> [His leadership] touched many other points of the spectrum . . . he went from a leader to a great leader . . . I think César even surpassed being a great leader because he became a leader who went beyond his immediate group. He reached a status of international focus.

From Alvarez's perspective, Chávez was internationally recognized as a man of peace and a humanist concerned with the welfare of those who work for their sustenance. For Alvarez and other leaders, Chávez was an accurate representation of the farm working person he struggled to defend. For example, Alvarez observed, Chávez did not expend much energy promoting his particular ethnic identification, yet he was able to represent his ethnicity in the ways he carried himself and in his actions with and for his people. Alvarez continued,

his identity as a Chicano, being Mexicano, being Indio, or being part of the ancestry of the people from here was clear, even though he didn't go around bang-
ing that drum. He didn't have to tell you that he was brown; he was brown. He
didn't have to tell you that he thought in Indian ways because he acted in an
Indian way.

Clearly Alvarez did not perceive Chávez as a monotypic leader who professed
merely to have the influence and authority of a union president. In Alvarez's
reflections on the man as a leader, Chávez did not autocratically dictate the
direction of his movement, but guided it using humility, commitment to
change, and investment in the workers whom Chávez considered the most
dispossessed of our society. As Alvarez saw it, Chávez directly and indirectly
influenced many by his life, his vision, and his actions. García agreed with this
perception of Chávez because for him Chávez "was a model, a prototype for
all of us, somebody who met all criteria of leadership—a wonderful leader."

WHAT DID HE REPRESENT?

> *Your myth shall grow upward, like the tree of life*
> *and you shall give light and shade to all of humanity.*
> *For you shall always lead us, my brother.*
> —Luis Valdez[8]

For many people, including me, Chávez was a figure of mythic proportions. Chávez embodied hope because he engendered in us—the idealists of
the late '60s and early '70s—a sense of power, by inspiring us with his call
to resist all that is unjust and unfair. From Chávez, I learned to struggle for
justice and to allow myself to evolve into someone who is committed to social
change and who non-violently pursues equality and fairness for the dispossessed of our society.

Many of those I interviewed remembered Chávez as a humble person who
actively refused to pursue material goods for himself. Mendoza spoke of him
as a person of humble beginnings with the will to struggle for his beliefs:

When you think back to your own culture and think back to your original roots,
I just think of César as a warrior who wasn't tainted by anything. He did things
because he had to do them. He never lived in fancy homes. He never had fancy
things. He was with the people. He was extremely intelligent.

In Mendoza's view, Chávez acted out his values and beliefs, even when not
in public view. For example, Mendoza recalled being there with him in one
of his many fasts. "I remember going to see him. He was in a little building
even without a bed, just a mattress on the floor. He would tell us 'Don't give
up.'" Working with César was one of Mendoza's greatest satisfactions in life,
because she was part of the movement from the beginning.

According to Mendoza, Chávez had no more and maybe even less than
the workers he so avidly supported. Hermelinda Sapien, a well-respected

and active deputy director of a vocational training center, spoke of mourning César's passing; she recalled a sense of loss that she can not get over and reflected that "César was in a class by himself." She said, "I cannot get over it! Seeing his coffin taken away was probably the saddest moment that I've ever lived."

Ernestina García said that Chávez epitomized someone with genuine qualities of leadership:

> . . . leaders are *como* Cesar Chavez; and he's still our leader, and he'll be the only leader that I would recognize, I guess, in my life. Leader *es Diosito; primero Dios, y luego mi padre y madre*—those are leaders, and Cesar Chavez.

Once again, García lauded Chávez's humanity and revered him for what he represented. She made a connection to his humble beginning as a farmworker, and expressed an appreciation for his leadership in improving conditions for all who worked in the field.

> César Chávez and I come from the roots of working in the fields, *antes que hubiera any union de César Chávez se sufria mucho en los files, y el fue el que* took the role, took the stand *y se quedo en el fil*, took the stand and stuck with it, stuck with it *pa' que se hicieran unos cambios. . . .*[9]

Chávez's perseverance and tenacity are implicitly embedded in García's description of his commitment to farm workers. She feels a reverence for him beyond that of any other leader who struggled for the rights of Mexicano and Chicano workers. But, to the community activists and leaders in my study, Chávez's example and call to leadership was not limited to the agricultural fields. According to Gónzalez, García, and Alvarez, in the urban setting where Chicanos began to fend off race and class oppression, Chávez also inspired students and other activists to pursue the struggle for justice and equality. He showed them and many of their contemporaries that you can stand up against injustice, regardless of your station in life. Robinson, an organizer and activist, recalled a Chávez whose "crusade embodied humility, [and who] didn't kowtow to anybody." In her statement, she emphasized the strength of his convictions and commitment to what he believed, which was an inspiration and a call to struggle. Josie Romero, long-time supporter of the UFW and a political activist, spoke of Latinos' beliefs that only educated or professional people can engage in social change and advocacy, beliefs that she felt were prevalent before Chávez rose to prominence. She contended that

> César Chávez has shown us that you don't need to be professionally educated to be a leader. He also showed us that you don't have to have millions of dollars to create change.

Notions of leadership and who could be leaders in our communities were reshaped by Chávez and his followers. Chávez inspired many to take on the struggle to improve the rights of those who work to harvest the food that ends up on our tables. He supported women in leadership by recognizing

and bringing them into the fold of the UFW; he included those who were
economically better off; he recruited leaders of national stature like Bobby
Kennedy and other Kennedy family members; and he enveloped other racial
and cultural minorities in the movement for farm workers' rights. Ernestina
García recalled

> César worked with all kinds of people—*de todos colores. El no distinguía que
> porque tu eres negro, que to eres chino, o tu eres gringo, o lo que sea. El lo hacía por
> la humanidad por eso pudo trabajar a diferentes niveles. La visión de César era todo el
> tiempo por la humanidad.*[10]

García reflected on Chávez's ability to attract people from many walks of
life. In her leadership interactions, she saw Chávez forming coalitions with
people who had never before been able to work in unity for the same objective. Women became a strong part of the movement. Also Filipinos, Jews, and
liberal whites answered his call for justice in the fields. García noted that before coalitional politics were in fashion, Chávez amassed a multiethnic, multi-
classed, and two-gendered coalition to work toward a common objective. For
García, Chávez—the simple man, the humble man, the pacifist, and the farm
worker—was able to inspire action on the part of many who prior to this call
had remained content with the status quo. As Eugene García put it:

> I don't think many of us will achieve the kinds of ability or respect or apprecia-
> tion that César Chávez received. There's only a few people who can rise to that.
> We need Césars but we need a lot more Genes and Josies who are just out there
> doing their work; and I'm not expecting anyone to remember us.

While García's statement underscores Chávez's contributions and his greatness, there are more general principles implicit here. For one, leaders and activists in the Latino community must continue to work for the betterment of the
people, not to achieve the greatness of Chávez, but to advance a better quality
of life. For another, work must be done because it is the "right thing to do." Like
Chávez, we must do the work because we have to, without the expectation of
fame, or a place in history. Whether we get the credit or the recognition is not
the point. The point is that there is much work to be done; the one lesson we
all learned from César was to get the work done regardless of the cost. As Alvarado insightfully noted, "had this gentle giant been part of the upper crust,
the revolution inspired by Chávez would have called for the writing of many
volumes to document the brilliant strategist and tactician that he was." Many
doubt whether we will ever again see a leader of Chávez's stature, but all those
I interviewed shared the knowledge that he inspired many to begin as well as
to continue the struggle for Chicana and Latino rights.

HOW WAS HE PERCEIVED?

The testimonials of those leaders who worked with Chávez or for his struggle reflect a man of much humanity, who embodied goodness and possessed
a generous heart. Without exception, all perceived Chávez as the spark of the

movimiento and a leader without equal. From their perspective, Chávez was not simply a farm worker who rose to the rank of union president—he was a brilliant strategist, with the moral character and leadership qualities to move nation and government to recognize the rights of farm workers. In their eyes, while he is recognized as a champion of peace in the international world, the nation of his birth has yet to recognize fully the greatness of the man who died while waging a war against corporate greed and the inhumanity of multi-national corporations which strip Mexican workers of their dignity, then perceive them as unworthy of a decent living wage.

Without exception, organizers, activists, and leaders who knew and worked with Chávez, or supported his struggle, saw him as a leader. Kathy Chávez Napoli, a local businesswoman and supporter of the UFW union, stated that, "There are leaders that I feel are true leaders: people like César Chávez, people who really lead people into more benefits or more action."

To explain how Chávez reached this pinnacle of greatness, Alvarado suggested that

> Some people are born to be great musicians, some people are born to be great teachers, some people are born like César Chávez to lead a movement, and I don't know what it is about the personality. I don't know if it is something that is genetic, I don't know if it is something that is intuitive. I think that we are called for different things.

Though she attempted to explain Chávez's leadership in a variety of ways, Alvarado was forced to conclude only that all of us are called for a specific purpose in life.

HOW DID HE INFLUENCE LEADERSHIP AND ACTIVISM?

In one way or another, Chávez inspired many people to take on the struggle for farm-worker rights. He inspired their activism and directly and indirectly influenced their involvement in defense or promotion of Raza rights. Sofia Mendoza, who engaged in many door-to-door campaigns in Santa Clara County, recalled one direct lesson she learned from Chávez.

> I remember César used to tell me, "You gotta dress like the people. You gotta talk with the people. Don't even drive a car. Don't take a lunch. Let the people feed you." I learned a lot because he taught me that you have to be where the people are and start organizing where they're at.

Implicit in Chávez's directions are several leadership lessons. First, to organize people you have to understand how they experience the social world you are attempting to change.[11] Second, the one way to do that is to be in the same social surroundings, to be one of the people, and to work on an agenda that is based on the people's understanding of social reality. Jorge Gónzalez, President of Raza Si!, noted that "César Chávez has been an inspiration. I really didn't work with him. I worked with his organization. He's been an inspiration." Gónzalez speaks to the experiences of those who were involved in the secondary boycotts, who participated in the marches, and supported his cadre of organizers to bring about changes in the field. From these experiences, many of us learned different tactics and strategies for organizing in and outside the United Farm Worker's movement. For example, Hermelinda Sapien noted the many urban problems of poor working people, Mexicanos and Chicanos in particular and reflected that we can

> do anything [to create change] . . . if we can all agree on one issue and focus on that, really fight for that, like César Chávez did with the farm workers—it was one issue—that's why he was so identifiable, we will be better equipped to make a difference.

From Chávez, Ernestina García recalled learning qualities of leadership that have been useful in the struggles she wages. She said "I learned that you have to humble yourself to what other people want. I also learned *pacencia, respeto, y humildad*. I think *que César siempre se humillo no a un modo de que* 'I'm nobody.' *Se unio* humbly, *sin mandar sin violencia* to bring about change."[12]

The level of commitment and willingness to sacrifice all that you have for something you believe is a lesson that Alvarez also spoke about. He recalled that

> César said that "You have to be willing to give up your life for others." [It] doesn't mean to literally die in that sense. It means to dedicate your life to it, put your whole life into it. [To do this] takes . . . more *concientizacion* for people to begin to understand what that's about.

Alvarez's perception is that an effective leader is willing to give up everything for a cause. Such a leader acts out of belief, not to become famous, or to reap personal rewards.

The inspiration and the leadership lessons that these people learned from Chávez cut across the usual divisions in the activist community. For many, Chávez began with the labor movement and moved on to inspire those in the cities to struggle for educational rights, employment opportunities, and much more. Mike García, for example, President of SEIU Local 1877, spoke of Chávez's involvement as a labor leader:

> the community must try to understand the labor movement . . . some community people didn't even understand why labor was involved [in the march] . . . [but] he is a labor leader. They didn't even recognize César as a labor leader, which he was first and foremost. He was a labor leader, you know.

Once again, García pointed out that Chávez's contributions are clearly marked in our oral tradition, in labor history, and in the history of the Chicano Movement. Overall, these activists hoped that Chávez's death—the death of a humble man, a great leader, and an activist who was nominated for the Nobel Peace Prize in 1968—would reignite the quest for social change.

Some believed that, as a result, more young activists and leaders are involving themselves in a myriad of activities to foster social change.

CONCLUSION

When history writes its final chapter, he will be remembered
as a man who lived by his principles and who wasn't
afraid of taking uncomfortable positions.
— Paul Chávez[13]

As they examined their feelings, and their interactions with César Chávez, all leaders with whom I spoke agreed that Chávez was a man of principles and a man of honor. They saw him as an inspiring leader who did not lose his humanity in the process of reaching the prominence he achieved. In their view, Chávez maintained connections with those neighbors, leaders, organizers, and activists who chose to continue working in their own communities, because he knew they were staunch supporters of the struggle for farm workers' rights. As they reflected on Chávez's historical contributions, these leaders spoke of his great sense of justice, his belief in the dignity of workers, and his commitment to those who supported the struggle in and out of the fields. What they most admired about Chávez was his ability to disregard and disentangle barriers of race, class, and gender while building an organization of coalitions that will not easily be replicated again.

For those leaders who were inspired and initiated into the movement with the grape boycott, for those of us who mastered the secondary boycott as we stood in front of multi-national corporations to protest greed and inhumanity, and for those who participated in countless marches, Chávez represented an ideal of leadership. For all those I interviewed, and for myself, Chávez was the spark that motivated us to reach for the sky, while inspiring us to keep connected to our respective communities and maintain our activism. From Chávez, all learned that leadership is embedded in relationships, because they experienced his ability to foster and cultivate his relationships, never forgetting who he was and where he came from. As Elisa Gónzalez, a cultural activist and social worker, stated, with "César Chávez's death, we have a responsibility to pick up his *bandera* [flag] and keep it marching." If there is one lesson to garner from these recollections of Chávez, it is the reawakening of an individual's social and moral responsibility to create change.

NOTES

1. Quoted in "In San Jose, Diversity of Mourners Provides a Measure of the Man," *San Jose Mercury News* 29 Apr. 1993: 2,4A. I wish to thank Dr. Patricia Zavella, Dr. Herman Gray, and Dr. John Brown Childs and the Race and Ethnicity Research Council for their unending support, as well as Dr. Candace West for her editorial support. To those activists, organizers, and leaders who shared their reflections about César, I give my deepest and heartfelt thanks.

2. "César hasn't died; his spirit lives in the struggle."

3. Quotations are extracted from conversations with Chicana/Latino leaders in Santa Clara and Santa Cruz counties.

4. "Farm Organizer Chávez Dies at 66," *San Jose Mercury News* 23 Apr. 1993: 1A.

5. *Mercury News* 23 Apr. 1993: 1A.

6. "César Chávez looked out for the welfare of his neighbor; he wasn't looking for what was in it for him. He never became wealthy. And if he saw injustice he would tell you it right there; he would tell you, 'That's not right and correct it.'" (Translations mine.) I have left this and the following quotation in the original language in which they were spoken. Mrs. García has been struggling against language oppression and for the right to speak in the language with which she is most comfortable, in order to exercise her self-determination in social and political interactions.

7. "[He wasn't looking to get credit] and he didn't talk about people or expressed jealousy toward people . . . and if there were meetings of others, even if they weren't his, he would go, but he wouldn't go to instigate or to break the unity; he would sit and listen."

8. "Canto a César Chávez," *San Jose Mercury News* 2 May 1993: 1P.

9. ". . . and before there was a César Chávez union we suffered much in the fields, and he was the one that took the role, took the stand and he stayed in the fields took the stand and stuck with it, stuck with it so that there would be changes."

10. ". . . of all colors, he didn't make a distinction because you were black, or Chinese, or white, or whatever you are. What he did he did it for humanity because he could work at different levels. César's vision always was for humanity."

11. An integral part of his organizing strategy was door-to-door campaigns. Rudy Acuña says that "he built his union by going door-to-door in the barrios where the farm workers lived" (269).

12. "I also learned patience, respect, and humility. I think that César always humbled himself and not in a sense that 'I'm nobody.' He united humbly, without commanding, without violence, to bring about change."

13. "A 'Warrior for Justice' Mourned Nationwide," *San Jose Mercury News*, 24 Apr. 1993: 1A.

WORKS CITED

Acuña, Rudy. 1981. *Occupied America: A History of Chicanos*. New York: Harper and Row.

Valdez, Luis. "Canto a César Chávez." *San Jose Mercury News* 2 May 1993: 1P.

"Farm Organizer Chávez Dies at 66." *San Jose Mercury News* 23 Apr 1993: 1A.

"In San Jose, Diversity of Mourners Provides a Measure of the Man," *San Jose Mercury News*, 29 Apr. 1993: 2,4A.

Montiel, Miguel and De Ortego y Gasca. 1992. "Chicanos Community, and Change," *Community Organizing in a Diverse Society*. Ed. Felix G. Rivera and John L. Erlich. Boston: Ally and Bacon.

A Personal and Historical Testimony

Richard A. García

> The living spirit grows and even outgrows its earlier forms of expression; it freely chooses the men in whom it lives and who proclaim it. This living spirit is eternally renewed and pursues its goal in manifold and inconceivable ways throughout the history of mankind.
>
> —C. G. Jung

> When the genius of the people is released, it is a powerful force.
>
> —César Chávez

It is not often that any of us consciously participates in a historical event. I did on Thursday, April 29, 1993, when 35,000 people marched in Delano, California, to honor the memory of César Chávez. I was not quite sure what to expect, but I knew I had to go. I first met and supported Chávez and the Farm Workers Union in the late sixties. Consequently, personal memories, personal reflections, and the desire to be in the presence of César Chávez again drove me to pay my last respects.

Most of the thousands were there to "remember" their personal or public memories of Chávez, but countless others were there to experience "the end of an era" or were there to "liberate" and resurrect César Chávez from just being a union leader, a "Mexican American hero; or a "Chicano symbol." Many had already started to see him as a national metaphor of justice, humanity, equality, and freedom. It seemed to me that many of us were there consciously or not to place César Chávez in the pantheon of national and international American heroes. This was underscored by the statements sent by the Pope, the President of Mexico, and President Bill Clinton.

As I was marching, an image came to my mind: the image of John Adams when he was on his deathbed and was told that Jefferson had just died. Adams discounted the news of death. "Jefferson lives," he declared. Of course, he

---

Richard G. García: "A Personal and Historical Testimony," first published in *The Pacific Historical Review*, vol. 63, num. 2 (May 1994): 225–233.

meant in the soul of America. In a similar fashion, we were there, I felt, on April 29, marching down the dusty, hot streets of Delano not to acknowledge that Chávez was dead, but to proclaim that Chávez lives—in the Mexican and the American soul, as well as in the international soul.

The majority of the marchers were farmworkers and their families. They came because they were touched by Chávez's presence. There were also many of us, the old students and the old activists now turned academics and intellectuals. We were there to feel the innocence of the sixties, the fieriness of yesteryears' rebellion, and the *lumbre* (the fire) of Chávez's heart and will. We wanted that period back. In this essay, I want to explore Chávez's sense of his own historical presence, the sense of spirituality that he exuded, and the fire in his heart that he instilled in us.

In May 1969, I met César Chávez at a breakfast at a downtown hotel in El Paso, Texas. In attendance were a cross-section of the city's Mexicanos: representatives of the League of United Latin American Citizens (LULAC), the Mexican American Youth Organization (MAYO), the Movimiento Estudiantil Chicano de Aztlan (MECHA), the Allianza (a south El Paso barrio youth group with ties to Reies López Tijerina of New Mexico), Mexican American local politicians, university professors, local teachers, community leaders, students, and some farm workers, as well as Anglo American "friends" of the farmworkers. Chávez was seeking support for the United Farm Workers Organizing Committee which, with AFL-CIO help, had been engaged since 1964 in a protracted struggle with agribusiness. A more immediate goal of these populist meetings in which he had participated throughout the country was the grape strike and the promotion of his innovative secondary consumer boycotts.

The Mexican Americans at the breakfast were there not only to show their support for the boycotts, but also to meet the now famous Chávez, especially to "feel" his presence. For all of us, Chávez seemed to represent cultural solace and potential leadership in an alienated and powerless world. He seemed to represent our lost sensitivity of the land, our historical past, and our cultural traditions. Consequently, regardless of our ideological orientation, all of us at the meeting felt the "presence" of our lost *Mexicanidad*. Although nobody said it, many of us perceived a spiritual savior rather than a political leader.[1]

What all of us Mexican Americans, with our young Chicano sons and daughters, were experiencing at that meeting was what philosopher Philip Wheelright has called a "poetic consciousness" being recontextualized.[2] There we began to "see" and to "feel" from a new angle of vision that transcended the meeting. Each of us with our different perspectives entered the "world of Chávez," as one would enter a new text, and experienced, between our personal view and the new context, a new vision of reality.

Chávez uttered very little at that breakfast: "support, "agribusiness," "familia," "togetherness." His words were almost unnecessary since the message seemed so clear. Chávez liked to give facts and felt that each listener could read the truths of oppression from the litany. But the message for many of us was not so much in the "facts" than in the "presence" of Chávez. This was reminiscent of Christ's followers listening to him and his "word" and feeling his persona. Chávez's "presence" did not denote power, action, or political program, but rather something more akin to the Indian Juan Diego in Mexican history who was the messenger of Our Lady of Guadalupe in 1531—the humble innocence that is the bearer of the words of another world.

The atmosphere projected by Chávez's presence and persona was, metaphorically, of a new reality of trust, hope, love, and brotherhood. As a result, all of us Mexicanos felt the possibility of peace, not the chaos of the sixties; a stability of brotherhood, not the radicalization of the youth; and a world of consensus, not the turbulent world of radical politics, nor the cries of "Uncle Tom" or "Aztlán," or "revolución." The breakfast meeting engendered commonalities, not differences.[3]

For most of the Mexicanos attending the breakfast, the central configuration, consequently, was Chávez's spiritual "presence" which was intertwined with symbols: of religion and motherhood—Our Lady of Guadalupe (which Chávez promoted), the farm workers' flag (which became the symbol of the eternal campesino), and the atmosphere of a struggle for justice and dignity (which Chávez espoused). What we mythically felt was what anthropologist Octavio Romano has argued was the central core of our mexicanidad: indianism, immigration, spirituality, historical struggle, and the quest for freedom from oppression and ontological definition.[4] As essayist Richard Rodríguez wrote in 1992: "Chávez wielded a spiritual authority that, if it was political at all, it was not mundane and had to be exerted in large, priestly ways or it was squandered. César Chávez was a folk hero."[5]

With Chávez, Mexican Americans throughout the Southwest had stopped thinking of their own "self-constructed" worlds of individualism, egoism, racism, money, poverty, and barrios. Our private individualized worlds for a morning in 1969 had become responsive to our hearts and not to our heads. Chávez, that morning as he had done over the last number of years, had established what Wheelright has suggested is a new responsive-imaginative act which each Mexicano present at the meeting could feel: their separate but common "soul," historically, ontologically, and epistomologically. Chávez, throughout the Southwest, had become "la causa," and la causa was each Mexican's need for redemption from modernity. Chávez was a metaphor for our lost ethnic paradise. The problem was our interpretation of this "paradise." When the question was asked: "Cesar, when will you become the leader of the Chicano Movement?" The new responsive-imaginative presence was broken. The mood was now political, ideological, and temporal. Chávez's persona, with its dynamics of mystery, awe, and "presence" was broken at this point when the meeting turned to the concrete realities of issues, problems, theories, and ideologies.[6]

Nevertheless, Chávez's "presence" had touched all those in attendance. He had for a moment formed the living spirit of our existence and forged a regressive-progression Sarterian vision of hope, innocence, and possibilities. It was not Rudolfo "Corky" Gonzales's political-historical visions of "I am a Joaquin," nor the revolutionary visions of Reies López Tijerina's struggles for Tierra Amarilla, nor the pragmatic third party formulations of José Angel Gutiérrez's Raza Unida Party. Instead, it was a vision of a pastoral past blessed by la Virgen de Guadalupe. However, if Chávez's "presence" was enduring as a new symbolic representation of the Mexican American/Chicano "soul," his organizational strategies and ideological stances were open to criticism.[7]

As Richard Rodríguez has accurately pointed out, "by the late 1970s, Chávez had spent his energies in legislative maneuvers. His union got mixed up in a power struggle with the teamsters. Criticized in the liberal press for allowing his union to unravel, Chávez became a quixotic figure; Gandhi without an India."[8] Moreover, Chávez did not accept the poet Alurista's mythical Aztlán nor the militant Chicanos new ethnocentrism. Chávez was mythical without being mystic; he was ultimately a union leader in search of a vision. A vision that would be shaped by the 1960s sociopolitical context.

The context which set the stage for the "presence" of Chávez was established by the Mexican-American intellectuals in the early 1960s. In a conference headed by the leading Mexican-American intellectual, Julian Samora, the socioeconomic and intellectual conditions of the Mexican American community were analyzed, and ultimately resulted in the publication, *La Raza: Forgotten Americans* in 1966. Scholars and political leaders such as George Sánchez, Ernesto Galarza, Eduardo Quevedo, Eugene González, Bernardo Valéz, Julian Samora, and others met at Notre Dame University and later in San Francisco to help formulate the themes and ideas with which they wanted to shape the Spanish-speaking communities.[9]

Educator George Sánchez, for example, emphasized the need for the persistence of the Spanish language as key to gaining access to the consciousness of "Lo Mexicano." John A. Wagner, a clergyman, underscored three basic linkages within the Spanish-speaking mind: poverty, spirituality, and diversity of religious affiliation. Catholicism, he said, was predominant, but Protestantism of different variations was also central because it linked a ministry of spirituality with one of economic help. Wagner believed that Mexicanos found something lacking in the United States Catholic church; it did not meet the needs of their spirituality: an interrelationship of leadership, hope, and trust. Chávez, he felt, could fulfill that need.[10]

Political scientist John Martínez noted that, outside of union leadership, most of the Mexican-American leadership was middle class. Neither unions nor the viable political organizations such as the Mexican American Political Association (MAPA), the Political Association of Spanish Speaking Organization (PASSO), the Community Service Organization (CSO), GI Forum, or the League of United Latin American Citizens (LULAC), the oldest and strongest—seemed to possess a spiritual core or a philosophy that reached every Mexican American. LULAC had originally (1930s–1950s) seemed different, but by the late 1950s and early 1960s it had lost much of its "spiritual" and political potential.[11]

In short, these organizations and even the most prominent politicos of the early 1960s, such as Henry B. González of Texas, Edward Roybal of California, Kiki do la Garza of Texas, and Henry Montoya of New Mexico did not have the national or "ethnic" presence to be a major leader of the Mexican-American communities.[12] There were no Martin Luther King Jr.'s in Mexican American politics in the early 1960s. What the Samora group did was to forge a politics that crossed Tocquevillian pluralism with Mexico's traditional authoritarianism: the man on the white horse, but receptive to the issues in the community rather than to a political program. Chicanos envisioned a Mexican-American

Franklin D. Roosevelt who had the qualities of Lázaro Cárdenas. Ironically, this cry for a new leader and era sought community not individualism, leadership not civil servants, justice not welfare or political revolution, and meaningful integration not prideful separation. The Mexican-American intellectuals sought to return to an ethnicity based on "Lo Mexicano," not to incorporate a world nationalism. As the Samora group announced: "The Spanish-speaking population has reached a stage in its development where its influence is being felt in local, regional, and national matters. Private and public agencies at all levels are ready to listen to the ideas and even demands that [this group] is ready to express."[13] This new group of intellectuals was receptive to Chávez's spiritual leadership, and the new *grito* (cry) was for an ethnic "presence" especially in the person of the emerging Chicano youth.

By 1968, young Chicanos throughout the United States were accepting Chávez as their own. Stan Steiner, in his very popular and widely used book in Chicano studies courses, *La Raza: The Mexican American* (1969), sought to capture the attention of these Chicano voices.[14] Steiner's book became the text for young Chicanos, like José of California who argued on behalf of "Brown power" and who believed that Chávez was struggling for "family ties" and "tribal ties." Other youths, like those engaged in the Crusade for Justice in Colorado, supported Chávez because they believed he supported their cultural nationalism and antipolice sentiment. Still others saw Chávez as being in the tradition of a Mexican peasant or in the mold of a Mexican revolutionary such as Emiliano Zapata or Pancho Villa. He emerged as larger than life in the "Corrido of César Chávez" which lifted him from only a "temporal presence" to the "mythical presence" of a folk hero.[15]

Ironically, such sentiments caused growers to view the Chávez movement as racialist and separatist. Indeed, many of the youth also believed this. To the Chicano youth, Chávez was for La Raza—the people, the race. It was only a short leap of faith for the radicalizing barrio youth, the university students, and the nascent Chicano intelligentsia to believe that Chávez stood for separation, third world nationalism, and class (union) struggle. It was also only a short leap of historical fiction to link Chávez as the personification of the "Chicano" struggle that had gone on since the 1848 war with Mexico. Historian Rodolfo Acuña, for example, wrote that "César Chávez emerged as the central figure in the [farm workers'] strike [in 1965]. Events converted him into a Ghandi-like Mexican leader, although from the beginning it was emphasized that this was not a Mexican fight, but rather one for the rights of all humans." "Chávez," Acuña argued, was the right man to get the nationalistic Mexicans together with other workers and friends. Chávez put them all under the red flag with the distorted eagle and a banner of the Virgin de Guadalupe.[16] Chávez, in spite of the lens through which Chicano radicals perceived him, said, "La Raza? Why be racist? Our belief is to help everyone, not just one race. Humanity is our belief." Steiner observed that when Chávez told Chicanos this, "their faces fell" in disbelief. They had thought he was a nationalist, not a humanist.[17]

For Chávez, civil rights was linked to a fight for human rights. He would often say of Mexican Americans, specifically the farm workers: "We are weak.

And the weak have no rights, but [only] the right to sacrifice until they are strong." In the same way, the young Chicanos, especially through the voice of their radical journal *La Raza*, argued that they also wanted "the guarantee of our constitutional rights," but they felt that this meant our rights as a people who have their own culture, their own language, their own heritage, and their own way of life." They thought that Chávez believed the same. However, Chávez meant rights under the Constitution and the Bill of Rights. But for the youth of the barrios and the universities, Chávez's civil rights were interpreted as cultural rights, and as rights for a colonized people to self-determination, self-empowerment, and communal empowerment. Stan Steiner claimed that in the Chicano mind "civil rights became cultural rights."[18] Consequently, for the Chicanos of the sixties, the fiery cries of "Huelga! Huelga! Huelga!" and "Viva Chávez!" carried the whisper of a militant historical-cultural memory, a rhythm of political struggle, a sense of national pride, and a movement of radical activism. They felt that Chávez agreed with the codification of the ideas of Alurista's *Plan de Aztlán* which called for the "return" to the homeland of Aztlán. They accepted his "presence" and his spiritual leadership.

That morning in El Paso, Texas, as was happening throughout the Southwest, the Mexican Americans not only saw themselves in Chávez but felt the *lumbre espiritual* (the spiritual fire) that he radiated. They felt their right "to be" and not just exist without power and in sorrow. Chávez himself said it best: "It is a question of suffering with some kind of hope. That's better than suffering with no hope at all." We all sensed this lumbre in the presence of Chávez and tried to make it our own as we whispered quietly and reverently: "César," "César," "César" in almost mantra fashion. We found in Chávez the *lumbre por dentro* and through him—the messenger—found it in ourselves, regardless of class or age. Chávez was, metaphorically, our soul and our vision in a world of nothingness and chaos. Chávez was not only the soul, but the fire in our soul—the logos of the Chicano experience.[19]

In spite of his death, César Chávez still lives in his philosophy that cooperation is the aim of life, common respect is the basis of cooperation and happiness, and spirituality and humanism are the criteria of respect. As Chávez said, we need "a cultural revolution. And we need a cultural revolution among ourselves not only in art, but also in the realm of the spirit. As poor people and immigrants, all of us [Americans and Mexicans] have brought to this country some very important things of the spirit. . . . We must never forget that the human element is the most important thing we have—if we get away from this, we are certain to fail." César Chávez remains for the twenty-first century a mirror of our Mexican and American agrarian soul, our liberal and humanistic traditions, and our need to maintain justice as the philosophical cornerstone in a new world of diversity.[20]

NOTES

1. I took notes on my observations and reflections at the meeting. This essay is for Karina who helped me see beyond the dusty streets of Delano.

2. See Philip Wheelright, *Metaphor and Reality* (Bloomington, 1973), esp. chaps. 4–6.

3. For insights into Chávez and the 1960s and 1970s, we Jacques Levy, *César Chávez: Autobiography of La Causa* (New York, 1975) and Richard Griswold del Castillo and Richard A. García, *César Chávez: A Life of Struggle and Sacrifice* (Norman, 1995).

4. Richard A. García, "Creating a Consciousness, Memories and Expectations: The Burden of Octavio Romano," in Tatcho Mindiola, Jr. and Emilio Zamora, *Chicano Discourse* (Houston, 1992), 6–31.

5. Richard Rodríguez, *Days of Obligation: An Argument with My Mexican Father* (New York, 1992), 68.

6. I asked Chávez the question about leadership since many of us in 1969 wanted to know how he perceived his role beyond the farm workers struggle.

7. Richard A. García, "The Chicano Movement and the Mexican American Community, 1972–1978: An Interpretative Essay," *Socialist Review*, VIII (July–Oct. 1978), 117–136; Carlos Muñoz Jr., *Youth, Identity, Power: The Chicano Movement* (London, 1989).

8. Rodríguez, *Days of Obligation*, 68.

9. Julian Samora, ed., *La Raza: Forgotten Americans* (Notre Dame, Ind., 1966), v–xvii.

10. Ibid., 1–26, 27–46.

11. Ibid., 47–62.

12. Ibid.

13. Samora, *La Raza*, 211. See also Richard A. García, *Rise of the Mexican American Middle Class: San Antonio, 1929–1941* (College Station, Tex., 1991).

14. Stan Steiner, *La Raza: The Mexican Americans* (New York, 1970), 166.

15. Ibid., 120–121, 515.

16. Acuña, *Occupied America* (2nd ed. New York, 1981), 269–70.

17. Steiner, *La Raza*, 317.

18. These statements are taken from Steiner, *La Raza*, 170, 171.

19. Luis A. Solis-Garza, "César Chávez: The Chicano Messiah," in Edward Simmen, ed., *Pain and Promise: The Chicano Today* (New York, 1972), 298. The Chávez quote on hope is on p. 304.

20. Levy, *César Chávez*, 92, 163. For the influence of Dolores Huerta, see Richard A. García, "Dolores Huerta: Woman, Organizer, Symbol," *California History*, LXXII (Spring 1993), 56–72.

La Causa's Self-Destruction

Marco G. Prouty

By the end of the 1970s, the UFW appeared poised to become a major force in the AFL-CIO with a membership of more than one hundred thousand farmworkers; instead, the union atrophied over the next decade losing 80 percent of its organizational strength. Both internal and external factors contributed to the UFW's demise. Internally, Chávez failed to prepare his organization for its transition from a social movement/union to a union/social movement; externally, declining national interest in social causes and a corresponding rise of conservatism combined to exacerbate the internal ailments that wracked La Causa.

As the UFW matured, Chávez should have prepared La Causa to make the necessary transition from a social movement/union to a union/social movement—a process that required an efficient administrative apparatus rather than marching or fasting. Despite the fact that Higgins and Rausch had advised Chávez of the need for administrative reform, he did not undertake corrective action. Moreover, it appeared that Chávez did not wish to remedy the situation by becoming a conventional labor union; after observing traditional union officials "at the conventions in their gray pinstripe suits and red ties," Chávez noted with disdain that "they looked like the employers of their workers."[1]

Three principal factors contributed to the UFW's deterioration. First, Chávez reportedly possessed a charismatic yet authoritarian management style that ultimately made his union an unattractive long-term employer. Second, Chávez wanted to staff his organization with true believers and demanded a radical level of commitment (for example, accepting abysmally low pay for exceptionally long hours) that was not sustainable over a normal career span. Finally, Chávez did not establish an administrative structure capable of successfully functioning independent of his charismatic leadership.[2]

The union's deficiencies worsened as La Causa experienced its major victories during the late 1970s. Apparently, the UFW could only find peace in war. The March 1977 jurisdictional agreement with the Teamsters should have

Marco G. Prouty: "La Causa's Self-Destruction," from *César Chávez, The Catholic Bishops, and the Farmworkers' Struggle for Social Justice* by Marco G. Prouty. © 2006 The Arizona Board of Regents.

ushered in an era of sustained prosperity for the UFW. Instead of parlaying victories into better contracts for the farmworkers, union officials fought bitterly among themselves and La Causa imploded.[3]

Between 1977 and 1981, many of Chávez's most dedicated and competent employees resigned. The torrent of high-profile departures included Marshall Ganz, the fifteen-year UFW veteran and chief organizer; Gilbert Padilla, the UFW's secretary-treasurer and founding member of the NFWA; and perhaps most importantly from an administrative standpoint, Jerry Cohen, chief UFW legal counsel and director of the legal office for seventeen years. Making matters worse, an exodus of almost the entire UFW legal staff followed Cohen's departure.[4]

Jerry Cohen's resignation merits special attention because it indicated the extent of Chávez's inability, or unwillingness, to transform the UFW from a social cause to a conventional union. In 1979, Cohen asked the executive board to consider a proposal "to pay staff salaries rather than in-kind subsistence." Although seemingly a reasonable request—Cohen and his legal team performed a vital function for La Causa and deserved adequate compensation—Chávez opposed the idea and successfully persuaded the board to reject Jerry's proposal.[5] Although Cohen agreed to stay on until March 1981, the loss of legal talent devastated the union.

Monsignor Higgins, ever loyal to La Causa, defended Chávez throughout the UFW's disintegration. Dismissing critics of Chávez's authoritarian behavior, the Labor Priest attributed the union's reversal of fortunes to the overall weakening of labor's potency during the 1980s. Higgins maintained that "the farm workers, . . . like many other labor movements, have fallen on hard times," and "the question of whether the union is overly identified with a single 'charismatic' personality seem[ed] beside the point."[6]

Clearly, a social movement's success requires an appropriate national mood and an opportune political climate, but a suitable leader—Chávez in the UFW's case—must also emerge at the proper time. Therefore, because it is plausible to link the UFW's rise to Chávez, we must also consider it highly probable, despite Higgins's assessment, that Chávez bore at least partial responsibility for La Causa's decline.

Compadrazgo, the Mexican custom of serving as a personal friend and protector for individual workers, pervaded the UFW.[7] Accordingly, workers felt that Chávez should personally address their union-related problems.[8] The obvious flaw with this cult-of-personality approach is that compadrazgo "cannot be transferred to a cadre of administrators."[9] Ideally, Chávez would have used his charisma to launch the movement, and then by the late 1970s, when his union had an estimated one hundred thousand workers, he would have redirected the UFW's emphasis toward formal organizations with written rules and managerial hierarchies, including associating authority with offices instead of personal qualities and extraordinary abilities.[10]

As La Causa atrophied, critics openly assailed Chávez's management style as inflexible and autocratic.[11] Disgruntled UFW employees charged Chávez with centralizing power and mistreating staff members.[12] While the union skidded toward political and organizational oblivion, La Causa's leadership sank into paranoia over the presence of leftists and others who supposedly had their own agenda within the union.[13] Student volunteers, once critical to Chávez's success, were marginalized and not invited to participate in the union's policy decisions.[14] Additionally, allegations emerged that Chávez's union, with his brother, sister-in-law, and son-in-law sitting on the executive board, had essentially become a "family cartel."[15]

Aristeo Zambrano, a one-time union activist until fired by Chávez, remarked that "in the mid-seventies, when I became an activist, Chávez was making every decision in the union." For example, "if a car in Salinas needed a new tire . . . [the UFW staff] had to check with Chávez in La Paz. [Chávez] controlled every detail of union business. And nobody was allowed to say Chávez made a mistake, even when he had." Zambrano also contradicted reports of Chávez's characteristic humility. "[W]hen you talked to him you had to humble yourself," claimed Zambrano, "as if he were a King or the Pope." Apparently, Chávez "was incapable of sharing power," and according to Zambrano, Chávez believed that the "farmworkers were good for boycotting, or walking the picket lines, or paying union dues, but not for leading" the UFW. Finally, Zambrano maintained that "Chávez built the union and then . . . destroyed it. . . . When the Republicans came back in the 1980s and the growers moved against the union, there wasn't any farmworker movement left."[16]

In addition to ineffective management, the UFW's staff endured abysmally low salaries. Joining the UFW meant sacrificing both one's personal life and financial security. La Causa's weekly paychecks of five dollars plus room and board could not attract and retain career-minded professionals.[17] Admirably, Chávez and his top lieutenants shared in the same appalling compensation package; however, Chávez upbraided those who did not share his sense of sacrifice because he felt that they failed to exhibit sufficient dedication.[18] Many such supposedly "uncommitted" officials departed the union after devoting more than a decade to the movement.[19] Ironically, the same UFW employees who labored to bring, among other things, a living wage to the farmworkers did not earn one themselves.

The three internal factors that led to the UFW's decline occurred against the backdrop of a withering national interest in social causes and a flourishing conservative movement. These two external factors exacerbated the UFW's internal ailments and expedited La Causa's demise. Chávez's union thrived as the baby boomer generation came of age in the 1960s and early 1970s, but by 1976, as exemplified by the defeat of Proposition 14, La Causa's once vibrant public following began to fade.

Rarely can idealism be carried past youth. The demands of life—bills, children, and the pursuit of a means to provide for them—compelled the baby boomers to labor in and for the very system they once criticized. The level of commitment, and ensuing poverty, that Chávez demanded could not harmonize with the ethos of a generation that entered professional life during the late 1970s and 1980s.

In a final blow to La Causa, the domestic political climate by the 1980s turned conservative and decimated Chávez's political alliances. Monsignor Higgins acknowledged that during the "material" decade, "the plight of farm workers . . . [was] not uppermost in the minds of people."[20] As the nation's concern for the La Causa diminished, California's electorate lost interest in Chávez's most politically powerful ally, Jerry Brown. Republican (and future California governor) Pete Wilson's defeat of Brown in a 1982 senate race highlighted the UFW's protracted decline, and progrower Republican George Deukmejian's assumption of the governorship simply intensified the problem.

Chávez ascended on the liberal ethos of the 1960s and early 1970s, but stumbled as baby boomers traded their Birkenstocks for wingtips during the 1980s.[21] Because Chávez had not taken the time to develop a solid administrative structure during his years of political bounty, La Causa could not endure the cycle of reaction by vested interests against him that characterized the 1980s.[22] Instead of Jerry Brown, Chávez had to engage Deukmejian and Reagan—neither of whom expressed sympathy for organized labor.[23]

In his address to the UFW's seventh constitutional convention in September 1984, Chávez made clear his enmity for Reagan and Deukmejian by calling them "the enemies of the poor and the working classes" because they "give away millions of dollars in cash money to the richest corporate growers in America for not growing crops, while unemployment benefits for farm workers are cut and while food and medical care for the poor are reduced."[24] Chávez mocked Reagan's invocations of the Almighty, observing that "President Reagan sees a proper role for government and a proper role for God. It's very simple: Reagan's government helps the rich, and God helps the rest of us."[25]

As the 1980s wore on, Chávez repeatedly made serious miscalculations. In one glaring blunder, Chávez continued to place the UFW's emphasis on boycotts and fasts rather than on organizing the farmworkers. Like a fading movie star, Chávez doggedly clung to the formula that brought him success twenty years earlier, but the audience had moved on. His now ineffective boycotts took the best farmworker activists from the fields and placed them in major urban centers—a disastrous misstep from the standpoint of building farmworker membership.[26] By the time of Chávez's death in 1993, the UFW was not primarily a farmworker organization. Instead, it reportedly was "a fundraising operation . . . staffed by members of Chávez's extended family and using as its political capital, Chávez's legend, and the warm memories of millions of aging boycotters."[27]

Today the UFW still exists as the largest agricultural labor union in California with contracts that cover 70 percent of the mushroom workers on California's Central Coast and more than 50 percent of rose workers in California's Central Valley. Additionally, the UFW has an agreement with Coastal Berry, the largest U.S. employer of strawberry workers.[28] Under the majority of UFW contracts, farmworkers receive family medical care, job security, paid holidays, and vacations, as well as pensions and a host of other benefits.[29]

The UFW is still devoting considerable resources to activities beyond traditional organizing. For example, the union now has a goal of helping ten million Latinos and working families in ten years by expanding its radio network, building low-income housing, and developing educational programs for underprivileged children.[30] La Causa has also recently made progress on the legislative front. California's mandatory mediation law, SB 1736, took effect in 2002 and forced growers to agree to contracts after farmworkers have voted for union representation. The law favors the UFW and eliminated growers' ability to prolong the contract process indefinitely.[31] The union now represents approximately twenty-seven thousand farmworkers—a respectable improvement from its nadir of twenty thousand laborers, but far below its organization apogee of more than one hundred thousand members.[32]

Did César E. Chávez make a difference? Were the farmworkers better off after Chávez than before? Definitely.

By 1980, the UFW had brought farmworkers improvements in wages, benefits, and job security.[33] For example, between 1964 and 1980 farmworkers' real wages adjusted for inflation increased 70 percent.[34] The UFW built health care facilities for farmworkers, and created service centers where they could receive assistance such as workers' compensation and food stamps.[35] Monsignor Higgins unequivocally stated that the UFW had "significantly improved the lot of its members," and that "UFW workers['] . . . pay rates . . . [ran] well above those of other farm workers."[36]

In addition, Chávez's movement raised awareness of the farmworkers' plight and increased pressure on legislators to bring justice to California's valleys. In part because of Chávez's persistent efforts, lawmakers abolished the hated short-hoe (cortito), heightened regulations on pesticide use, and brought CALRA into force.[37] Farmworkers also experienced long deserved improvements in basic working conditions, which included two scheduled rest periods each day and cool, potable water and individual cups.[38]

One of the UFW's greatest legacies has been its practice of currying political favor to advance farmworker interests. Although this strategy backfired with the rise of conservatism in the 1980s, the union attained its most meaningful achievements, including CALRA, by developing powerful allies throughout the 1960s and 1970s.[39] Because the UFW could successfully apply political pressure, state and national elites did not automatically side with the growers.[40]

Chávez once said that "it is how we use our lives that determines what kind of people we are."[41] Accordingly, he was, as the late Senator Robert Kennedy noted, "one of the heroic figures of our time."[42]

Six days after Chávez died peacefully in his sleep on April 23, 1993, near Yuma, Arizona, more than fifty thousand people attended his funeral—the largest such gathering for any U.S. labor leader.[43]

In recognition of Chávez's contributions to social justice, President Bill Clinton in August 1994 posthumously awarded Chávez the Presidential Medal of Freedom, America's highest civilian honor. "Cesar Chávez left our world better than he found it," reflected President Clinton, "he was for his own people a Moses figure."[44] Acknowledging this contribution in bringing farmworkers closer to the promised land of fair wages and working conditions, California established March 31 as César Chávez Day—an official state holiday.[45]

César Chávez had led a revolution—a peaceful movement for social change—that, if only for a brief period during the early 1970s, prompted the American Catholic hierarchy to make social justice one of its highest priorities.

NOTES

1. Patrick Mooney and Theo Majka, *Farmers' and Farm Workers' Movements: Social Protest in American Agriculture* (New York: Twayne, 1995), 189.

2. Gerald Costello, *Without Fear or Favor: George Higgins on the Record* (Mystic, Conn.: Twenty-Third Publications, 1984), 116.

3. Mooney and Majka, *Farmers' and Farm Workers' Movements*, 186.

4. Ibid.

5. J. Craig Jenkins, *The Politics of Insurgency: The Farm Worker Movement in the 1960s* (New York: Columbia University Press, 1985), 205.

6. George G. Higgins with William Bole, *Organized Labor and the Church: Reflections of a "Labor Priest"* (New York: Paulist Press, 1993), 103.

7. Jenkins, *The Politics of Insurgency*, 206.

8. Ibid.

9. Ibid.

10. Mooney and Majka, *Farmers' and Farm Workers' Movements*, 188.

11. Jenkins, *The Politics of Insurgency*, 204.

12. Richard J. Jensen and John Hammerback, eds., *The Words of César Chávez* (College Station: Texas A&M University Press, 2002), 89.

13. Linda Majka and Theo Majka, *Farm Workers, Agribusiness, and the State* (Philadelphia: Temple University Press, 1982), 274.

14. Jenkins, *The Politics of Insurgency*, 206.

15. Jensen and Hammerback, *The Words of César Chávez*, 145.

16. Frank Bardacke, "Decline and Fall of the UFW: Cesar's Ghost," *The Nation* (July 26/August 2, 1993): 133–34.

17. Jenkins, *The Politics of Insurgency*, 206.

18. Ibid.

19. Mooney and Majka, *Farmers' and Farm Workers' Movements*, 164–65.

20. Higgins with Bole, *Organized Labor and the Church*, 104.

21. Jensen and Hammerback, *The Words of César Chávez*, 89.

22. Mooney and Majka, *Farmers' and Farm Workers' Movements*, 190–91.

23. Jensen and Hammerback, *The Words of César Chávez*, 111.

24. Ibid., 118.

25. Ibid.

26. Bardacke, "Decline and Fall of the UFW: Cesar's Ghost," 131.

27. Ibid., 130.

28. United Farm Workers Web site: www.ufw.org/asrbio.htm.

29. Ibid.

30. Matt Weiser, "UFW's New Path: Help Millions." *Rural Migration News*, May 12, 2004, Web site: http:/migration.ucdavis.edu/rmn/more.php?id 854b0b8p0

31. Ibid.

32. Nancy Cleeland, "Farm Workers Urge Davis to Sign Binding Arbitration Bill," *Los Angeles Times*, August 11 2002, United Farm Workers Web site: www.ufw.org/lat81102.htm

33. Stephen Sosnick, *Hired Hands, Seasonal Farm Workers in the United States* (Santa Barbara, Calif.: McNally, 1978), 351–52.

34. Jenkins, *The Politics of Insurgency*, 206.

35. Colin Austin, "The Struggle for Health in Times of Plenty," in *The Human Cost of Food: Farmworkers' Lives, Labor and Advocacy*, Charles D. Thompson Jr. and Melinda F. Wiggins, eds. (Austin: University of Texas Press, 2002), 212.

36. Higgins with Bole, *Organized Labor and the Church*, 106.

37. Jenkins, *The Politics of Insurgency*, 207.

38. Sosnick, *Hired Hands*, 350.

39. Jenkins, *The Politics of Insurgency*, 209.

40. Ibid.

41. Ricardo Ramirez, "What Cesar Chavez Believed," *Origins* 23 (May 1993): 19.

42. United Farm Workers Web site.

43. Ibid.

44. Ibid.

45. Presidential Medal of Freedom Web site.

FROM SAL SI PUEDES:
CESAR CHAVEZ AND THE
NEW AMERICAN REVOLUTION

Peter Matthiessen

For Cesar Chavez and his people, the dank winter in Delano has always been a time of low morale, and the winter of 1968–69 was darkened further by the Di Giorgio sale and by Chavez's physical inability to provide active leadership. When he came home from Santa Barbara in December, Cesar was still half crippled by pain, and finally the Union acquired another house next to its present headquarters, so that he could try to administer from bed. In mid-January he delivered an impassioned speech at Filipino Hall, asking the members for renewed sacrifice and dedication. There were plans to extend the Service Center to other cities in California, Texas, and Arizona, and to establish a retirement farm for the Filipino members. In Delano, Leroy Chatfield and Marion Moses were revitalizing the Union's health and welfare program, which now includes a medical insurance plan to which all Union ranches contribute. With the expansion of the clinic had come a need for a full-time doctor as well as a program of preventive medicine; too many of the clinic's patients were half dead by the time they came in for help. At a meeting of two hundred farm workers it was discovered that nine out of ten had never been to a dentist, and that only three had ever had X-rays of the chest. Most of the farm workers' complaints were based directly on deprivation, but the most serious illnesses were caused by exposure to agricultural chemicals. In early January, in a letter to the growers' organizations calling for negotiations to avoid a third year of boycott, Chavez said that the Union wished to negotiate this problem of "economic poisons . . . even if other labor relations problems have to wait."

The growers did not answer his letter, and on January 25, at a general meeting in Delano, plans were set up for an intensified boycott, as well as an effort to draw public attention to the irresponsible use of agricultural chemicals.

Peter Matthiessen: segment from "Sal Si Puedes: Cesar Chavez and the New American Revolution," first published in *Sal Si Puedes (Escape If You Can): Cesar Chavez and the New American Revolution,* by Peter Matthiessen © 2000.

Four days after this meeting in Delano, court hearings began in Bakersfield in response to a UFWOC suit demanding access to public records on the use of pesticides kept by the Kern County Agricultural Commission. In August 1968, because of numerous worker injuries in the Coachella and San Joaquin valleys, Jerry Cohen had gone to the commission and asked to see the records. "I went there at eleven in the morning. I was told to come back the next day. At one thirty-three the same day a temporary restraining order was issued preventing me from seeing the reports of the spray. That's one of the fastest injunctions ever issued in the Valley."

The county agricultural commissioner testified that "no farm workers have been injured by the application of economic poisons in Kern County to my knowledge," and his counsel supported this astonishing statement by fighting introduction of evidence to the contrary from the records of the state Department of Public Health. The assistant state director of agriculture, a recognized authority on pesticides, also refuted the commissioner: he referred repeatedly to poisoning cases in Kern County, including an episode in Delano in which sixteen out of twenty-four workers who entered a field more than a month after it had been sprayed were hospitalized for parathion poisoning.

For want of a better defense, the growers had called on the crop-dusting companies to fight public identification of the "economic poisons" on the grounds that the poisons were "trade secrets." But one crop duster testified that four of the five men who mixed his chemicals had been too sick to work at one time or another during the past year, and another acknowledged that his company abandoned the use of TEPP (tetraethyl pyrophosphate) after he himself had become very ill from exposure to it. The hearings were recessed after one week at the request of the crop dusters' attorney. A few days later, at hearings of the state Department of Agriculture at Tulare, a department expert, noting that California used more pesticides than any other state, admitted that his department made no tests on these products, preferring to accept the word of the chemical companies. This policy was vigorously attacked by a Los Angeles physician, Dr. Bravo, who owns a ranch in the Imperial Valley and is a member of the state Board of Agriculture: in his opinion, the word of the chemical companies isn't nearly good enough. Accusing them of fraud in labeling their fertilizer and pesticide products, he declared that their prices were exorbitant—one common pesticide, he said, sells at a 3,000 percent profit—and that the labels were misleading in regard to the dangers of the products; research on the immediate and long-term effects had been totally inadequate. "Seven or eight hundred persons per year," he understood, "are injured from these chemicals. The mortality rate is high." It was also brought out that much pesticide use was inspired by unscrupulous advertising campaigns rather than a real need. Since the chemical companies had failed to regulate their own ethics, the doctor called for legislation of the kind that had been imposed on the drug companies, which like so many other American industries had failed miserably in its responsibilities to the people who made it prosperous.

On March 14 (in the *Medical World News*), there appeared a preliminary report on a five-year study by the National Cancer Institute which declared that many common pesticides act as carcinogens; the institute felt obliged to deny that it was under pressure from the chemical industry when, at the last minute, the five-year study was withdrawn as inconclusive. Meanwhile, at the hearings in Bakersfield, a Public Health Department report was cited to the effect that among ninety-four agricultural workers reported injured by pesticides in Kern County in 1968, fifty-four were farm laborers, and Judge George Browne of the Kern County Superior Court, in a decision handed down on March 27, acknowledged that "many commonly used pesticides—particularly the organic phosphate and chlorinated hydrocarbons—are highly toxic and can constitute a hazard to human health and welfare, including death, if not properly regulated and used." Nevertheless, Judge Browne prohibited disclosure of the public records on pesticide use, basing his decision on the pesticide industry's economic importance to the state and on the growers' contention, which he dutifully accepted, that UFWOC's "efforts to organize agricultural workers, and the grape strike and the boycott having been unsuccessful, the intervenor's [i.e., Jerry Cohen and UFWOC] motive and purpose are not in fact as herein above stated, but are to use the information acquired to keep alive controversy with the growers, to assist in selling unionization to workers, and to invoke public sympathy and support and to force unionization not only through publicity but by using the information to commence and prosecute groundless lawsuits for alleged pesticide injuries against growers and owners."

Though it called the Superior Court decision "appalling," the Union had won a propaganda victory. To keep the issue alive, it appealed the decision, and in April filed a series of suits with the declared intention of forbidding further use of DDT in California, where over 1,300,000 pounds of this long-lived poison are still used annually in the San Joaquin Valley alone. In Washington, Senator Gaylord Nelson of Wisconsin was calling for a national ban on DDT ("The accumulation of DDT in our environment . . . is reaching catastrophic proportions"), citing the recent confiscation by the FDA of ten tons of contaminated salmon from Lake Michigan, and the Department of Health, Education, and Welfare announced that the average American diet contains 10 percent more DDT than the limits set down by the World Health Organization. California's leading newspapers, the conservative Los Angeles *Times* and San Francisco *Chronicle*, were also clamoring for regulation of the pesticides which had grossly polluted California's rivers and were threatening the fisheries. Under the circumstances, the California Farm Bureau Federation thought it best to join the hue and cry against DDT, which it did officially on May 25.

The growers' troubles were just beginning. Under the Landrum-Griffin Act of 1959, all new labor groups must file a report on their organization with the U.S. Department of Labor, and on February 22—eight months late—the report of the Agricultural Workers Freedom to Work Association was finally filed by its president, Gilbert Rubio, and Shirley Fetalvero, its secretary-treasurer. The report declared that AWFWA was and had been from the beginning an organization set up by the growers, with the support of the John Birch Society, to fight the effect of Chavez's union by disrupting UFWOC efforts to organize and boycott, to seek worker support for AWFWA (propaganda, free picnics, no dues), to obtain information on UFWOC sympathizers, activities, and future plans, and so forth. The AWFWA staff was paid through a front outfit that called itself "Mexican-Americans for Democratic Action," and was furnished office space and typewriters at the Edison Highway headquarters of the Giumarra corporations in Bakersfield; use of mimeograph machines, office supplies, and the like, were furnished by the Di Giorgio ranch at Arvin, despite a clause in Di Giorgio's contract with UFWOC that prohibits activities tending to undermine the Union.

The report also stated that AWFWA was set up originally at a lunch meeting in Sambo's Restaurant in Bakersfield, in May 1968. At this meeting it was decided that Gilbert Rubio and Joe Mendoza would be hired at $120 a week to oppose Chavez, and that a number of growers not present at the meeting would be solicited for support. "Several meetings involving many persons were held but only John Giumarra, Jr., Robert Sabovich and Jack Pandol gave orders to Mendoza and AWFWA."

In early March, UFWOC announced that court action would be filed in Bakersfield against the John Birch Society, the National Freedom to Work Committee, and a group of growers on grounds of conspiracy to form an illegal employer-dominated union; a separate suit would be filed against the Di Giorgio Fruit Corporation for intentional subversion of its Union contract. Meanwhile Mendoza, claiming that AWFWA no longer existed, had been sent on an anti-boycott lecture tour of the Eastern cities by the National Right to Work Committee, and appeared at a committee banquet in Washington, D.C., where he was presented with an award by Senator Everett Dirksen for his efforts on behalf of American farm workers.

On March 7, two weeks after he had filed the AWFWA report, Gilbert Rubio was haled into the Delano court for his part in the October disturbance for which his gang had been arrested. Although his probation report had recommended a maximum of thirty days, he was given a sentence of three months. (After a week the Union got him freed on a technicality, but the jail term is still pending. Since then, the luckless Gilbert had been hospitalized with head injuries suffered in a fall, and has been arrested once again, charged with drunken driving.)

If its own report is true, AWFWA was nothing more than an inept right-wing conspiracy whose founders undertook to destroy a legitimate organization and smear the reputation of its leader, Cesar Chavez. The usual cheap Americanism was invoked, and the law of the land purposely broken, for no worthier cause than their own wallets. In the list of sponsors of this enterprise, most of the names are predictable enough: I was sorry to see "John J. Kovacevich" among them.

During the winter the Union had maintained the boycott pressure. Except for the Gristede chain, New York City was reported "clean" of grapes by January, and in Chicago the wholesalers acknowledged that the warehouses held fifty thousand boxes, still unsold. In California, storage grapes were sold off for wine at the disastrous price of $26 a ton. The boycott had even taken hold in the big cities of the South; in Atlanta the campaign was led by Dr. Martin Luther King Sr., in recognition of the esteem in which Chavez had been held by his late son. In London, on February 12, British stevedores refused to unload a grape shipment of seventy thousand pounds, and their protest spread to other ports in England, Sweden, Norway and Finland. The following day, February 13, Jack Pandol and Martin Zaninovich declared at a public meeting of the state Board of Agriculture in Tulare that no strike existed and that the boycott had had no effect.

This was too much for Lionel Steinberg, the Coachella grower who is thought of as the "liberal" on the Board; most of Steinberg's workers had gone out on strike in June 1968, after his refusal to hold elections or negotiate with the Union, and another Coachella grower, Harry Carrian, had declared bankruptcy. Steinberg said it was "short-sighted" of the Board to pretend that no strike existed. He was also annoyed that the rice farmers, dairymen and others on the Board, in the hope of deferring their own confrontation with the Union, were crying fiercely for a "fight to the death" against Chavez; it was the grape growers, after all, who were doing all the fighting, and it was the grape growers who were faced with death in 1969. The harvest season in Coachella was only a few months away, and markets all over the country were pleading with the growers to resolve the boycott crisis before the start of the new season.

Of all the supermarkets, the most intransigent was Safeway, which has well over two thousand stores and is the largest buyer of table grapes in the West. The interlocking business interests of Safeway's board of directors give a vivid idea of what is meant by "agribusiness." One director, J. G. Boswell, is also president of J. G. Boswell, Inc., one of the largest cotton growers in California—it owns 135,000 acres in California alone—and the largest grape grower in Arizona: in 1968, for *not* growing cotton, Boswell received over four million of the taxpayers' dollars in subsidies from the U.S. government. Another director is Ernest Arbuckle, who is also a director of the Kern County Land Company; KCL received $838,000 in cotton subsidies. Other board members own, direct or have large financial holdings in sugar plantations, the Southern Pacific Railroad, Del Monte canned foods, the 168,000-acre Tejon Ranch, and other huge components of California agribusiness. (Compared with agribusinessmen like these, the Giumarras are small farmers, having received but $278,000 in cotton subsidies in 1968.)

Nevertheless, Safeway styled itself "neutral" in the grape dispute, stating its intention to protect the consumer by offering grapes as it has always done. Robert Magowan, the company's chairman of the board, declared that "there has been flagrant injustice for the Mexican migrant worker . . . but we are not a party to the dispute. That is between the growers and the Union." The chairman is a director of the J. G. Boswell farm empire as well as of such huge agribusiness corporations as Del Monte, Southern Pacific, and Caterpillar Tractor: his recognition of "flagrant injustice" and his simultaneous refusal to act on it call to mind the signs that appeared this winter in East Los Angeles, after one of the street kids was killed by a policeman: GRINGO JUSTICE IS SPELLED M-O-N-E-Y.

In early March, Chavez was visited by Dr. Janet Travell, whose treatment had worked so well for President Kennedy. Dr. Travell discovered that

Chavez's "disc trouble" was actually a painful muscle spasm: his right leg is shorter than his left, one side of his pelvis is smaller, and he has what is known as a "transitional vertebra"; in consequence, the muscles on his right side were doing all the work. As he grew older and less resilient, these muscles could no longer compensate, and spasms developed which gradually became constant. "She is really phenomenal," Marion Moses wrote me on March 20. "By a few simple mechanical adjustments, using books, scissors, paste and felt, she got him where he was comfortable. Then she uses a spray technique with a surface anesthesia which relaxes the muscle so it can be stretched to relieve the spasm. Today for the first time in years Cesar said that he woke up without pain. He looks much better, most of the pain lines are gone from his face most of the time—and most importantly of all, he is following the treatment very faithfully. He really is very anxious to get well and start organizing again." In fact, he was anxious to go to the Coachella Valley, but Manuel Chavez and many others were dead set against it: the strong possibility of victory should not be endangered by the increased tension that Cesar's presence there would bring.

The growers, expecting sympathy from a Nixon Administration, were lobbying for new farm labor legislation, and on April 16 Dolores Huerta, Jerry Cohen and Robert McMillen, the Union's legislative representative in Washington, appeared before the Subcommittee on Labor of the Senate Committee on Labor and Public Welfare, which was holding hearings on a new bill to include farm workers under the National Labor Relations Act. Other farm workers, from Wisconsin, Texas, Florida, and Colorado, also testified. Mrs. Huerta read a general statement by Chavez, who could not be present; he was concerned about the illusory protection that the NLRA would give to farm workers unless the new union was at least temporarily exempted from the Taft-Hartley and Landrum-Griffin amendments, which would deprive it of the only weapons at its disposal, and thus legislate it out of existence. "Under the complex and time-consuming procedures of the National Labor Relations Board, growers can litigate us to death; forced at last by court order to bargain with us in good faith, they can bargain in good faith—around the calendar if need be—unless we are allowed to apply sufficient economic power to make it worth their while to sign.

"We want to be recognized, yes, but not with a glowing epitaph on our tombstone."

Unfortunately, the Union had not publicized its position on the NLRA before the hearings, and Chavez's resistance was misunderstood and resented, even by some segments of the press that had been sympathetic. Inevitably, the growers and their spokesmen ridiculed his fear that the "protection" of the NLRA might legislate his union out of existence. "By opposing various measures newly introduced in Congress to improve the bargaining position of farm workers, the head of UFWOC has shown up his cause for what it is: neither peace-loving nor compassionate, but a ruthless grab for power," cried an editorial in *Barron's* on June 2; in this same issue, three months after AWFWA had been exposed as a disreputable fake, *Barron's* was still taking it seriously. Meanwhile the growers were spending hundreds of thousands of dollars on anti-Chavez propaganda prepared by expensive advertising firms, including an attack by the president of the California Grape and Tree Fruit League which blamed UFWOC for "the terror tactics visited upon the grocery outlets of this nation"; he referred to the fire bombings at A&P stores in New York City in October 1968 which the Union long ago admitted were probably the work of misguided sympathizers. Out of context, *Barron's* quoted from Chavez's "Marxist" response to the League's attack: "'While we do not belittle or underestimate our adversaries, for they are the rich and the powerful and possess the land, we are not afraid or cringe from the confrontation. We welcome it! We have planned for it. We know that our cause is just, that history is a story of social revolution, and that the poor shall inherit the land.'" The word "revolution" is the key to *Barron's* uneasiness, but the truth is that the United Farm Workers have never asked for land reforms, nor considered revolt against the American Way of Life; they ask only for a share in it.

An example of what *Barron's* means by legislation "newly introduced in Congress to improve the bargaining position of farm workers" is the "Food Profits Protection Act," sponsored by a legislator who has called the farm workers' strike "dishonest."

> Washington, Apr. 30 [1969] (AP)—Senator George Murphy (Rep., Cal.) Tuesday unveiled a plan that he said would protect customers and agriculture from persons he called "of narrow interest, limited vision," such as organizers of the California grape boycott . . .
>
> Murphy said his bill would safeguard production and marketing of food products from labor disputes and provide "an orderly system within which agricultural workers may organize and bargain collectively."
>
> He would prohibit secondary boycotts, efforts to persuade a farmer to join a union or employer organization or to recognize or bargain with an uncertified union, picketing at retail stores, and inducements to employees not to handle or work on an agricultural commodity after it leaves the farm.
>
> "Strikes at farms are not permitted if the strike may reasonably be expected to result in permanent loss or damage to the crop," Murphy said.
>
> He said that he expects to get President Nixon's endorsement of his plan but has not solicited it . . .

President Nixon endorsed instead a plan attributed to his Secretary of Labor, Mr. Schultz, under the terms of which farm workers would remain excluded from the jurisdiction and protection of the NLRB but would be subject to the strike-killing provisions of the Taft-Hartley amendment that forbid secondary boycotts and organizational picketing; a special "Farm Labor's Relations Board" could delay any strike at harvest time (in farm labor disputes, a strike at any other time is a waste of effort) with a thirty-day period of grace that could be invoked at the discretion of the grower. After thirty days, when the harvest in any given field would be largely completed, the workers could strike to their heart's content.

The Nixon plan was strongly criticized by Senator Walter Mondale of Minnesota, who had taken over from Senator Harrison Williams as head of the

Subcommittee on Migratory Labor, and by Senator Edward Kennedy, who had inherited a vested interest in *la causa* from his brothers. Mondale and Kennedy led the dignitaries who assembled, on May 18, to greet a company of strikers who had trudged one hundred miles in a 100-degree heat from Coachella to Calexico, to dramatize their protest against the unrestrained importation of poor Mexicans to swamp their own efforts to better their lot. Cesar Chavez addressed the rally in Calexico, and so did Senator Kennedy: a country that could spend $30 billion every year on a senseless war, send men to the moon and present rich farmers with millions of dollars in subsidies for crops they do not grow, Kennedy said, could afford to raise the standard of living of the poor who fed the nation. Both Kennedy and Mondale pledged themselves to a fight for new green-card legislation.

The strike in Coachella began ten days later, on May 28. Over one hundred local workers manned the picket lines, and though the harvest had scarcely started, another two hundred walked out in the first two days. Many signed affidavits of the sort required to certify a strike, and thereby make illegal the importation of scab labor into that field, but this year the two observers from Mr. Schultz's Department of Labor refused to interview striking workers or inspect their affidavits. When David Averbuck, the Union attorney, protested to the department's regional director, he was told that "orders from Washington" forbade the Labor officials to investigate or certify strikes: unless the strikes are decreed official, there is no legal recourse against the wholesale importation of Mexican strikebreakers. Since an estimated fifty thousand workers are available in this border region, with only three thousand needed to harvest the grapes, the strikers would be giving up their jobs for nothing.

Averbuck was also told that the federal men would make no investigations whatever but would base all decisions on the reports of inspectors sent by Governor Reagan. One of the latter declared frankly that the state men would not interview the strikers either. They were willing to accept signed affidavits, which would then be made available to the growers; if the growers used the affidavits to compose a blacklist, that was no concern of theirs.

Averbuck, a cynical young man not easily surprised by perfidy, was stunned. "It's a Nixon-Reagan conspiracy to screw the farm workers and to help the growers recruit workers illegally," he said. "It's so blatant it's unbelievable."

In any case, the Coachella strike got off to a slow start, and the growers, emboldened by open federal and state support, were making the same old arguments. "If my workers wanted me to sit down at the negotiating table, I would," said a Coachella grower interviewed by a *New York Times* reporter in early June. "But my workers don't want Union recognition. If they did, they would have walked out and joined the strike."

But one of his workers, interviewed in the same report, refuted him. "I belong to the Union but I'm working here because I have bills to pay. The Union can't pay them and I can't work anywhere else. A lot of people like me are forced to do this. How can you stand on a picket line when your family is hungry! It's hard for me to work here when the Union is out there picketing, but I can't help it."

By the time I returned to Delano in late July 1969, the strikers were back from the Coachella Valley and were preparing for the harvest in Lamont. Dave Averbuck was convinced that the campaign in Coachella had been a great success, whereas Jim Drake, while acknowledging progress on all fronts (including fair treatment from the Riverside County police, who did much to prevent the violence of the previous year's campaign), was sorry to come back without a contract. Everyone agreed, however, that most or all of the Coachella Valley would be under Union contract before a single grape was harvested in 1970, and although much the same thing was said last year, the evidence for this year's confidence is much better. Grape sales were off 15 percent, and even those chain stores that were still selling grapes have used the boycott as an excuse for paying the growers so little that many grapes were left unharvested. As a group, the Coachella growers were admitting that they had been badly hurt, though a few still refused to be led from the burning barn. "The Union's boycott has failed," Mike "Bozo" Bozick declared manfully on July 11, the day after the local agricultural commissioner estimated that 750,000 boxes of Coachella grapes had been left in the fields to rot, and one week after eighty-one of his fellow grape growers filed suit against UFWOC, claiming boycott damages of $25 million.

A turning point, not only in the Coachella campaign but in the four-year strike, was a sit-in, in early June, by Filipino strikers at Bozick's Bagdasarian Grape Company's labor camp Number 2 that led to a wave of sit-ins at other ranches. By the time Bozick had the last holdouts evicted and arrested a few days later, the Union had won its most significant victory since the Schenley capitulation in 1966, and Dolores Huerta gave much credit for this to the Filipinos of Bagdasarian. "Their courage, their actions, may have been the final straw that scared the growers into opening discussions," she said.

On Friday the thirteenth of June, ten growers, who claimed to represent 15 percent of the state's table-grape production, held a press conference at Indio at which they declared willingness to negotiate with the Union. Their spokesman was Lionel Steinberg, whose Douglas Freedman Ranch is the biggest in Coachella. Steinberg, acknowledging publicly that the boycott had been costly, said, "If we have a conference and discussions with the Union and we see that there is a give-and-take attitude on their part, there is no question that we are prepared to recognize UFWOC as the collective-bargaining agent."

Five of the growers were from Arvin-Lamont, the next area to be harvested, and the spokesman for the Arvin group was John J. Kovacevich, who had been holding private talks with Jerry Cohen ever since March. Publicly Kovacevich was still fulminating about the "illegal and immoral boycott," but this did not spare him the damnation of the Delano growers, led by Martin Zaninovich and Jack Pandol, who said that the 93 percent of the table-grape industry that they spoke for would fight Chavez to the end rather than sell out the consumer. The actions of the ten, according to Pandol, were "un-American and un-Christian," an opinion apparently shared by the Christians unknown who attempted to gouge out the eye of one of the ten, William Mosesian, in a night attack outside his house, and burned a stack of wooden grape boxes belonging to another, Milton Karahadian, in the Coachella Valley. Grower Howard Marguleas was warned not to set foot in Delano, John Kovacevich was snubbed by friends in Top's Coffee Shop in Lamont, and Lionel Steinberg, after years of membership, resigned from the California Grape and Tree Fruit League due to the viciousness of the League's attempts to defame the ten growers and sabotage the negotiations.

The Union, of course, had welcomed the meetings, which began on June 20 in the Federal Building in Los Angeles; the negotiations were supervised by three officials of the Federal Mediation and Conciliation Service of the Department of Labor, whose job it was to keep them from breaking down. Most of the ten growers were present at most of the meetings, which continued until July 3; the Union was represented by Jerry Cohen, Dolores Huerta, Larry Itliong and Philip Vera Cruz, and by Irvin de Shettler, an observer for the AFL-CIO. At the last conference, on July 3, the ten were joined by Bruno Dispoto of Delano. Dispoto had been hurt that spring in Arizona, but many Union people felt that he had been sent in by other Delano growers to find out what was going on. Bruno, introduced to Dolores before the meeting, said, "I haven't seen you since the old days on the picket line."

The talks were recessed for the Fourth of July and have not been resumed. There had been inevitable differences (wage scales, Union hiring halls, jurisdiction of workers, safety clauses, and other matters), but the one that derailed the talks was the matter of pesticides. The growers agreed to abide by the lax state and federal laws regarding the use of dangerous chemicals so long as the Union did "not embark on any program which will in any way harm the industry to which the employer is a member." This clause, which also gave immunity to the non-negotiating growers, would stifle all campaigns by the Union against pesticide abuses, including the matter of chemical residues on grapes; it was presented in the form of an ultimatum by the growers' negotiator, a fruit wholesaler named Al Kaplan, and was promptly rejected by the Union. The growers retired to think things over. At a press conference a week later, they denounced the Union for its bad faith and demanded a new "fact-finding commission," to be appointed by President Nixon. (The growers' charges were excited, but it is true that the Union was not overly accommodating: except on very favorable terms, a settlement with a small part of the industry was simply not worth the inevitable weakening of the boycott.)

The bad news was received in the Union offices with a certain levity—"We were very upset," Cesar says, "but what could we do? We just made jokes." The growers' demand seemed to bear out certain people in the Union who suspected that the breakdown of negotiations had been planned from the start as an excuse to go to the Nixon Administration for help. But Dolores Huerta was convinced that most of the ten growers were serious, and so was Jerry Cohen. "One night, you know, like it was maybe two in the morning, and everybody was worn out, and Kaplan was still abusing us with all this bullshit, and there was this popcorn on the table, so I started to eat popcorn. And finally the things he was saying got so stupid that I started to crunch the popcorn, and the stupider he got, the louder I crunched, you know, just to bug him. Well, our side was trying like hell not to laugh, especially Dolores, and

Kaplan was beginning to get sore, and finally this grower named Howard Marguleas couldn't stand it any more—he flipped. He said, 'How can you be so rude! Here we are trying to settle something which is very serious, and you sit there eating popcorn that way, and all you Union people smirking!' So there was this silence for a minute, I was sitting there like I had lockjaw, and then I said, 'Can I swallow, Howard?' Well, this just about broke Dolores up, and the meeting too, but anyway, Howard is usually a pretty calm guy, and the incident told me a lot about the strain they were under and about how serious they were about finding a solution."

In mid-July, as the negotiations broke down, Senator Mondale's subcommittee was advised in Washington that the Department of Defense, by its own estimate, would ship eight times as many grapes to Vietnam in 1969 as in any previous year. Like the chain stores, the Defense Department was getting a bargain on the grapes, but in the opinion of the Union, this was no more the reason for the incredible jump in grape consumption than the dehumanized excuse of "increased troop acceptance" that issued like a machine chit from the Pentagon. Claiming the usual collusion within the military-industrial establishment, the Union filed suit against the Defense Department for taking sides in a labor dispute in contravention of its own stated policies: in effect, using public funds to offer a "market of last resort" to a special-interest group.

The Mondale hearings, which continued until August 1, later heard testimony from Jerry Cohen that the growers were using dangerous chemicals in dangerous ways and in dangerous amounts, among them Thiodan, which caused the recent fish kill in the Rhine, and Amino Triazole, residues of which, ten years before in New Jersey, caused the confiscation of wholesale lots of cranberries. By common estimate, it had taken the cranberry industry nine years to recover from the public scare, and the Union did not introduce this evidence without having given the growers a chance to regulate their own practices and come to some satisfactory arrangement about pesticides without being committed to a Union contract. But the growers had not bothered to respond to this offer from Chavez in January, and when, after negotiations had fallen apart on the pesticide issue, Cohen called John Kovacevich to advise him of his intention to bring up the use of Amino Triazole at the Senate hearings, Kovacevich thanked him for the warning but could not bring the growers to act on it. As Averbuck says, "Sometimes they seem to want us to do exactly what we don't want to do, which is to put them out of business."

Cohen told the senators about reports from Micronesia of decreased cannibal acceptance of American missionaries; the poisonous residues in American bodies had become so great, he said, pointing a finger at Senator Henry Bellmon of Oklahoma, that "you are no longer fit for human consumption." Subsequently, an official of the FDA testified that Mr. Cohen's remarks were accurate enough, but that his agency was ready and able to protect the public against grapes with chemical residues that exceeded the federal tolerance level. Asked by Senator Mondale for the tolerance level on the pesticide known as aldrin, he said, "One tenth of a part per million." The senator then submitted a laboratory report obtained by the Union on two batches of grapes purchased the day before at a Safeway store in Washington, D.C. One batch, carrying the label of Bozo Bozick's Bagdasarian Fruit Company, contained aldrin residues of 1.4 parts per million, or fourteen times the permissible amount; another batch from Bianco Fruit Company carried eighteen parts, or one hundred and eighty times the federal tolerance level.

"They won't understand that we will not compromise on the pesticide issue, that we will give up wage increases first," Chavez said. "They're just not ready yet to negotiate seriously; they need more pressure, and they're going to get it. But I think some of them were serious. Jerry and John Kovacevich were able to talk like human beings, right from the start; if Kovacevich had done their negotiating for them, we might have hammered out a contract in two days."

Like all his people, Chavez was upset by the damage that the growers' recalcitrance is doing to the industry. "The longer the boycott continues, the more damage will be done. We *still* hear of people boycotting Schenley, you know, even after they are told that the Schenley boycott has been over for two and half years."

As of early August, Union people agree that a meaningful settlement of the California grape strike is unlikely in 1969, since contracts could not be written in time to help the growers; even the ones most likely to sign would probably prefer to hold out until the spring of 1970, in the hope of legislative help from the Nixon Administration. If that help is not forthcoming, however, the Coachella growers will probably give in, and once Coachella falls, the Arvin-Lamont area will fall too. The Delano growers have a longer season and are better equipped with cold-storage sheds, but it seems doubtful, even so, that they could compete indefinitely with Union competitors who are not harassed by the boycott (although how the boycott will be made selective without losing its impact remains a problem). And if Delano falls, so will all the ranches to the north, because Delano is the heart of the resistance to its own foremost citizen, Cesar Chavez.

Even if the present talks remain suspended, their implications are momentous for the Union. The precedent for negotiation is a gaping crack in the monolithic wall that the growers have shored up for four years, and that crack can only erode faster and faster. *Hay más tiempo que vida*, as Chavez says, and time is on his side.

Cesar, though still based in bed, was sitting in a chair most of the day. He looked much better than he had eight months before; the pain lines and grayness were gone from his face, and the gaiety had returned to it, and he had taken up photography again. His therapy of massage and exercises was working; also, he was using a shoe correction and a pillow under his hip to adjust the imbalance of his weight. He hoped to be fully active by the end of the year. Meanwhile he was working twelve hours a day, talking to aides and visitors, directing strategies, discussing plans; he ate the regular meals that Helen prepared for him in the bungalow kitchen, but he did not stop talking or listening. By his side was a young German shepherd named Boycott,

who was very uneasy when more than a few feet from Cesar and already extremely protective of him. There was another dog outside. "That one is *mean*,"
Cesar said. "He can't seem to learn who are my friends. But Boycott is really
very nice." He paused a moment to scratch the ears and neck of the first dog
he has ever owned. "The one thing that really bothers him is a stranger coming in with something in his hand—you know, a swinging purse or something—he doesn't like that. It's instinct, I think. And even when he sleeps, he
wakes right up when something changes in the room; when I'm in my chair,
he lies against it, so that he will wake up if I move."

Cesar was out of bed almost all the next day, running a series of meetings with his board. When the meetings were finished, he sat still for a liver-
extract shot from Marion Moses, who was now his nurse. As Marion finished,
I looked up from an article that concluded ". . . the involvement of Soviet
agents (and their dupes) in the Chavez operation deserves our attention before they succeed, not after," and said, "I didn't realize how dangerous you
were." Cesar, arms extended, had begun a slow painful kneebend, his pajama
bottoms poking out from beneath his trousers and Boycott's leash draped
around his neck. "Ex-*treme*-ly dangerous," he said, scowling dangerously.
Watching the man, I could appreciate the feelings that Marion has when she
administers to him: "How often I've thought," she says, "that this whole thing
is held together by this small piece of skin and these few bones." Yet this
small man is very, very tough.

Cesar's son Babo came in to play with Boycott, and soon after that, Fer-
nando, or "Polly." In the past year Polly's face had matured, and so had his
whole manner. This spring, after refusing induction into the Army, he had
gone with Manuel to Arizona and worked there as an organizer. "One morning," Cesar said, "he just announced, 'I don't think I'll go,' and he meant it."
Father Mark Day, who accompanied Polly to the induction office in Fresno,
said that the boy had given the matter a lot of thought before he decided that
he was a conscientious objector. He had been influenced by his father's fast,
and said that any kind of violence made him sick. A mass for nonviolence,
given by Father Day outside the induction office, was duly photographed
by FBI agents attracted to this subversive event by a newspaper report on
Chavez's son's decision. "I got some awful letters," Cesar said, "even from
some of the membership. But I believed in him, and I couldn't forsake him out
of expedience. Finally, I held a meeting about it. 'When we started this union,'
I said, 'I told you you were welcome to everything I had, even my life. Well,
now I am going to take something back. You are welcome to my life, but not
to my principles.'"

When he said this, Cesar was at home in bed after a workday that had
ended at ten in the evening. His children came and took his shoes off, and
he lay back in the hot summer night behind drawn shades, his mezuzah glis-
tening on his chest. Outside, in the living room, the girls fiddled with one
another's hair, and Boycott lay at the foot of the bed, watching the door.

I was just back from Africa, and Cesar asked me about the death of Tom
Mboya, and about Julius Nyerere of Tanzania; he was pleased to hear a high
opinion of Nyerere, whose picture has joined the gallery in his office. We dis-

cussed sharks and his earthworm population (the worms were prospering on a diet of oatmeal), and many other things. The subjects didn't matter; Cesar is so intensely present that talking to him is like going to a source, a mountain spring; one comes away refreshed. At one point we spoke of the oil damage at Santa Barbara—"I thought of you the minute it happened!" Cesar grinned, referring to my impassioned speeches on environmental pollution of the autumn before—and I recalled a speech made on April 6, 1969, at Stanford University by Professor Richard Falk of Princeton, who is working on a research project "devoted to world order in the 1990's." Professor Falk recommended making people "angry at what is happening to their environment, and the prospect for themselves and their children as a consequence of allowing so much public policy to be determined by the selfish interests of individuals, corporations, nations, and even regions of the world. I think the kind of community reaction that occurred in Santa Barbara recently, as a consequence of the oil slick, is the sort of thing that is going to happen more frequently and more dramatically in the years ahead. When it is understood that these occurrences are not isolated disorders but threads in the pattern of disaster, then a more coherent response will begin to emerge . . . A movement toward a new system of world order will be a serious part of the political life of the community when people are willing to go to jail on its behalf and are put there by those who fear the challenge. The outcome of this confrontation will shape the future of planetary history—in fact, determine whether the planet is to have a future in history."

In the past year, the interior of Cesar's house had changed a little. Helen had an enormous collection of strike, peace and political buttons mounted on a burlap sheet on which was painted in plump psychedelic lettering, WOW LOVE WOW!, and Cesar showed me a big cartoon of an astronaut aghast at finding a striker on the moon. The striker, strolling past the lunar vehicle, was carrying a sign that read BOYCOTT GRAPES. "Look at him!" Cesar laughed, delighted. "He doesn't even need a space suit!"

Outside, the house had not changed at all. A year later, the old Volvo was still there, and the leaky hose, gleaming in the summer moonlight, and the faded old stickers on the windows. But as I left, a little after midnight, a man rose from a chair in the house shadows and watched me go. Chavez had become a national figure, and his door was no longer open to any stranger. It was not Chavez who had changed but the limited nature of his struggle, which had taken on a significance far beyond the confines of the Valley. That autumn, when he left California for the first time since his fast, in 1968, he had recognized that la causa was no longer separable from the new American revolution. On September 28, in a speech at the Washington Cathedral to a dedicated gathering of twenty-five hundred, he enlisted his campesinos in the great strike for peace-in-Vietnam to be held on October 15, and the following morning, in testimony at hearings of the Senate Subcommittee on Migratory Labor, he attacked irresponsible use of farm poisons as a threat not only to human beings but to the despoiled American environment. Under the hard lights of national television, the small clear-voiced, wide-eyed man in a green sweater contrasted strangely with Senator Murphy of California, who sat stiff as a puppet on the high rostrum, coached from behind by an attorney for the growers: the senator, wearing silver hair and enormous dark glasses, was insinuating in sepulchral tones that farm worker Manuel Vasquez, seated beside Cesar on the witness stand, might have tampered with the aldrin-tainted grape samples from Safeway (even though Safeway, after running its own tests, had suspended further grape shipments from Bianco Fruit Company). Later I asked Manuel, the one-time co-captain of the Sacramento march, if he had felt nervous as a witness, and Manuel, whose spirit is typical of these strikers, who have been away from home for a year or more without complaint, laughed at the question. "Why be nervous? All I had to do was say the truth!"

Senators Mondale, Kennedy, and Cranston were sympathetic to Chavez, and Mondale attacked as partial and unfair the testimony of the FDA that questioned the laboratory reports of aldrin residues on the Safeway grapes. But that testimony stood: the government agencies, as Chavez had claimed the night before at the cathedral, were siding with the growers.

"This is the last time I'll ever testify," Cesar said. In pain after three hours on the witness stand, he was resting in the camper-truck that would carry him on a six-week fund-raising circuit of the Eastern cities, and he took no pleasure in the white citadels of American law and justice that glistened in the blue September sky on Capitol Hill. "I'm tired of all the promises and all the words. I've never known anything in Washington but anger and frustration and disappointment." From here, he would go eventually to New York, where Mayor John Lindsay was anxious to present him with a key to the city. The resultant publicity would be useful to them both, but the emptiness of such a ceremony made him shake his head. "I remember once they gave us the key to somewhere else. We thought it looked beautiful, shining in its box, but you know, it was only tinfoil. By evening, it had already fallen to pieces." He laughed, and his face cleared again. "Maybe this one will be made of wood," he said, as if refusing to give up hope for a new America.

But under the Nixon Administration, an American renaissance had been deferred, and every passing year increased the likelihood that renaissance would take the form of revolution. Chavez's cause had become a holding action for change that was inevitable, a clash of citizens versus consumers, quality versus quantity, freedom versus conformism and fear. And sooner or later the new citizens would win, for the same reason that other new Americans won, two centuries ago, because time and history are on their side, and passion.

CESAR'S GHOST

Frank Bardacke

Cesar, who was always good at symbols, saved his best for last: a simple pine box, fashioned by his brother's hands, carried unceremoniously through the Central Valley town he made famous. With some 35,000 people looking on.

Here was meaning enough, both for those who need it blunt and for those who like it subtle. No one—especially not the newspaper and TV reporters whose liberal sympathies had been one of his main assets—could fail to hear that pine box speak: Cesar Chavez's commitment to voluntary poverty extended even unto death. And perhaps a few among the crowd would get the deeper reference. Burial insurance had been Cesar's first organizing tool in building the National Farmworkers Association back in 1962. Many farmworkers, then and now, die so badly in debt that they can't afford to be buried. By joining up with Cesar and paying dues to the association, workers earned the right to take their final rest in a pine box, built by brother Richard.

The funeral march and picnic were near perfect. The friendly crowd was primarily Chicano, people who had driven a couple of hours up and over the Grapevine from Los Angeles to honor the man who was the authentic representative of their political coming of age in postwar America. Martin Luther King is the standard comparison, but Cesar Chavez was King and Jackie Robinson, too. Chicanos and Mexicans had played well in their own leagues—they built a lot of power in the railroad, mining, and factory unions of the Southwest—but Cesar forced his way into the political big leagues, where Chicanos had always been excluded. And, like Robinson, he played on his own terms.

Not only Chicanos but all manner of farmworker supporters marched at the funeral: liberal politicians, celebrities, Catholic priests, grape and lettuce boycotters. This was fitting too, as Chavez had always insisted that his greatest contribution to the farmworker movement was the consumer boycott. The boycott, he argued, ended the debilitating isolation of farmworkers that had doomed their earlier organizing. And so it was right that the boycotters marched at Cesar's funeral, and it was their buttons (the word "grapes" or "uvas"[1] with a ghostbuster line through it) that everyone wore.

Frank Bardacke: "Cesar's Ghost," reprinted with permission from the July 26, 1993 issue of *The Nation*.

What the march lacked was farmworkers, at least in mass numbers. Several buses had come down from the Salinas Valley, and farmworkers from the immediate area were well represented, but as a group, farmworkers added little weight to the funeral. I saw no banners from UFW locals, nor did I see a single button or sign proclaiming the idea of farmworker power. And this, too, was symbolically perfect, for at the time of Cesar Chavez's death, the UFW was not primarily a farmworker organization. It was a fundraising operation, run out of a deserted tuberculosis sanitarium in the Tehachapi Mountains, far from the fields of famous Delano, staffed by members of Cesar's extended family and using as its political capital Cesar's legend and the warm memories of millions of aging boycotters.

It was my second funeral march for Cesar Chavez. The first had been two days earlier, back home in Watsonville, in the Pajaro Valley, four and a half hours by car from Delano. Throughout the 1970s, Watsonville, together with nearby Salinas, had been a center of UFW strength. Back then, most of the major growers (the two valleys specialize in vegetable row crops) were signed up with either the UFW or the Teamsters, and pushed by the militancy of several hundred Chavistas, the two unions had won increasingly better contracts. In the 1980s the entry-level hourly wage moved up over $7, and working conditions on UFW crews significantly improved. But by the end of the decade that had all come apart. In Watsonville, the UFW now has only a couple of apple contracts, covering no more than a few hundred workers. In Salinas, the Teamsters still have a contract with the giant Bud Antle/Dole, but for most workers, unions have been replaced by farm labor contractors, and average hourly wages have fallen to around $5.

So I was surprised by the farmworker presence at that first funeral march. Fewer than 200 people had shown up, but a good number of them were field workers. I ran into my old friend Roberto Fernandez,[2] the man who taught me how to pack celery in the mid-seventies and who helped me make it on a piece-rate celery crew, where on good days we made over $15 an hour. Roberto came to California first as a bracero in the early 1960s and later as an illegal. We worked side by side for three years, and I have a lot of memories of Roberto, but my fondest is when we were on a picket line together, trying to prevent a helicopter from spraying a struck field. We were with a group of other strikers, half-jokingly using slings to throw rocks at the helicopter as it flew past. Suddenly, Roberto ran into the field, directly at the oncoming helicopter, a baseball-size rock twirling in the sling above his head, screaming a warrior's roar. The rest of us were astounded; God knows what the pilot thought as he yanked the helicopter straight up and away from the kamikaze attack.

Roberto, his 6-year-old daughter, and I walked a short while on the march together, and when the other folks went into Asunción Church to pray, the three of us walked back into town. I had seen Roberto off and on since I left our celery crew after the 1979 strike, but we had avoided discussing farmworker politics. Roberto is a committed Chavista and always could be counted on to give the official UFW line. He was currently working on one of the few union contracts in town—not with the UFW but with a rival independent union, as the UFW no longer has any celery workers under contract. I asked him what went wrong in the fields.

"The Republicans replaced the Democrats and ruined the law, and we no longer had any support in Sacramento."

"That's it? All the power we had, gone just because Deukmejian replaced Brown?"

"The people were too ignorant."

"What do you mean?"

"We got swamped by people coming from small ranchos in Mexico who didn't know anything about unions. When the companies were letting our contracts expire and bringing in the labor contractors, we would go out to the people in the fields and try to explain to them about the union. But they didn't get it. They just wanted to work."

"I don't believe that. We had people from ranchos in Mexico on our UFW crews. They were strong unionists; unions are not such a hard thing to understand."

"Well, Frank, you aren't ever going to believe that the workers were at fault, but I was there and I talked to them, and you weren't."

I never could beat Roberto in an argument, and although I like to think I would have had a better chance in English, probably not. Two days later I drove to Delano with another old friend, Cruz Gomez. Cruz's father was a farmworker—a year-round employee on a good-size farm outside Santa Barbara. The family was relatively well off compared with the braceros and the other seasonals who worked on the ranch. Nevertheless, her father worked thirty-seven years without a paid vacation, his body slowly breaking down as he passed middle age. As we were driving, I asked Cruz about Chavez.

"For me, Chavez was it, that's all, just it. He was the main main. I remember when I met him. It was 1967 or '68, I was a college student at the University of California at Santa Barbara. I was divorced and had two small children, a kind of mother figure in the MEChA [Movimiento Estuddiantil Chicano de Aztlan] student organization. We went up to Delano as a group, and sat around and talked with him. It was very informal, but he was all there. He gave us his full attention."

When Cruz returned to UCSB she, as they say, had been organized. She soon switched majors from biology to sociology where a few influential teachers taught her that it was her obligation to "give back to the community." In 1971 she found herself working in a local community organization. She has been doing the same kind of work ever since, moving to Watsonville is 1978, spending her days listening to the problems of migrant farmworkers.

Unlike so many others with similar backgrounds, Cruz had never gone to work in Delano or even spent much time working in a boycott organization. From her contact with farmworkers she was well aware that the UFW had become pretty much a nonfactor in the Pajaro and Salinas valleys, but she had no idea why. She asked me what had happened.

Roberto and the UFW are not far wrong. The virtual destruction of a unionized work force in the fields of California in the 1980s was due finally to the overwhelming social, financial, and political power of the biggest business in our Golden State. The weight of the internal errors of the UFW is secondary to the longstanding anti-union policies of the people who own and operate the most powerful agro-export industry in the world.

Nevertheless, in the late seventies, at the height of the UFW's strength among farmworkers, some in California agribusiness had come to the conclusion that Chavez's victory was inevitable and that they would have to learn to live with the UFW Why wasn't the union—with perhaps 50,000 workers under contract and hundreds of militant activists among them—able to seize this historic opportunity?

The short answer is that within the UFW the boycott tail came to wag the farmworker dog. While it was not wrong of Chavez to seek as much support as possible, this support work, primarily the boycott, became the essential activity of the union. Ultimately, it interfered with organizing in the fields.

It was an easy mistake to fall into, especially as the failure of the first grape strikes was followed so stunningly by the success of the first grape boycott. The very best farmworker activists, the strongest Chavistas, were removed from the fields and direct contact with farmworkers, so that they could be sent to work in the boycott offices of major cities. From the point of view of building the boycott, it was a genius decision. But from the point of view of spreading the union among farmworkers themselves, it was a disaster.

The manipulative use of farmworkers gave the union boycott its texture and feel. In the mid-1970s a story circulated in Salinas about a union meeting in the Imperial Valley called to recruit workers to go to a press conference in Los Angeles to support one of the boycotts. For the workers it meant a ten-hour round-trip drive on one of their days off, but many of them were willing to do it. These particular farmworkers were mostly young piece-rate lettuce cutters who earned relatively high wages, and who, like a lot of working-class people able to afford it, put their money into clothes and cars which they sported on their days off. They were proud people, volunteering to spend a weekend in Los Angeles organizing support for their movement. As the meeting closed, Marshall Ganz—one of the union's top officials at the time—had a final request. At the press conference everybody should wear their *work* clothes.

The union officials didn't want farmworkers to appear as regular working people appealing for solidarity. They had to be poor and suffering, hats in hand, asking for charity. It may have made a good press conference, but the people who told the story were angered and shamed.

What the UFW called publicity strikes hurt quite a bit too. Typically, the union would enter a small spontaneous walkout (a tactic California farmworkers have been using for more than a hundred years to drive up wages at harvest time), escalate local demands as a way of publicizing the overall plight of farmworkers and then leave. This played well enough in New York and Chicago, but made it more difficult for farmworkers to win these local battles.

The union's strategy after passage of California's Agricultural [Labor] Relations Act in 1975 was similar. The union would aim to win as many certification elections as possible, thereby demonstrating to Governor Jerry Brown, allies in the California legislature, boycott supporters around the world, and even agribusiness that it had the allegiance of a large majority of California farmworkers. The UFW hoped that this would result in some sort of state-wide master agreement, imposed from above, that would cover farmworkers in most of the larger agribusiness companies.

As with the publicity strikes, the UFW came onto a ranch with its high-powered organizing techniques, explained how important it was for people to vote for the union, usually won the elections and then left. Less than a third of the elections resulted in union contracts, however; too many workers felt used and deserted; and opposition to the UFW grew in the fields.

Just how out of touch the UFW was with farmworker sentiment is per-haps best illustrated by its approach to the question of undocumented work-ers. Most all California farmworkers have people in their families who have trouble with their legal status, so any union trying to organize them cannot risk taking the side of the INS [Immigration and Naturalization Service], the hated *migra*. Yet the UFW sometimes supported the use of the *migra* against scabs, sacrificing long-term respect for a possible short-term gain.

It was the lack of strength among farmworkers that made the 1983 change in the Governor's office and the weakening of boycott support so devastating. Some of the biggest ranches reorganized their operations and replaced union contracts with labor contractors. Others let their UFW contracts expire and refused to renegotiate them. In both cases, the union was powerless to stop them; the years of neglecting farmworker organizing finally took their toll.

A natural question arises: How could a farmworker organization staffed by so many intelligent people of good will, and led by one of the heroes of our time, make so many mistakes? The answer is just as direct. Structurally, the UFW is one of the least democratic unions in the country. Officials in the local field offices are not elected by the workers under contract in those areas, as they are in most other unions. They are appointed by the UFW executive board and were under the direct control of Cesar.

This meant that local farmworker leadership had no way of advancing within the union, other than by being personally loyal to Cesar or other high-level officials. Complaints about the union and its practices, although freely discussed among workers on the job, could not influence union policy.

This criticism does not fall from some idealized heaven of union democ-racy. Many staff members, who either resigned or were purged from the union, have complained privately about Chavez's authoritarian style and the lack of democracy within the UFW They have rarely gone public, however, because they believed that any criticism of the UFW would only help the growers, and because they were intimidated into silence by Chavez himself or by others on the UFW staff. Even now people are reluctant to speak for fear of reprisals.

Philip Vera Cruz, onetime vice president of the union, who worked in the grapes for twenty years before Chavez came along, is the only staff member who put his criticism into print. Vera Cruz, who could not be guilt-tripped into silence, describes in an oral history, taken by Craig Scharlin and Lilia Villanueva, a UFW staff where "power was held by Cesar alone." His conclusion is straightforward:

> One thing the union would never allow was for people to criticize Cesar. If a union leader is built up as a symbol and he talks like he was God, then there is no way you can have true democracy in the union because the members are just generally deprived of their right to reason for themselves.

The most critical UFW purge was not against the union staff but against its own farmworker members—people who dared to give the union some alternative, middle-level leadership. The trouble began when the 1979 contracts provided for full-time union grievers, elected by the workers, to handle specific complaints from the work crews. Some of the people elected in Salinas, the first workers in the hierarchy to have any real power independent of Chavez, regularly criticized several internal union policies.

At the union's 1981 convention in Fresno these men and women supported three independent candidates, not previously approved by Chavez, for election to the UFW's executive board. Afterward, they were fired from their jobs back in Salinas. Although they eventually won a nearly five-year court battle against Chavez and the union, the damage was done. No secondary leadership emerging from the ranks would be tolerated in the UFW.

I talked to one of the men, Aristeo Zambrano, a few weeks after the funeral. Aristeo was one of eleven children born to a farmworker family in Chavinda, Michoacán. His father worked as a bracero between 1945 and 1960, and after getting his papers fixed, he brought his son, then 14, to Hayward, California, in 1969. Aristeo moved to Salinas in 1974 and got a job cutting broccoli at a UFW-organized company—Associated Produce. He was elected to the ranch committee in 1976; for the next six years he was an active unionist, re-elected to the committee every year and then to the position of paid representative, until he was fired by Chavez.

I asked him the same question I had asked Roberto Fernandez. What went wrong? How did the union fall so far so fast? His answer took several hours. Here are a few minutes of it.

"The problem developed way before we were fired in 1982. In the mid-seventies, when I became an activist, Chavez was making every decision in the union. If a car in Salinas needed a new tire, we had to check with Cesar in La Paz. He controlled every detail of union business. And nobody was allowed to say Chavez made a mistake, even when he had. And when you talked to him you had to humble yourself, as if he were a King or the Pope. . . .

"I remember in particular a closed meeting during the strike, just before the Salinas convention in 1979. He called together about twenty of us—the elected picket captains and strike coordinators—and told us that he was going to call off the strike and send us on the boycott. We refused, and we told him so. We thought the strike should be extended, not called off. And we damn sure were not going on any boycott.

"Well, he couldn't call off the strike without our support, and we did continue to fight and we won. Which made us stronger. That meeting, and its aftermath, was a political challenge to Cesar. It meant that the situation in the union had changed. He was going to have to deal with us—with the direct representatives of the workers—and, in some way or other, share power with us.

"And that was what he couldn't do. He was incapable of sharing power. So after the 1982 convention—the first UFW convention that was not simply a staged show, the first convention where true disagreements came to the floor—he fired us. First he tried to organize recall elections, so that farmworkers would replace us. But he couldn't do it. We had too much support in the field.

"We went back to the fields, and tried to continue organizing, but it was impossible. The damage had been done. People were scared or gave up on the union. They could see that the union did not belong to the workers, that it was Chavez's own personal business, and that he would run his business as he pleased. Farmworkers were good for boycotting, or walking the picket lines, or paying union dues, but not for leading our union. . . .

"Chavez built the union and then he destroyed it. The UFW self-destructed. When the Republicans came back in the 1980s and the growers moved against the union, there wasn't any farmworker movement left."

What happens next? There was a feeling of optimism at the funeral. So many people together again, united by their respect for Chavez, pledging themselves to renewed effort. In her own fashion, Dolores Huerta, one of the founders of the union, expressed the hope of the crowd in her eulogy. "Cesar," she said, "died in peace, in good health, with a serene look on his face. It was as if he had chosen to die at this time . . . at this Easter time. . . . He died so that we would wake up. He died so that the union might live."

In the several weeks since the funeral, I have pondered Dolores's image of Chavez as the UFW's Christ, dying so that we might live. In one way, it is perfect. All the talk of [Saul] Alinsky and community organizing aside, Cesar Chavez was essentially a lay Catholic leader. His deepest origins were not in Alinsky's radical Community Service Organization but in the *cursillos de Cristiandad* movement, the intense encounters of Catholic lay people, first developed by the clergy in Franco's Spain and transplanted to the New World in the 1950s. The song they brought with them was "De Colores," and their ideology was a combination of anticommunism and personal commitment of ordinary lay people to the Gospel's version of social justice. Chavez, throughout his public life, remained true to that commitment. What many of the liberals and radicals on the staff of the union could never understand was that all the fasts, the long marches, the insistence on personal sacrifice and the flirting with sainthood were not only publicity gimmicks, they were the essential Chavez.

Chavez died so that the union might live? What Dolores seems to have meant was that people, inspired by Chavez's life, would now rejoin the cause and rebuild the union. That might happen, but rebuilding the union *among farmworkers* will require a complete break with the recent past by the people who now control the UFW.

The UFW is no longer the only group trying to organize in the fields of California. Teamster Local 890 in Salinas, with more than 7,000 field workers under contract, recently has been taken over by reformers with long experience in the Chicano and Mexican cannery worker movement. They would like to begin a new organizing drive in the Salinas Valley. In Stockton, Luis Magaña and the Organización Laboral Agrícola de California have established close contacts with the newest migrant stream in California agriculture, the Mixtec and Zapotec Indians from Oaxaca. In many areas small community groups have gone beyond simply providing services to farmworkers and have helped them organize to fight for better housing, better schooling for their kids, and against violations of labor laws by farmworker contractors.

Up until now, these small beginnings have had an uneasy relationship with the UFW. Viewing them as competitive organizations, Chavez often tried to block their activities, even when the UFW was not organizing in the same areas. Now that Chavez is gone, could the UFW learn to cooperate with these other groups? Could people who were originally inspired by the heroic example of Chavez's life, and who now no longer have Cesar around to interfere with their work, make a hundred flowers bloom in the California fields?

Sí se puede.[3]

NOTES

1. *uvas*: Spanish word for grapes
2. A pseudonym.
3. *Sí se puede*: Yes, it can happen.

FROM DELANO: THE STORY OF THE CALIFORNIA GRAPE STRIKE

John Gregory Dunne

Three months after the strike began, Chavez found the stratagem to focus nationwide attention on Delano. The tactic was economic boycott.

Though grapes might not seem to lend themselves to boycott, the two biggest ranches in Delano did. The DiGiorgio Corporation, with 4,400 acres in Delano, and Schenley Industries, Inc., with 3,350 acres, were absentee landlords only minimally interested in farming. Less than ten percent of DiGiorgio's $232 million annual revenues came from farming; the bulk came from the processing and sale of canned goods. Similarly, only a fraction of Schenley's $500 million annual sales, mostly in distilled spirits, derived from its farming properties. For both companies, the profits from agriculture were marginal, if any; DiGiorgio's farming operation, for example, has lost money three out of the five preceding years.

The situation of both companies appealed to Chavez. No other ranches in Delano could afford him the means to tell the NFWA's story so effectively. Both DiGiorgio and Schenley distributed their products through outlets across the nation. Both had scores of contracts with other unions that they could not afford to compromise by behaving cavalierly with the NFWA. In addition, it was unlikely that either company wanted to jeopardize its consumer sales on behalf of an agricultural operation that barely paid its way. Early in December, Chavez's boycott plans were given a boost when the AFL-CIO convention in San Francisco, after some assiduous backstage lobbying for the NFWA, passed a resolution supporting the grape strike. The next day, Walter Reuther himself came to Delano to bestow the AFL-CIO's official blessing. The town was in an ugly mood. Outside the Filipino Hall on the West Side, a fight nearly broke out between strikers and townspeople carrying placards reading, "You Are Not Welcome Here, Mr. Reuther," and "We Can Take Care of Our Own Problems." The mayor of Delano arranged a secret meeting between Reuther and a contingent of local growers, but it broke up with both sides intractable. "We will put the full support of organized labor behind your boycott and this

---

John Gregory Dunne: from "Delano: The Story of the California Grape Strike."

is a powerful economic weapon," Reuther told the strikers. "You are making history here and we will march here together, we will fight here together, and we will win here together."

From the beginning, Chavez decided to concentrate the boycott on Schenley. "It was a simple decision," he told me one day. "In the first place, booze is easier to boycott. And then it is usually the man who goes to the liquor store and he's more sympathetic to labor as a rule than his wife." From an atlas, Chavez picked thirteen major cities across the United States as boycott centers, and then raised a boycott staff, all under twenty-five, from workers and volunteers who had impressed him on the picket line. They left Delano penniless and hitchhiked or rode the rails to the various cities where they were to set up shop. Chavez gave the boycott staff no money, both out of necessity and to prove a theory. He reasoned that if a person could not put his hands on enough money to maintain himself on a subsistence level, then he would be of little use raising money for the boycott and setting up an organization. In most cities, the boycott staffers went to union locals and begged room, board, an office, a telephone, and whatever help was available. Across the country, they recruited some 10,000 people to pass out leaflets or to telephone neighbors, friends, churches, and stores, urging support of the boycott. (In Los Angeles, I came out of a supermarket one day to find, stuck under the windshield wiper of my car, a leaflet that said: "Steve Allen and the Los Angeles friends of the grape strikers urge you not to buy (1) Schenley Products (2) Delano grapes." A few days later, the supermarket put up a sign: "We do not handle Delano grapes.")

The staffers were seldom at a loss for ingenuity. In Boston, one staged a Boston Grape Party. He bought several lugs of Delano grapes, organized a march, and paraded his charges through town to the waterfront where, with attendant publicity, the grapes were dumped into Massachusetts Bay. In New York, another talked the Transport Workers Union into printing and passing out one million boycott leaflets in the city's subways. In all, fifty million leaflets were distributed throughout the country.

In Delano, the NFWA even arranged to boycott the freight-car loads of table grapes that rolled out of town by rail to markets around the nation. Contacting SNCC and CORE, Chavez rounded up a cadre of volunteers who had ridden the rails before. "We'd slip them on the trains right here in Delano," he told me. "We'd cover the yard with pickets and create a big scene, maybe start a fight or something, and then when everyone was looking the other way, they'd hop on the train. Sometimes a train would make six or seven stops, and at each one our people would slip off and contact our local organization to tell them a load of Delano grapes was in town. The local people would then set up the pickets." One volunteer team rode the rods with a load of grapes all the way from Delano to Hoboken, New Jersey. Another was apprehended by a railroad employee as their train was crossing one of the snow-covered Western mountain ranges. Telling them they would freeze to death if they stayed on the train, the railroad man bought them bus tickets to the first stop on the other side of the mountains, where he told them they could get back on board. He was a good union man, he said, and this was his contribution to the Delano strike. "We even had girl volunteers who wanted to ride the rails," Chavez told me. "But I wouldn't let them. They were really upset."

Though the economic effects of the boycott were negligible (despite the grandiose claims of the NFWA), the adverse publicity began to worry executives of both Schenley and DiGiorgio. Chavez was well aware of their concern, as secret information was constantly passed to him from informants inside both companies. The NFWA's man at Schenley was a disgruntled employee passed over for promotion, but the identity of the DiGiorgio informant was unknown. He would neither meet with the NFWA nor talk to the union over the telephone. His information came by mail to a postal box in Delano, and the NFWA got in touch with him in the same way. Fully cognizant of the situation within both companies, Chavez decided to publicize the boycott even further.

He chose to do it by means of a *peregrinación*, or pilgrimage, from Delano to the state capital at Sacramento. The notion was first born shortly after the strike started, when Schenley ranch crews sprayed pickets with insecticides and fertilizer. Outraged, some NFWA members proposed that five striking families make a protest pilgrimage across the country from Delano to Schenley's corporate headquarters in New York. The march to New York was clearly unfeasible, but the idea of a *peregrinación* stuck. Chavez was well aware of the emotional impact of the Selma civil-rights march in the South, and after much discussion it was decided that the march should terminate on Easter Sunday at the steps of the capitol building in Sacramento: The choice of Sacramento was calculated. Up to that point, both the state legislature and the then governor, Edmund G. ("Pat") Brown, had been indifferent to the strike. Early in the walkout, when Pat Brown was asked if he intended to take any action, he had replied, "What can a governor do to end a strike?" A *peregrinación* would not only embarrass Schenley and DiGiorgio but also put pressure on Pat Brown.

Late in February, the NFWA began signing up marchers for the 250-mile hike to Sacramento. Only a limited number of pickets were allowed to sign on, since picketing and the operation of the nursery school, clinic, store, soup kitchen, and NFWA office in Delano had to continue. Of the one hundred names on the initial list, doctors struck off all those with diabetes, bad feet, high blood pressure, and sick wives at home. The rest received their assignments, some to drive the luggage and toilet trucks, others to act as advance men, visiting towns ahead of the marchers, arranging meals, halls for meetings, places to sleep.

The *peregrinación* was scheduled to begin on March 17, but it very nearly did not make it out of Delano. "We knew the march was coming up," Chief Ailes told me. "There was a report about it in *Newsweek* magazine. They just acted as if nothing was going to happen, but we were monitoring their radios, just like they were monitoring ours, and we heard them asking for bedding, tents, food, stuff like that." A day or so before the start, Chief Ailes said, Alex Hoffman told him that the marchers were going to walk down Albany Street, which is the city line, and then on out of town. But on March 17, the marchers, with Chavez leading them, changed their plans and prepared to walk through the center of Delano. "They didn't have no permit to do that,"

Chief Ailes said. Immediately a line of police blocked their route of march. So many reporters and television cameramen were on the scene that Ailes and Delano's city manager, Louis Shepard, decided to avoid an incident and let the marchers go through town. "They wanted us to arrest them," Chief Ailes said. "But that was one time we just lucked out. They were all down on their knees with their priests saying all their words and what not. It would have made them look good if we arrested them with all that press and TV there. No, I got to say we just lucked out."

For twenty-five days, the marchers straggled up through the Valley behind the banner of the Virgin of Gaudalupe, who symbolized the Mexico of the poor and the humble. The first night, when they stopped to rest, one of the marchers discovered a seven-year-old boy who had skipped school, eluded his mother, and was intent on trekking to Sacramento. He was reluctantly sent home, and sixty-seven marched on. Every night, feet were soaked and blisters treated. Peggy McGivern, the NFWA's nurse, lanced so many blisters that one night she dreamed that one burst and its serum gushed out in a tidal wave, engulfing her. At each town, the ranks of the marchers swelled as farm workers joined the *peregrinación* for a mile or an hour or even a whole day. Scores of new members signed with the NFWA, and their families gave the marchers rosaries, mass cards, fruit, tea, and food. In the evening, rallies were held which were like religious revivals. At each rally, the NFWA's plan of Delano was read: "We are suffering . . . We shall unite . . . We shall strike . . . We shall overcome . . . Our pilgrimage is the match that will light our cause for all farm workers to see what is happening here, so that they may do as we have done."

To the delight of the rally audiences, El Teatro Campesino (The Farm Workers' Theater, an adjunct of the NFWA set up to raise money and to publicize the strike throughout the state) nightly performed broad, neo-Brechtian skits about *esquiroles* (scabs), *contratistas* (contractors), *patroncitos* (growers), and *huelguistas* (strikers). The most successful playlet involved the DiGiorgio Corporation.

"When the time for the Teatro came," says Luis Valdez, the group's founder and director, "the DiGiorgio character—complete with sign, dark glasses, and cigar—leaped onto the truck used as a stage for the rallies and was booed and reviled by the audience. Threatening them with the loss of their jobs, black-balling, and deportation, 'DiGiorgio' blustered and guffawed his way through all the booing, and announced that his old school buddy, the governor, was coming to speak to them that same night, and in Spanish. At this point, a car with a siren and loudspeaker drove up behind the audience, honking and moving toward the platform. An authoritative voice commanded the workers to move out of the way, and the outside rally was momentarily halted as 'Governor Brown' was pulled out of the car by his cronies and pushed on to the stage.

"'No huelga,' they exhorted, 'just say *no huelga.*'

"And *no boycoteo*,' insisted DiGiorgio.

"The governor not only spoke Spanish, he spoke so ardently that he turned into a Mexican. This is the turning point of the *acto*. DiGiorgio and his friends were forced to drag the metamorphosed governor off the stage as he shouted, '*Huelga, huelga*.'"

Easter Sunday, the marchers paraded into Sacramento. I was standing on the balcony of the capitol building and it was like watching newsreels of de Gaulle marching into Paris in 1944. Below, on the mall, thousands of people were cheering and weeping and waving Mexican flags. "Clear away the dignitaries," a Spanish-accented voice commanded over the loudspeaker. "Clear away the dignitaries. The platform is reserved for the *originales*"—the fifty-seven marchers who had walked the entire distance between Delano and Sacramento. The villain of the day was neither Schenley nor DiGiorgio but Pat Brown. The governor had declined to meet with the strikers, saying that he had a previous engagement to spend the holiday with his family. With ill-concealed delight, the NFWA announced that the setting for the governor's family holiday was the Palm Springs home of Frank Sinatra.

As the afternoon wore on, it started to rain and the excitement began to ebb. Ponderousness replaced the throbbing revivalist flavor of the march. Speech followed interminable speech, each rendered in both Spanish and English. Priests and ministers compared the *peregrinación* with the Passion, rabbis the Passion with Passover. If Passover was a mystery to the *campesinos*, it was less so than the peroration delivered by the director of the Migrant Ministry, the Reverend Hartmire, who chose as his text relevant passages from the works of Albert Camus. All that saved the day was the residual excitement from an announcement made a few days before: Schenley had capitulated.

Less than a month before, Schenley had stated categorically that it would not recognize the NFWA. What troubled the company was the fear of stockholder reaction if it recognized a union so ardently supported by the radical left, in particular Students for a Democratic Society and the W. E. B. DuBois clubs. The publicity generated by the boycott undermined the company's determination. Clergymen denounced Schenley from the pulpit, and letters of protest poured in from over forty states. Otherwise completely organized, the company began to feel pressure from the unions with which it had contracts. The Teamsters refused to cross an NFWA picket line outside the warehouse of Schenley's major distributor in San Francisco and threatened to stop serving a supermarket chain that carried Schenley products.

Clearly up against it, Schenley retained Sidney Korshak, a Los Angeles attorney, to get the company out of its corner. Korshak's negotiations were proceeding nowhere when a piece of misinformation brought matters to a head. The misinformation arrived via Herman "Blackie" Leavitt, the head of the Bartenders' Union in Los Angeles. Not long before, the NFWA had asked Leavitt to help the strike by declaring a bartenders' boycott on Schenley products. Leavitt refused, but after some persuasion reluctantly agreed to help the NFWA by picking up the cost of a mailing. In the telling, however, the story got turned around, and word filtered back to Korshak that the bartenders were about to boycott Schenley products. The threat of a boycott was the lever that Korshak sought. He contacted Leavitt and asked him not to do anything for a while. "Since I wasn't doing anything anyway," Leavitt told a friend, "it was easy to agree to keep on doing nothing."

Korshak next got in touch with Lewis Solon Rosensteil, then Schenley's seventy-five-year-old board chairman and chief stockholder. Noted for his contentiousness, Rosensteil had for years feuded with the liquor industry over its marketing practices and more recently had spent a large part of his time in court fighting with, among others, his estranged fourth wife, his daughter, one of his lawyers, and his neighbors in Greenwich, Connecticut. Korshak told Rosensteil about the rumors (false) of the bartenders' boycott. The strike, however, did not loom as large in Rosensteil's thinking as it did in Cesar Chavez's or in the minds of the growers of Delano, and Korshak had to bring him up to date. When informed that only 200 grape pickers were involved, Rosensteil told Korshak that he was not a farmer but was in the liquor business, and ordered him to sell the Schenley properties in Delano. As an alternative, Korshak suggested that Schenley could avoid the bartenders' boycott by recognizing the NFWA, thus coming out of the dispute with its tarnished image buffed up. Rosensteil finally agreed and gave Korshak carte blanche in settling the strike. So a bartenders' boycott that was never even contemplated brought Schenley in line, and, on April 6, an agreement was signed that left the NFWA free to concentrate its attack on DiGiorgio.

Selected Bibliography

Dalton, Frederick John. *The Moral Vision of Cesar Chavez*. Maryknoll, N.Y.: Orbis Books, 2003.

Dunne, John Gregory. Delano: *The Story of the California Grape Strike*. Berkeley: University of California Press, 2008.

Ferriss, Susan, with Ricardo Sandoval. *The Fight in the Fields: Cesar Chavez and the Farmworkers Movement*. New York: Mariner Books, 1998.

García, Ignacio M. *Chicanismo: The Forging of a Militant Ethos among Mexican Americans*. Tucson: University of Arizona Press, 1993.

Hammerback, John C., with Richard J. Jensen, eds. *The Rhetorical Career of Cesar Chavez*. College Station, Texas: Texas A&M University Press, 1998.

———, eds. *The Words of Cesar Chavez*. College Station, Texas: Texas A&M University Press, 2002.

Levy, Jacques E. *Cesar Chavez: Autobiography of La Causa*. Introduction by Fred Ross Jr. Minneapolis: University of Minnesota Press, 2007.

Matthiessen, Peter. *Sal Si Puedes: Cesar Chavez and the New American Revolution*. Introduction by Ilan Stavans. Berkeley and London: University of California Press, 2001.

Prouty, Marco G. *The Catholic Bishops, and the Farmworkers' Struggle for Social Justice*. Tucson: University of Arizona Press, 2006.

Ross, Fred. *Conquering Goliath: Cesar Chavez at the Beginning*, by Fred Ross. Keene, Calif.: El Taller Gráfico Press/United Farm Workers, 1989.

Stavans, Ilan, ed. *Cesar Chavez: An Organizer's Tale*. New York: Penguin Classics, 2008.

Steinbacher, John. *Bitter Harvest*. Whittier, Calif.: Change Tree Press, 1970.

Yinger, Winthrop. *Cesar Chavez: The Rhetoric of Nonviolence*. New York: Exposition Press, 1975.

INDEX

About the Editor and Contributors

EDITOR

Ilan Stavans is Lewis-Sebring Professor in Latin American and Latino Culture and Five College-Fortieth Anniversary Professor at Amherst College. A native from Mexico, he received his doctorate in Latin American Literature from Columbia University. Stavans' books include *The Hispanic Condition* (HarperCollins, 1995), *On Borrowed Words* (Viking, 2001), *Spanglish* (HarperCollins, 2003), *Dictionary Days* (Graywolf, 2005), *The Disappearance* (TriQuarterly, 2006), *Love and Language* (Yale, 2007), *Resurrecting Hebrew* (Nextbook, 2008), *Mr. Spic Goes to Washington* (Soft Skull, 2008), *A Critic's Journey* (Michigan, 2009), and *Gabriel García Márquez: Sleepless in Macondo* (Palgrave, 2009). He has edited *The Oxford Book of Jewish Stories* (Oxford, 1998), *The Poetry of Pablo Neruda* (Farrar, Straus and Giroux, 2004), *Isaac Bashevis Singer: Collected Stories* (3 vols., Library of America, 2004), *The Schocken Book of Sephardic Literature* (Schocken, 2005), *Cesar Chavez: An Organizer's Tale* (Penguin, 2008), and *Becoming Americans: Four Centuries of Immigrant Writing* (Library of America, 2009). His play *The Disappearance*, performed by the theater troupe Double Edge, premiered at the Skirball Cultural Center in Los Angeles and has been shown around the country. His story *"Morirse está en hebreo"* was made into the award-winning movie *My Mexican Shivah* (2007), produced by John Sayles. Stavans has received numerous awards, among them a Guggenheim Fellowship, the National Jewish Book Award, an Emmy nomination, the Latino Book Award, Chile's Presidential Medal, and the Rubén Darío Distinction. His work has been translated into a dozen languages.

CONTRIBUTORS

Frank Bardacke was a public-school teacher in California. He is the author, with Alexander Cockburn, of *Good Liberals and Blue Herons* (1994) and co-translator of *Shadows of Tender Fury: The Letters and Communiqués of Subcomandante Marcos and the Zapatista Army of National Liberation* (1995).

John Gregory Dunne (1932–2003) is the author of *Delano: The Story of the California Grape Strike* (1967), *A Star Is Born* (1976), *True Confessions* (1981), *The Red White and Blue* (1987), among other books.

Richard G. García teaches Ethnic Studies at California State University, Hayward. He is co-author, with Richard Griswold del Castillo, of *Cesar Chavez: Triumph of Spirit* (1997). His books include *El Político: The Mexican American Elected Official* (1972), *A Gringo Manual on How to Handle Mexicans* (1974), and *The Making of a Chicano Militant: Lessons from Cristal* (1998).

Richard Griswold del Castillo is Professor of Chicana and Chicano Studies and chair of the department at San Diego State University. He is the author of, among other books, *Los Angeles Barrio 1850–1890: A Social History* (1980) and *Chicano San Diego: Cultural Space and the Struggle for Justice* (2007), and co-author, with Richard G. García, of *Competing Visions: A History of California* (1997).

José Angel Gutiérrez teaches at the University of Texas, Arlington. He is a founder of the Mexican American Youth Organization (MAYO) as well as the Raza Unida Party.

John C. Hammerback teaches in the Department of Communication at North Carolina State University, Raleigh. He co-edited, with Richard J. Jensen, *The Rhetorical Career of Cesar Chavez* (1998) and *The Words of Cesar Chavez* (2002).

Luis D. León teaches in the Department of Religious Studies at the University of Denver. He is the author of *La Llorona's Children: Religion, Life, and Death in the United States–Mexican Borderlands* (2004), and co-editor, with Gary Laderman, of the *Encyclopedia of Religion and American Cultures* (2003).

Jorge Mariscal is director of the Chicano/a–Latino/a Arts and Humanities Program at the University of California, San Diego.

Peter Matthiessen is the author of, among other books of fiction and nonfiction, *At Play in the Fields of the Lord* (1965), *Sal Si Puedes: Cesar Chavez and the New American Revolution* (1969), *The Snow Leopard* (1978), *In the Spirit of Crazy Horse* (1983), *East of Lo Monthang* (1995), and *Shadow Country* (2008).

Josephine Méndez-Negrete is Associate Professor in the College of Education and Human Development at the University of Texas at San Antonio. She is the author of *Las hijas de Juan: Daughters betrayed* (2002).

Marco G. Prouty is the author of *The Catholic Bishops, and the Farmworkers' Struggle for Social Justice* (2006).